BRITISH ROYAL AND JAPANESE IMPERIAL RELATIONS
1868–2018

At the back of the Enryōkan, Tokyo, 1881. Front row (from left to right): Prince George, Prince Higashi-Fushimi, Prince Albert Victor; back row: Matsumura Junzō, Dr Alexander Turnbull, Suzuki Kenzō, unknown, Prince Karim (*sic*, probably Prince Kan'in Kotohito), Maruoka Kanji, Prince Yamashina Kikumaro (1873–1908), unknown, Rev. John Dalton, unknown. [See Pl. 9]

THE JAPAN SOCIETY

British Royal and Japanese Imperial Relations, 1868–2018

150 YEARS OF ASSOCIATION, ENGAGEMENT AND CELEBRATION

by

Peter Kornicki, Antony Best & Hugh Cortazzi

Routledge
Taylor & Francis Group
LONDON AND NEW YORK

BRITISH ROYAL AND JAPANESE IMPERIAL RELATIONS, 1868–2018
150 YEARS OF ASSOCIATION, ENGAGEMENT AND CELEBRATION

First published in 2019 by RENAISSANCE BOOKS

Published 2025 by Routledge
4 Park Square, Milton Park, Abingdon, Oxon OX14 4RN
605 Third Avenue, New York, NY 10158

Routledge is an imprint of the Taylor & Francis Group, an informa business

British Library Cataloguing in Publication Data
A catalogue record for this book is available from the British Library

ISBN: 9781898823865 (hbk)
ISBN: 9781041176459 (pbk)
ISBN: 9781003691945 (ebk)

SPECIAL THANKS

The Chairman and Trustees of the Japan Society, together with the Publishers, wish to express their thanks to the Great-Britain Sasakawa Foundation for their support in the making of this book

This book is dedicated with great respect and affection
to the memory of our co-author, friend and mentor,
Sir Hugh Cortazzi (1924–2018)

Contents

Plate section faces page 138

Usages and Abbreviations

IN THIS BOOK we have followed the Japanese style of putting the family name first. The following abbreviations appear in the text and the endnotes.

ANA	All Nippon Airways
BC	Blair Castle, Blair Atholl
BL	British Library, London
BP	Buckingham Palace
BUL	Birmingham University Library (Birmingham)
DNI	Director of Naval Intelligence, Admiralty
FBI	Federation of British Industry
FCO	Foreign and Commonwealth Office
FE	Far Eastern Department, Foreign Office
FEPOWS	Far East Prisoners of War
FO	Foreign Office
GCB	Knight Grand Cross of the Order of the Bath
GCMG	Knight Grand Cross of the Order of St Michael and St George
GCVO	Knight Grand Cross of the Victorian Order
GGS	Gaimushō Gaikō Shiryōkan (Tokyo)
GOV HK	Governor, Hong Kong
GVD	King George V's Diary (in the Royal Archives)
HC	House of Commons
HIH	Her/His Imperial Highness
HRH	Her/His Royal Highness
IJA	Imperial Japanese Army
IJN	Imperial Japanese Navy
IOLR	India Office Library and Records, British Library, London
JET	Japan Exchange and Teaching (Programme)
KCB	Knight Companion of the Order of the Bath

KK	Kunai Kōbunshokan (Tokyo)
KKB	Kokuritsu Kōbunshokan (Tokyo)
KPS	King's Private Secretary
LCO	Lord Chamberlain's Office
MC	Master of Ceremonies
NA	Naval Attaché
NRO	Northamptonshire Record Office (Northampton)
OM	Order of Merit
POW	Prisoner of War
PUS	Permanent Under-Secretary
RA	Royal Archives, Windsor
RVC	Royal Victorian Chain
SOAS	School of Oriental and African Studies, London
TNA	The National Archives, Kew
WO	War Office
WSRO	Wiltshire and Swindon Record Office (Chippenham)
WWF	World Wide Fund for Nature

Foreword

by

DAVID WARREN

Chairman, The Japan Society (2012–2018)

THE POLITICAL AND economic links between Britain and Japan since the Meiji Restoration of 1868 have stimulated much historical analysis. This is the first collection of essays focusing specifically on the connections between the British royal and Japanese imperial families. It illuminates how the two countries' status as hereditary monarchies has been reflected in the ebb and flow of their bilateral relationship.

As Professor Peter Kornicki explains in his essay on the period from the accession of Emperor Meiji in 1868 to the Anglo-Japanese alliance in 1902, at the time of their first encounter the two countries had profoundly different conceptions of monarchy. Britain was ruled by a queen who had succeeded to the throne in her own right and presided over an empire (indeed, was to assume the title of Empress of India in 1876). Japan was ruled by an emperor who claimed to have a (virtually) unbroken line of descent through the male line; and while his predecessors had reigned in quasi-hermitic seclusion for centuries, the restoration of the institution under Emperor Meiji represented a new, outward-looking Japan about to convert itself from a feudal society to a world industrial power.

Britain and the other great powers had already forced the Japanese to open up to trade. But when, in his first contacts with the emperor, Sir Harry Parkes treated the Japanese Court by the standards of the Treaty of Vienna of 1815 (which regarded all states as equal irrespective of style of government), he effectively forced a new form of diplomatic contact and protocol on the nascent Japanese government, and paved the way for the emperor's public role to evolve over the coming years and resemble that of European monarchies. In due course, royal visits ensued, playing an important role in helping both to normalise the relationship with Japan as it entered the community of nations, and beginning to promote closer links with Britain (though other Powers quickly followed suit); and members of the imperial family visited Britain, initially more for study than ceremony. But relations between the two families and households were not close. And protocol was always fraught, not least because of the British reluctance to honour the emperor with the Knighthood of the Garter, which the queen had bestowed on other foreign heads of state, but was deemed inappropriate for an Eastern monarch.

As British/Japanese relations developed in the twentieth century, so did the nature of royal/imperial links. Dr Antony Best tells this story in his essay, covering the period from the alliance to the outbreak of the Pacific War in 1941. The impetus for the alliance came from concern about Russian imperial ambitions in North-East Asia. But although King Edward VII supported it, it was in no sense seen as an arrangement between equals. It took another four years for the Garter to be bestowed upon the emperor. British sympathies for Japan during the Russo-Japanese War, while neutrality was maintained according to the terms of the alliance, were reflected in royal as well as official channels of communication. The momentum of reciprocal visits increased over the next ten years, culminating in the ceremonial exchanges following the deaths of Edward VII and Emperor Meiji, and the accessions of George V (who had visited Japan as Duke of York in 1881) and Emperor Taishō. By the time of the First World War, in which Japan was a combatant on the Allied side, as Dr Best writes: 'there was a sense that the royal relationship was now in good fettle'.

The strength of contacts, both formal and informal, continued after the war, with the crown prince's visit in 1921, the Prince of Wales's in 1922, and the bestowal of the Garter on the new emperor, Hirohito, in 1929. But it was during this era that the alliance and indeed the political relationship began to deteriorate as Japan began to assert its imperial ambitions. The attempts of individual members of both families to maintain cordial links made little impact as the world crisis deepened, and British public opinion turned against Japan with its 1937 invasion of China. With the outbreak of war in 1941, the relationship ceased for the duration.

The post-war story is told by the late Sir Hugh Cortazzi in the third essay in this collection, which sets out how the relations between the two households were restored after the war, starting with the visit of Crown Prince Akihito to the Coronation in 1953. The political and constitutional background to this relationship had already begun to evolve by 1945, and was to see more fundamental change over the ensuing decades. Hostility to Japan and to the Japanese emperor personally, because of the war, persisted for many years in Britain. Public attitudes towards both families changed. In Britain, there has been a general decline of deference and respect for hierarchies. The aristocracy is of diminishing social relevance. And people's views of the modern and media-friendly royal family are ambivalent: affection from some, particularly for the queen, indifference and hostility from others. In Japan, the Emperor Shōwa's renunciation of his divinity and the constrained and symbolic role that the imperial family is able to play in the life of the nation (as well as the maintenance of a purely male line of succession, because of resistance to reform from extreme nationalists) create a very different environment. Nevertheless, continued visits and contacts play a role in the 'soft power' that Britain and Japan deploy around the world. Indeed, the number of such visits has sharply increased: over 70 in the last 65 years. And in the sense that monarchies can be stabilising factors at times of flux and crisis, the perceived affinities between Britain and Japan in this area can also be significant.

We are on the cusp of a historical moment of change. With the abdication of the emperor in 2019, Japan enters on a new era – literally, as the era of Heisei will close with the emperor's stepping down. This is a significant moment. In Britain, respect for Her Majesty The Queen precludes public discussion of the future of the monarchy in the decades ahead. But the essays in this book show how the relations between monarchical systems both reflect and on occasion influence political and diplomatic relations between countries. The extent to which the royal/imperial relationship will remain an element in future links between Britain and Japan, as these change and evolve in a changing and evolving world, is an open question.

The idea for this book was Hugh Cortazzi's. His indefatigable scholarship and energy helped to produce countless volumes of historical and biographical essays on Britain and Japan, which the Japan Society has had the privilege of helping to co-publish over many years. He was working on his account of post-World War Two royal/imperial exchanges up to a few days before his death, at the age of 94, in August 2018. He was a diplomat and Japanologist of great distinction and is much missed by all his many friends. This volume is a tribute to his memory and achievements.

Preface

by

KOJI TSURUOKA

Ambassador of Japan in the United Kingdom

THIS BOOK, BY three distinguished scholars with profound knowledge and experience of Japan, is a comprehensive and illuminating account of the history of exchange and friendship between the Japanese Imperial and British Royal Families. As the book reveals, the close relationship between the two countries' monarchies, notwithstanding the very different circumstances in which they have evolved, has done much to underpin our bilateral ties and to foster cordial relations between our peoples.

It is most timely that this book is being published in Spring 2019, coinciding with the abdication of His Majesty Emperor Akihito and the accession to the throne of His Imperial Highness the Crown Prince. Their Imperial Highnesses the Crown Prince and the Crown Princess both studied at the University of Oxford and have developed deep connections with the United Kingdom. I am convinced that the links between the Japanese Imperial and British Royal Families will continue to flourish in the new era.

The essay in the book by the late Sir Hugh Cortazzi was the last piece of work from the prodigious volume of scholarly output he contributed throughout his life. Indeed, he was one of the architects of the close friendship that developed between Japan and the United Kingdom in the post-war period. The publication of this new work is a most appropriate occasion for me to express anew my deep appreciation of the passion and dedication Sir Hugh brought to both his diplomatic and his intellectual endeavours.

Koji Tsuruoka
Ambassador of Japan in the United Kingdom

Acknowledgements

WE ACKNOWLEDGE WITH gratitude the gracious permission of Her Majesty the Queen to draw upon material contained in the Royal Archives in Windsor and that of the Imperial Family in Japan to draw upon material contained in the archives of the Imperial Household Agency. We are also most grateful to the Imperial Household Agency for their assistance in preparing the chronology (see pages 221–225) of Imperial Visits to the UK. His Grace the Duke of Buccleuch and Queensberry has kindly given permission for use of material kept at Drumlanrig Castle or on deposit at Northamptonshire Record Office. Quotations from the papers of Sir Herbert Warren and Magdalen College appear by kind permission of the President and Fellows of Magdalen College Oxford.

There are many others to whom we would like to express our thanks for assistance and advice freely given. They include HRH The Duke of Gloucester; HRH The Duke of Kent; The Viscount Trenchard; former British ambassadors to Japan, Sir Tim Hitchens, Sir David Warren, Sir John Whitehead, and Sir David Wright; Charlotte Berry, the Archivist at Magdalen College, Oxford; Damien Burke, the Archivist at the Irish Jesuit Archives in Dublin; Allison Derrett and her staff at the Royal Archives; Keren Guthrie, the Archivist to the Duke of Atholl at Blair Castle; Sandra Howat and Crispin Powell, respectively Private Secretary and Archivist to The Duke of Buccleuch & Queensberry; Rachel Peat of the Royal Collection Trust; Danny Howell, historian of Warminster; Keiko Itoh, historian of the Japanese community in Britain; Professor Jane Ridley of the University of Buckingham; Professor Nicole Rousmaniere, IFAC Handa Curator of Japanese Art in the Department of Asia at the British Museum; Mr Kiyohisa Komatsu of Ise City, and Phillida Purvis and Ben Thorne who assisted Sir Hugh Cortazzi with his chapter. We would also like to thank the Japan Society, and especially Sir David Warren and Heidi Potter, for having sponsored this book and given us every encouragement.

Our publisher, Paul Norbury, began publishing Sir Hugh's books in 1998, and when Hugh proposed this book to him in December 2016, while both were attending the celebration of the Emperor's birthday at the Japanese Embassy in London, Paul eagerly took it on. We are all three greatly indebted to him for his enthusiasm and his support for this book. Finally, it is a pleasure to acknowledge here the warm support given to this project by Lady Elizabeth Cortazzi, who frequently welcomed Antony and Peter to her home when Hugh wanted to confer with us.

List of Contributors

ANTONY BEST is an Associate Professor in International History at the London School of Economics. His most recent single-authored book is *British Intelligence and the Japanese Challenge in Asia, 1914–1941* (Basingstoke: Palgrave 2002), and he is one of the co-authors of *International History of the Twentieth Century and Beyond*, 3rd edition (London: Routledge, 2015). He is currently completing a manuscript on British interactions with Japan between 1854 and 1922.

HUGH CORTAZZI was British ambassador to Japan between 1980 and 1984 and chairman of the Japan Society between 1985 and 1995. He wrote, edited and contributed to many books and chapters on the history of modern Japan and on Anglo-Japanese relations. His writings include *Victorians in Japan: In and Around the Treaty Ports* (London: Continuum, 1987) and *The Japanese Achievement: A Short History of Japan and Japanese Culture* (London: Sidgwick and Jackson (1990). His most recent book (co-edited with Antony Best) was *British Foreign Secretaries and Japan 1850–1990: Aspects of the Evolution of British Foreign Policy* (Folkestone: Renaissance Books, 2018).

PETER KORNICKI retired as Professor of Japanese at the University of Cambridge in 2014. He had been teaching at Cambridge since 1985 and prior to that had been teaching at the University of Tasmania and Kyoto University. At Cambridge he served as head of the Department of East Asian Studies and Chairman of the Faculty Board of Oriental Studies. He is the author of numerous books and articles, most recently *Languages, Scripts, and Chinese Texts in East Asia* (Oxford: Oxford University Press, 2018) and *Umi o watatta Nihon shoseki* (Tokyo: Heibonsha, 2018), and was the co-editor with Hugh Cortazzi of *Japanese Studies in Britain: A Survey and History* (Folkestone: Renaissance Books, 2016).

List of Plates

Plate

PART ONE

Northamptonshire Record Office) with the kind permission of the Duke of Buccleuch & Queensbury KT KBE.

9 The two princes photographed with their party at the back of the Enryōkan in Tokyo, 1881. Front row (from left to right): Prince George, Prince Higashi-Fushimi, Prince Albert Victor; back row: Matsumura Junzō, Dr Alexander Turnbull, Suzuki Kenzō, unknown, Prince Karim (*sic*, probably Prince Kan'in Kotohito), Maruoka Kanji, Prince Yamashina Kikumaro (1873-1908), unknown, Rev. John Dalton, unknown. Matsumura Junzō (1842-1919), later a baron and vice-admiral in the Imperial Japanese Navy, had studied in England and America from 1865 to 1873; Maruoka Kanji (1836-1898) was a high-ranking bureaucrat. Some of the names are given beneath the photograph. Royal Collection Trust, © Her Majesty Queen Elizabeth II 2018.

10 The two princes and their party at the Nishi-Honganji temple in Kyoto. Front row (from left to right): Sannomiya Yoshitane, Prince Albert Victor, Hattori Senzō, Prince Higashi-Fushimi, Prince George, Lord Francis Osborne; back row: Arthur Christian, Rev. John Dalton, Suzuki Kenzō, Charles Napier, Nagasaki Seijō, Ernest Satow, Matsumura Junzō, Dr Alexander Turnbull. (These identifications are based on names written under an identical photograph in the H.M.S. *Bacchante* album (Box 24, Lady Scott Archive, Northamptonshire Record Office). Most of the people present are mentioned in the text, but Hattori Senzō (1850-1886) was an officer in the Imperial Japanese Navy who had studied in England from 1867 to 1873. Suzuki Kenzō and Nagasaki Seijō are identified as 'secretaries', i.e. government officials, in notes included in the H.M.S. *Bacchante* album (Box 24, Lady Scott Archive, Northamptonshire Record Office). Royal Collection Trust, © Her Majesty Queen Elizabeth II 2018.

11 From *The Graphic*: 'In Japan, 1881: Prince George and the tattooing artist. Everybody was, it seems, tattooed, whether belonging to the ward-room, gun-room, or lower deck, including, of course, both the Princes, a dragon in blue and red writing down the arm being the favourite design.'

12 Letter from the imperial palace inviting the two princes to dinner on 26 ????. Reproduced from the original in the H.M.S. *Bacchante* album (Box 24, Lady Scott Archive, Northamptonshire Record Office) with the kind permission of the Duke of Buccleuch & Queensbury KT KBE.

13 From *The Graphic*, 14 June 1890: 'The Duke and Duchess of Connaught buying furs at Nikko.'

14 Prince Arisugawa Takehito and his suite attending the Diamond Jubilee of Queen Victoria in 1897. From left to right: K. Nabeshima, R. F. Synge (Foreign Office), Itō Hirobumi, R. Funaki, Prince Arisugawa Takehito, Kido Takamasa, T. Saitō, Captain L. A. Beaumont RN, A. Murata, S. Katō. Reproduced with the kind permission of the Japan Society, London.

PART TWO

15 The conferring of the Order of the Garter by Prince Connaught on Emperor Meiji, 20 February 1906 – from a contemporary Japanese print.

16 Cover of the Programme of Entertainment given in honour of His Royal Highness Prince Arthur of Connaught at the Kabukiza, Saturday 24 February 1906.

PART THREE

32 Princess Alexandra during an official visit to Japan in October 1961 photographed on a duck-netting expedition with Prince Hitachi at one of the imperial preserves near Tokyo where a lunch of wild duck and sake was served. Photographer unknown.
33 Ambassador John Pilcher at Haneda airport to welcome Prince Charles on an official visit to Japan, April 1970 in connection with Expo '70 in Osaka. Elizabeth Cortazzi is introduced to Prince Charles (pictured) with Hugh Cortazzi immediately behind her. Photographer unknown.
34 Ambassador John Pilcher introduces Prince Charles to a leading Kabuki actor (*onna-gata*) at the British Embassy, Tokyo, during the Prince's official visit to Japan, April 1970. Photographer unknown.
35 Queen Elizabeth II rides with Emperor Hirohito in the state carriage during the state visit of the Emperor and Empress, May 1971. Photographer unknown.
36 Formal portrait taken during the imperial visit to Britain, May 1971. From left to right: Prince Philip, Duke of Edinburgh, Queen Elizabeth, the Queen Mother, Empress Nagako, Emperor Hirohito, Queen Elizabeth II. Photographer unknown.
37 The Emperor and Empress visiting Kew Gardens. Photographer unknown.
38 The Emperor lays a wreath at the Tomb of the Unknown Warrior, Westminster Abbey, September 1971. Photographer unknown.
39 Emperor Hirohito and Empress Nagako with Queen Elizabeth II and the Duke of Edinburgh before the banquet given by the Queen at the British Embassy, Tokyo, marking the state visit in May 1975. Photographer unknown.
40 The Queen making her address at the banquet she hosted at the British Embassy, Tokyo, during the state visit in May 1975. Photographer unknown.
41 Queen Elizabeth II plants a commemorative oak tree at the Akasaka Detached Palace, Tokyo, during her state visit to Japan in May 1975. The Akasaka Detached Palace is an Imperial Palace in Tokyo, originally built as an official residence for the Crown Prince.at the beginning of the twentieth century. Photographer unknown.
42 The Queen and Duke of Edinburgh watch women divers collecting pearl oysters at the Toba pearl farm, near Ise, Mie Prefecture, during the state visit, May 1975.
43 The Crown Prince and Princess visit Stoke Poges church, scene of Gray's *Elegy Written in a Country Churchyard*, during a visit to Windsor in June 1976.
44 Dressed in miner's overalls and helmet, Crown Prince Akihito visits the Deep Navigation Coal Mine in South Wales, June 1976.
45 The Crown Prince and Princess arriving at Ascot, accompanied by members of the royal family, June 1976.
46 The Crown Prince and Princess attend a dinner at Trinity House, London, given by the Secretary of State for Foreign Affairs Anthony Crosland and his wife, 19 June 1976. Also featured are Sir Hugh and Lady Cortazzi. Photo: FCO.
47 Photograph of Prince Hiro (Naruhito) with Dr Highfield at a lock on the River Thames, 1984, during the time he was studying at Oxford. (Photo: Prince Naruhito). Inset: Prince Hiro attends an event at the University of Essex.
48 Prince Philip, the Duke of Edinburgh, welcomes the Crown Prince and Princess to a reception hosted by Ambassador Cortazzi at the British Embassy, during a visit on behalf of the World Wildlife Fund, November 1982. Photo: H. Cortazzi.

PART ONE

First Encounters: From 1868 to 1902

PETER KORNICKI

INTRODUCTION

THE FIRST EUROPEANS to set foot in Japan were Portuguese traders and missionaries in the middle of the sixteenth century, but more than seventy years were to pass before Britain first came into contact with Japan. In 1613 the East India Company of London opened a trading post in Hirado, which was then a small port in the north-western part of Kyushu, but for various reasons it did not prosper and it was closed down in 1623. From that time until 1854, when the Anglo-Japanese Friendship Treaty was signed, contacts between Britain and Japan were negligible and British officials for the most part considered Japan to be unimportant. It was, therefore, only after 1854 that Britain and Japan began to enjoy formal diplomatic relations. In 1868 the sovereigns of the two countries came into direct communication with each other for the first time and this was followed just one year later by the first meeting between members of the British royal and Japanese imperial families. What had happened since 1850 to make these startling developments possible in such a short space of time?

The Tokugawa shoguns had ruled Japan for more than 250 years when, early in 1868, the last of the shoguns, Tokugawa Yoshinobu (Keiki), informed the imperial court in Kyoto that he was surrendering his powers to the emperor. In this undramatic way, the Bakufu, the government of the Tokugawa shoguns, came to a sudden end. It was not violently overthrown; rather, it had been brought to its knees by a combination of domestic crises and pressure from foreign powers. In 1853, the American Commodore Perry and the Russian Admiral Putyatin had both travelled to Japan to seek access to Japanese ports, and they were followed in 1854 by Admiral James Stirling of Britain. These visits resulted in the conclusion of the Anglo-Japanese Friendship Treaty and similar treaties with the USA and Russia, but these treaties did not permit trade. The treaties did, however, permit foreign diplomatic representatives to reside in Japan and they continued to put pressure upon Japan to allow a trading relationship to develop.

In 1858 the Bakufu took the desperate step of yielding to the pressure applied by the Western powers and signing new treaties with the United States, Russia, Britain, France and the Netherlands which provided for the opening of Japanese ports to trade and foreign residence, low tariffs and a system of extraterritoriality that made foreigners exempt from the provisions of Japanese law. The Bakufu signed the treaties without first securing the formal agreement of the imperial court in Kyoto, a step that had unforeseen consequences. Divided loyalties immediately came into the open: supporters of the Bakufu considered that the might of the Western powers gave Japan no realistic alternative but to sign the treaties, while supporters of the court considered that the Bakufu had overreached itself and pressed the Bakufu to cancel the treaties or to delay their implementation. One of the tactics used by opponents of the Bakufu was to attack foreigners in Japan so as to embarrass the Bakufu in its relations with the foreign powers. These tactics succeeded, and the Bakufu inevitably found itself in increasing difficulties.[1]

The surrender of his powers by the shogun in 1868 was the key moment in what is now called the Meiji Restoration, and it brought the emperor onto the political stage and into the limelight for the first time for many centuries. This happened at a time when there were many more monarchies in the world than there are now. There was an emperor of China, a king of Korea and a tsar of Russia, and more European nations were monarchies than were not. At the time, then, monarchy itself was unremarkable, but the conventions of the European monarchies and the roles they played in international relations were entirely alien to Japan. Consequently, before there could be any thought of royal visits or other contacts with the sovereigns of other nations, the Japanese imperial institution would have to abandon long-established usages and undergo enormous changes. Would it be willing to do so?

For centuries, reigning emperors had been confined to the palace compound in Kyoto. Their material needs were provided for by the Bakufu, but their domain was limited to the court and they had no say whatsoever in the governance of the land. That began to change in 1853, when Commodore Matthew C. Perry, the commander of the US expedition to Japan, submitted a letter to the shogun urging that Japan's isolation be ended and that Japanese ports be opened for the procurement of coal and provisions, and ultimately for trade. Since the letter was backed up by a naval flotilla, the shogun consulted Emperor Kōmei (r. 1846–1867) and his court about the course of action to be followed. In 1854, the Bakufu signed a treaty with the United States and then with Britain, and in 1855 with Russia, but it was the more extensive treaties that were signed in 1858 that did not have the sanction of the court. In due course, foreign merchants began to arrive and foreign communities sprang up in Yokohama, Kobe, Nagasaki and Hakodate.

Emperor Kōmei, who was Emperor Meiji's father, was vigorously opposed to the presence of foreigners on Japanese soil and made no secret of his views. Iwakura Tomomi, one of the leading members of the government, said in 1871 that Kōmei 'would rather have had the whole of Japan burnt into a cinder than that foreigners should be permitted to live on its soil'.[2] From this time onwards, Kōmei and his court began to flex their long-dormant political muscles, to the increasing discomfort of the Bakufu, and it became ever more apparent to the foreign diplomatic representatives in Japan that they were mistaken in assuming that temporal power was the monopoly of the shoguns. The end result, after fifteen years of growing political strife, was the collapse of the Bakufu in 1868 followed by the Meiji Restoration, the formal restitution of power to the emperor.[3]

Emperor Kōmei had in fact died in early 1867, rather conveniently for those who considered that there was no future in anti-foreign sentiments. Indeed, it has frequently been suggested that he was assassinated, but there is no hard evidence.[4] He was succeeded by his son, Mutsuhito, who has posthumously been known as Emperor Meiji. At the beginning of 1868, Meiji was just fifteen years of age, and he had seen little of Japan beyond the court in Kyoto, to say nothing of the world over the seas. In that same year, however, he became the first reigning emperor for two centuries to go far from the precincts of the palace and the first to meet foreigners from beyond East Asia.

Early in January 1868 the foreign envoys resident in Japan received the following message:

> The emperor of Japan announces to the sovereigns of all countries and to their subjects that permission has been granted to the Shōgun Tokugawa Yoshinobu to return the governing power in accordance with his own request [to the emperor].[5]

In this way, the change of regime that we know as the Meiji Restoration first became known to the wider world, but what is significant about this message is that it took the form of an announcement from Emperor Meiji to the sovereigns of all other countries and this, it must be assumed, was a deliberate choice. The implication was that Meiji (or at least his advisors) not only recognised the need to engage with foreign countries but also accepted that Emperor Meiji was no different from other sovereigns. This may seem unremarkable, but the notion that the emperors of Japan were on a par with other sovereigns was anathema to thinkers such as Ōkuni Takamasa (1793–1871): he considered the emperor to be a 'global super-emperor' (*bankoku sōtei*) who was superior to all other monarchs.[6] Ōkuni himself was not against the 'opening' of Japan, for he saw it as the first step in gaining global recognition for the supremacy of the Japanese emperor, but others considered that the imperial palace would be defiled if foreigners were to set foot in it. As the British minister in Japan, Sir Harry Parkes (1828–1885), was to discover later in the year, there were in Kyoto men who were ready to use their swords to prevent such defilement.

The implications of the message issued to the foreign envoys were translated into action in March 1868 when the French and Dutch ministers were granted an audience at the palace in Kyoto. Before that could happen, however, those at court who were dismayed by the idea of the emperor consorting with foreigners had to be brought around or overruled, and it was Iwakura Tomomi whose arguments for change won the day. When the French and Dutch ministers had their audiences, the emperor remained behind a screen, but he did address a few words to them in Japanese. Sir Harry Parkes was to have followed them, but his party were attacked by swordsmen on the way to the Palace, so it was not until April that Parkes, together with Algernon Mitford (1837–1916) as interpreter, had his audience with Meiji. Parkes made sure that the protocol on this occasion followed European practice as closely as possible, for, like most European diplomats, he considered European diplomatic practice to be normative. Diplomatic practice in Europe was based on the Treaty of Vienna of 1815, which posited that all states were to be considered of equal status irrespective of the nature of their system of government. Naturally, Japan was not a signatory to the Treaty of Vienna and it is unlikely that there was anybody in Japan at this time who was familiar with its provisions. Nevertheless, Parkes, like his fellow diplomats from other nations, considered those provisions to be universally applicable and in effect forced them on the Bakufu.[7]

On the occasion of Parkes' audience, Meiji was not behind a screen, so Parkes and Mitford were the first foreigners to have the opportunity to see him face to face. At this stage he was still wearing Japanese dress, his teeth were blackened, and he spoke extremely quietly. It was in this form, then, that the emperor made himself accessible and visible to the foreign envoys, just as every European monarch did, and this was, it must be remembered, in spite of strong currents of opinion in Kyoto that were resolutely opposed to the presence of foreigners in the palace at all.[8]

Other developments in 1868 and subsequent years brought Meiji's public persona closer to that of European monarchs. First of all, he left the palace to travel to Osaka, where he stayed for more than a month and saw the sea for the first time. In 1870 he rode five miles on a horse from the palace to review his troops and was openly visible to the public for the first time; and in 1872 he embarked on the first of six lengthy tours of his country and in this way acquired first-hand familiarity with the geography and social conditions of Japan. For a Japanese emperor, these were unprecedented, but they were a commonplace in European monarchies.[9]

While Emperor Meiji was in Osaka in 1868, Parkes was granted a second audience on 18 May. On this occasion he was accompanied by Vice-Admiral Sir Henry Keppel, who was commander-in-chief of British naval forces in East Asia, and by other naval officers under his command. Parkes took with him two interpreters, Mitford and Ernest Mason Satow (1843–1929), who served as Japanese Secretary to the Legation until 1883. Parkes introduced the members of his suite and placed his letter of credence, which was personally signed by Queen Victoria, in Meiji's hands. This was, of course, a normal part of European diplomatic protocol, but it had the effect of bringing Meiji into direct communication with another monarch for the first time.[10]

Subsequently, after Emperor Meiji moved to Tokyo late in 1868, Parkes had yet another audience with him on 4 January 1869. This convinced Parkes that he had 'succeeded in gaining the confidence of the present government and that the friendship of England is properly appreciated by them'. Parkes also had a conversation with Iwakura Tomomi, who 'acknowledged the support derived by the Mikado's [emperor's] government from England'.[11] Whether Parkes' optimistic assessment was accurate or not, it is clear that he had frequent access to the leaders of the government as well as to the emperor himself. These audiences with Emperor Meiji were routine diplomatic formalities in much of the world, but for Japan they represented a revolutionary change in protocol. The same was true of the exchange of letters with the sovereigns of foreign countries: the first was an exchange initiated by the Austro-Hungarian Emperor Franz-Joseph I in late 1868 with a response from Meiji in 1869. And in 1869 another European practice was adopted when the foreign diplomatic representatives were invited to a reception to mark the emperor's birthday.[12]

Parkes, it should be noted here, was far from alone in referring to the Japanese emperor as the Mikado. The word 'Mikado' is an honorific term for a palace gate and was occasionally used metonymically as an indirect way of referring to the emperor. In English it was evidently popularised as a term for the emperor by Scheuchzer's translation of Engelbert Kaempfer's *History of Japan* (1727) and for some years 'Mikado' remained the standard term used by foreign diplomats and journalists to denote the Emperor Meiji and his predecessors.[13] In Japan, he was either referred to as *Tennō heika* (His Majesty the Emperor) or as *Nihonkoku kōtei* (Emperor of Japan), appropriating the Chinese word for emperor (Ch. *huangdi*, J. *kōtei*), but how to refer to him in English was a problem. Commodore Perry considered that there were two 'emperors' in Japan, one being the Mikado and the other the shogun, and the Anglo-Japanese Friendship Treaty negotiated by Admiral Stirling in 1854 was presented as a treaty between the queen and the emperor of Japan, without making it clear whether the Mikado or the shogun was intended. Later, a report written by a member of the British consular service in 1864, after interviewing three Japanese students in London, used both Mikado and emperor, and when Parkes wrote to the Japanese authorities he used the term emperor as well as Mikado. It seems, then, that the choice of 'emperor' as the word to denote the sovereign of Japan originated outside Japan.[14]

Since *huangdi* was customarily translated as 'emperor' in the Chinese context, it was perhaps inevitable that the same translation would be used in Japan, given that the Chinese term was now being used to denote the Japanese sovereign. The use of 'emperor' in English and 'empereur' in French was consciously adopted by the Japanese government in 1870 and they became standard in the twentieth century. The suitability of this translation has often been debated; it has been suggested that the Japanese term *tennō* be retained, as is the case with the Tsar of Russia, the German Kaiser and the Shah of Iran, and in fact Parkes did occasionally refer to the emperor in this way.[15]

For Japanese, on the other hand, there was a problem about how to refer to Queen Victoria. In accordance with Japanese practice, which avoided use of the reigning emperor's given name, her name was rarely used in Japan and instead she was referred to as 'Eikoku *kōtei*' (emperor/empress of Britain), using the Chinese word for 'emperor'. This had nothing to do with the title of Empress of India which Victoria assumed in 1876, for Parkes had insisted on this appellation ever since 1867 so as to ensure that Queen Victoria was perceived to be of the same high standing as the Japanese emperor.[16] Sometimes she was referred to as *jotei* (woman emperor), but the term *joō* (woman king) was avoided. However, *joō* is now the standard term used for Queen Elizabeth II, while the title used for her male predecessors is *kokuō* (king of the country).[17]

At the time when Parkes was having his audiences with the new emperor in 1868, Queen Victoria had already been on the throne for more than thirty years, ever since her accession in 1837. She was, by the end of 1868, the only reigning woman in Europe, for Queen Isabella II of Spain was deposed in September of that year. Victoria had been married and she had children who would eventually succeed her. By contrast, the most recent woman emperor in Japan was Go-Sakuramachi, who reigned from 1762 to 1770, who never married and who was succeeded by her nephew. The encounter between Britain and Japan in the Meiji period was, therefore, not simply an encounter between two monarchies, but also between one in which a woman was on the throne who was to be succeeded by her eldest son and one which claimed to have an unbroken line of descent through the male line. What is more, it was also an encounter between a nation that was taking its first hesitant steps on the world stage and one that had soundly defeated China in the Opium War and was at the apogee of its global power.

What did Queen Victoria know of Japan? There are a few references to Japan in her published letters and in her journal for this period. In 1858 she noted that Lord Elgin was 'now to proceed to Japan, to see if a Treaty can be negotiated there' and in 1862 that she had talked of Japan with Lord Russell, the foreign secretary.[18] Soon after this conversation, in September 1862, Charles Lenox Richardson, a British merchant who had been based in Shanghai but was passing through Japan on his way home, was cut down and killed by samurai from Satsuma while on a sightseeing trip near Yokohama, and two of his companions were seriously wounded. The queen was evidently informed of these events, and Sir Charles Phipps, who was assisting the queen's private secretary, wrote on her behalf to recommend caution before going to war with Japan over the death of Richardson. 'Her Majesty would be quite ready to agree to measures of reprisal for the protection of her subjects in these distant and wild countries, and to enforce punishment for the savage crimes committed; but the Queen strongly thinks that the opinion of the whole of her Ministers should be ascertained before the country is committed to demand a reparation which the Government of Japan may have no power to enforce.'[19] This last point indicates that she had some understanding of the current power vacuum in Japan, but because attempts to secure reparations and punishment of those responsible were unsuccessful, the Royal Navy bombarded Kagoshima in 1863.

Victoria is said to have regretted the need for these measures, and they doubtless did little to persuade her that Japan was anything other than a 'distant and wild' country. Throughout the troubled 1860s, she received memoranda from the Foreign Office, the confidential Foreign Office prints, summaries of despatches from Japan, and some decrypted telegrams. If she had read all of this she would indeed have been well informed about contemporary Japan, but there are no comments written on the papers she received, and it is unclear if she paid them much attention.[20]

The first Japanese person that Queen Victoria met was Tokugawa Akitake, the younger half-brother of the shogun, when he came for an audience on 4 December 1867. The opinions she confided to her diary were unfavourable and dismissive: 'an ugly little youth of 16, with his black hair combed back and tied up in a sort of chignon. He wore a long petticoat, belt and sword, and sandals on his feet'.[21] Although she showed no interest in Japan, Victoria was kept apprised of events: she was present, for example, when the Privy Council approved the removal of references to the Tycoon (i.e. shogun) in treaties and state papers and their replacement by the word Mikado, a change that recognised the political changes that had taken place in Japan.[22]

Queen Victoria's journals and published letters contain no other references to Japan in the 1860s, and do not even mention the visit of her second son, Prince Alfred, to Japan in 1869. It is certain, however, that she knew of the success of this visit, for Prime Minister Gladstone later wrote to the Foreign Office as follows:

> The Queen is not very well today but I think she gave me sufficient authority to approve of your sending a complimentary message of acknowledgement to the Mikado of Japan. The terms may deserve some consideration. This opening of the door to friendly intercourse is an event of some importance. … it would be a very good thing to have some intelligent Japanese here, and to use them liberally on the part of the country [i.e. treat them generously].[23]

Gladstone may well have stretched his interpretation of the queen's response to his report, as he himself implies, but his wish to send an appreciative message to the emperor reflects his sense of the importance of developing a closer relationship with Japan. Earlier that same year Parkes had sent notification to London of the emperor's marriage and the foreign secretary instructed him 'to convey Her Majesty's cordial congratulations on this occasion'.[24]

In Japan, on the other hand, the shoguns had been kept well aware of current events in Europe by means of the annual reports which they required the Dutch East India Company to provide. In the 1840s these mentioned the fact that the 'king of England' had been succeeded by his daughter Victoria and gave detailed information about the Opium War and the Treaty of Nanking signed by Victoria and the Emperor of China.[25] How much of the information which the Bakufu acquired in this way actually percolated through to the court in Kyoto is uncertain, but probably very little until the 1860s. When Lord Elgin visited Japan in 1858 in order to negotiate a trade treaty, he took with him a steam yacht which was presented to the shogun as a gift from Queen Victoria, and the Treaty of Yedo that resulted from his visit was one between the Queen and the 'Tycoon'; it was also to the Queen that the shogun wrote in 1861 and 1862 when seeking a delay in the opening of the treaty ports.[26]

Did the court in Kyoto have knowledge of these matters? Probably not. Some members of the court may have read a history of England published under the title *Eikokushi* in 1861, which started with Queen Victoria's family tree and thus made it obvious that the reigning sovereign was a woman.[27] By 1866, however, this fact was certainly common knowledge, for it was in that year that Fukuzawa Yukichi's *Conditions in the West* (*Seiyō jijō*) was first published. This extremely popular book was based on his travels to America and Europe in 1860 and 1862, and the section on British history ends with an unequivocal statement that the current British monarch was a queen by the name of Victoria.[28] So when Sir Harry Parkes presented his credentials in 1868, it cannot have come as a surprise to Meiji and his court that they came from Queen Victoria. Indeed, Parkes' intention was to impress upon them 'a just sense of the rank and dignity of the Queen and also of the power of the nation which is the first to offer to Japan this proof of friendship'.[29]

It is not clear when Emperor Meiji first saw a likeness of the queen. It may not have been until 1882, when a portrait was presented to him by Parkes. The portrait seems to have been a copy of one that had been made somewhat earlier, before the death of the prince consort, and it was sent out to Japan with Parkes when he was returning from home leave as a gesture of thanks for the hospitality rendered to the queen's grandsons when they visited Japan in 1881.[30]

What did Japanese make of Queen Victoria? The members of the Bakufu mission of 1862 were unable to meet her owing to the fact that she was still in mourning for Prince Albert, who had died the previous year. The first Japanese supposed to have seen her were members of a group of Bakufu students who went to the theatre in the West End in Japanese dress early in 1867 and reported that the queen was present. However, they were most likely mistaken, for no visit by the queen to any theatre is recorded in the court pages of *The Times* in 1867. It is probable that they saw either Princess Beatrice, who was at the Olympic Theatre on 8 March, or a party consisting of Princess Louise, Prince Arthur and Prince Leopold, who were at the Lyceum Theatre on the same day.[31]

Later that year, a troupe of Japanese performers were presented to the Prince of Wales and then performed at Windsor Castle before several of the queen's children. The first Japanese to be presented to the queen was Tokugawa Akitake, as mentioned above. He had travelled to France leading the official delegation to the Exposition Internationale in Paris in 1867, and in the course of his travels he met Napoleon III, King William III of the Netherlands, King Victor Emmanuel II of Italy and King Leopold II of Belgium. He also visited England and was presented to the queen on 4 December 1867 along with figures described as 'the Minister Plenipotentiary of Japan in Paris', and the 'Chamberlain of the Tycoon'.[32]

There is no sign that either the old or the new rulers of Japan were surprised that a woman reigned over what was then one of the most powerful nations in the world. No members of the Japanese imperial family met the queen until Prince Higashi-Fushimi was granted an audience in 1871, and there are few traces left to indicate the level of knowledge and interest in the queen before that. Members of the government may have had their first sense of the role that the queen played in Britain when, on 23 May 1868, several high-ranking Japanese were invited by Vice-Admiral Keppel to a celebration of the queen's birthday (which was actually on 24 May) on board HMS *Rodney*.[33] Most of them probably shared the puzzlement of Nakamura Masanao (1832–1891), a Confucian scholar who studied in Britain from 1866 to 1868 and later translated Samuel Smiles' *Self-Help* into Japanese. He commented that the *Illustrated treatise on the maritime kingdoms* (*Haiguo tuzhi*), a Chinese work that was widely read in Japan in the 1850s for the information it provided about the rest of the world, 'had not prepared him to understand how such a tiny nation, let alone one ruled by a woman, could have humbled the Middle Kingdom in war'.[34]

By contrast, much more information about Japan was available in contemporary Britain, both in the form of published books and in the form of articles in popular journals such as the *Illustrated London News* and *The Graphic*. Nevertheless, Mutsuhito/Meiji was unheard of in Britain when he ascended the throne in 1867, and for many years he was consistently referred to simply as the Mikado, both in diplomatic despatches and in the press. The *Illustrated London News* published in 1872 an engraving showing the emperor, in traditional court attire, arriving at Yokohama station from Shinbashi to inaugurate the first railway in Japan, but there was no image of his facial appearance available to the British public until March 1875, when *The Graphic* published an article on 'The Mikado and the Empress of Japan' and included engravings based on photographs.[35]

When Parkes presented his credentials to Emperor Meiji in 1868, it was an act that was unremarkable from the point of view of European diplomacy. For Japan, however, and particularly for the new government and for Meiji himself, it marked a dramatic shift. Just one year later Meiji came face to face for the first time with a member of a foreign royal family when Queen Victoria's second son visited Japan, and the prospect of this encounter forced the new government to make some difficult decisions about Meiji's public status as a monarch. John Breen has remarked that 'imperial audiences granted to British and other diplomats in the 1860s and 1870s were of definitive importance in the creation of the Meiji monarch in all his complexity', and face to face meetings with other royals were similarly instrumental in creating the public persona of the emperor.[36] For this reason, that first visit by Queen Victoria's son merits close examination and will be the subject of the next section. While that visit has already attracted some attention from Japanese scholars, the same cannot be said of the first lengthy visit of a member of the Japanese imperial family to Britain, that of Prince Higashi-Fushimi, who resided in Britain in the early 1870s: his visit will be the subject of the third section. Later sections will deal with subsequent visits by British royals to Japan and by members of the imperial family to Britain, albeit in rather less detail.

THE VISIT OF THE DUKE OF EDINBURGH IN 1869

The first member of the British royal family to visit Japan was Prince Alfred Ernest Albert (1844–1900), and he was in fact the first member of any foreign royal family to set foot in Japan. Prince Alfred was the second son and the fourth child of Queen Victoria and Prince Albert, and until 1864 he was second in line to the throne behind his elder brother, Edward Prince of Wales, who finally succeeded to the throne in 1901 as Edward VII. In 1866, Prince Alfred had been given the title of Duke of Edinburgh, so it was by this title that he was known while he was in Japan and for many years afterwards until, in 1893, he succeeded his uncle, Ernest II, as the reigning Duke of Saxe-Coburg and Gotha, a duchy in the German Empire.

The proposed visit of the Duke of Edinburgh to Japan forced the new Meiji government to confront some difficult problems. What was at issue was how the young emperor would be presented to foreign royal families and the terms on which any face-to-face encounters would take place. In the event, the visit proved satisfying to all parties, and it undoubtedly paved the way for closer relations between Britain and Japan and their royal families up to the end of the Meiji period and beyond. Some of the personal connections that were made in 1869 lasted for decades and were revived on subsequent royal visits.

In 1858, Prince Alfred (hereafter referred to as the duke) joined the Royal Navy at the age of fourteen. In January 1867, at the absurdly young age of twenty-three, he was promoted to the rank of Captain and was given command of HMS *Galatea*, which left Plymouth later that month for a voyage around the world. The *Galatea*, launched in 1859, was a 26-gun steam frigate with a substantial crew of 530 officers, seamen, boys and marines: since the duke lacked sufficient naval experience, it is probable that the effective command of the ship lay in the hands of Commander Edward Stanley Adeane (1836–1902), who was promoted on the duke's recommendation at the end of the voyage and later became an admiral.[37]

The *Galatea* called in first at Cape Town and then went on to Australia. The duke was the first member of the royal family to visit the several Australian colonies, which in 1901 were to combine to form the Commonwealth of Australia. His long stay in Melbourne resulted in negative newspaper comments about his ill-concealed boredom with ceremonial and particularly about what one called his 'record of immorality'. He later travelled on to Sydney, where, on 12 March 1868, a disturbed Irishman with strong nationalist sympathies fired a gun at his back. Extraordinarily, the bullet missed all his vital organs. Having recovered from his injuries, he resumed command of his ship and returned to England in June 1868.[38] In November, the *Galatea* set out again to complete its voyage around the world, and in the course of it the duke became the first member of the royal family to visit both New Zealand and Japan. The *Galatea* reached Yokohama on 29 August 1869 and stayed in Japanese waters for a little over a month before departing for China.[39]

The duke's arrival in Japan did not, of course, come as a surprise to the Japanese government, for in April 1869 Sir Harry Parkes, the British minister in Japan (the post was only upgraded to ambassador in 1905), had informed the new Meiji government that the duke would be visiting Japan. It was by no means a foregone conclusion, however, that the Meiji government would treat him as an official visitor, particularly since the government was beset with pressing problems. In a letter to his wife on 25 June, Parkes wrote:

> It is not yet settled whether his reception at Yedo will be a private or official one. In the latter case he would be the Mikado's guest. I shall accept that arrangement if the Mikado would treat him properly as an equal, but unless this can be arranged it would be better that his visit should be private. At Peking it is already so arranged [i.e. that the visit would be private].[40]

The biggest problem confronting the Japanese government at this time was the continuing conflict with the supporters of the defunct Bakufu, who had established themselves in Hokkaido. That conflict did not come to an end until the last days of June, so the government had to deal with the prospect of a royal visit at a time when its survival was not yet assured.

The news of the proposed visit provoked vigorous debate in the Japanese government over the question of exposing the emperor to foreign royalty. Parkes reported as follows:

> About two months have intervened since I first spoke of the Prince's visit … but in the meantime no small amount of discussion has taken place among the Japanese ministers and nobles as to the manner in which this visit should be noticed by the Mikado. The progressive party maintained that the reception by His Majesty should conform as far as the circumstances of Japan would permit to the usages of other nations; while their opponents were as ready to denounce as injurious to the Mikado's dignity any advance on His Majesty's part that could be regarded as an admission of equal rank between a Foreign Prince of the Blood Royal and the Imperial and Heavenly descended family of Japan.[41]

Later, Parkes reported what he had heard from Iwakura, namely that 'the reception of the Prince had caused the government much anxious consideration' but that '[a]n intelligent majority of the advisers of the Mikado had … seen that the occasion was one that should be profited by to mark their friendly feelings towards Foreign Powers, and their readiness to promote more intimate relations with them although at a sacrifice of old ideas and usages'. It 'afforded them gratification', Iwakura said, 'to feel that these compliments would be paid in the first instance to an English Prince, and would form therefore some acknowledgement of the various proofs they had received of the goodwill of England and Her Majesty's Government'.[42]

No documents appear to survive that would enable us to trace these internal government debates, but from Parkes' account it seems that there was a conflict between the views of Iwakura and others who were open to engagement with the West and the views of others who could not accept the idea of parity between the emperor of Japan and other sovereigns. At any rate, it was two full months before the government finally reached a decision, which is perhaps some indication of the division of opinion which the proposed visit provoked.

Finally, on 15 July, Date Munenari (1818–1892), the foreign minister, informed Parkes as follows:

> His Majesty the Emperor having been apprised that your honourable country's Prince, on his tour to the many countries of the East, also intends visiting Japan, has been delighted beyond measure; and although our country can offer but poor hospitality, His Majesty would be intensely pleased if your Prince would consent to take up his abode in the gardens of Hama-go-ten, the seaside palace of His Majesty.[43]

From this it was clear that the government had decided to treat this as a state visit. In fact, a very similar draft of this communication survives which shows that, two months before it was sent, the broad outlines of the foreign minister's response were already fixed, but a note attached to this draft makes it clear that there were objections from some quarters and so there was a postponement while more discussions took place.[44]

What role the young Emperor Meiji himself had played in the debates is unclear. Delight is attributed to him, but that may have been no more than a rhetorical device to undermine any remaining opposition to the visit. At any rate, the letter sent to Parkes was couched in terms of monarchical friendliness and must have reassured Parkes. Equally reassuring must have been the set of regulations issued by the government, which indicated how seriously it was taking the visit.[45]

Parkes had undoubtedly put pressure on the government that it was not in a position to resist. At the same time, however, it was true that the government saw definite advantages accruing from the visit and therefore decided to put every effort into ensuring it was a success, without begrudging substantial expenditure at a time when the new government's finances were still in a parlous state. In the long run, that decision can be seen to have formed the foundation stone of a closer relationship between Britain and Japan.

What was the 'seaside palace' that was to serve as the duke's home in Tokyo? The Hamagoten had been the property of the Tokugawa shoguns, but it began functioning as a detached palace for the emperor after he moved to Edo (Tokyo) in 1868, and he stayed there at the end of 1868 and on several occasions in 1869.[46] In 1867, a stone building had been constructed in the grounds of the Hamagoten to serve as the headquarters of the Bakufu's navy, and this was now adapted to become the official guest house, which was to be used by the duke in the first instance. Work was undertaken straight away to make it suitable, resulting in an amalgam of Japanese and Western styles of architecture. The newly refurbished structure was named the Enryōkan, meaning 'building to welcome people from afar', and it remained in use until 1890, when it was torn down. The Hamagoten was later taken over as an imperial detached palace and the site is now known as the Hama Rikyū Gardens: it is bordered by highways and overlooked by tall buildings, but in 1869 it was a secluded spot with extensive gardens and it faced onto the open sea.[47]

The government wished to make every effort to make the Enryōkan comfortable for the duke, and for this purpose enlisted the help of Algernon Mitford, who was later ennobled as Baron Redesdale and was the grandfather of the Mitford sisters. He had been serving as second secretary at the British Legation since 1866 and, owing to his command of Japanese, he had a key role to play in the visit. He moved into the Enryōkan for a month and, since he was to act as interpreter, he was coached in court language and etiquette for the duke's audience with the emperor. He also helped the government to procure furniture and other items, including thirty-two cases of wines and spirits, considered 'necessary to European ideas of comfort'. As Parkes acknowledged, this put the government to no small expense, but he expected the government to meet the entire cost of the visit. Just how big an expense all this was is clear from correspondence between the Foreign Ministry and the fledgling Ministry of Finance, which was severely short of money and found it difficult to produce the necessary cash for the purchases. The wares of the furniture dealers of Hong Kong had, in Mitford's view, 'a strong flavour of Tottenham Court Road', but the acquisition of the very considerable amount of furniture needed proved to be very profitable for the British merchants in Yokohama. Many of the internal decorations were Japanese, however, including paintings executed by Kanō Shōsen'in Tadanobu (1823–1879) which alone cost the government 12,000 *ryō* (equivalent to about £250,000 in 2018), but in the eyes of Mitford, the European furniture 'jarred piteously with the imaginative poetry of the Japanese artists'.[48]

For the finished state of the Enryōkan we can turn to a description by John William Ramsay (1847–1887), who was later to serve as equerry to the Duke of Edinburgh from 1874 to 1876 and to succeed his father as 13th Earl of Dalhousie in 1880. He was serving as a lieutenant on the *Galatea* and had the chance to explore the Enryōkan just before the duke arrived:

> The house was certainly provided with every convenience, baths (of wood) and bathrooms etc. about a dozen altogether, bedrooms large lofty and airy with large iron bedsteads, hard beds with white mosquito curtains and the floors with Japanese bamboo matting looking altogether very nice and cool.

He was particularly impressed by the duke's suite of rooms and the reception rooms:

> [They] were very gorgeous indeed – magnificent carpets, lacquer tables and cabinets and the walls covered with beautiful fantastic Japanese paintings on the paper representing different scenes; the dining room for instance was covered with illustrations of the national sport – hawking; the drawing room with fans of every possible pattern and design and in every degree of shut and open.[49]

It was clear to him that a great deal of effort had gone into the preparation of a comfortable place for the duke and his party to stay whilst they were in Tokyo.

Until almost the last moment, however, Parkes remained cautious. As he reported to the Foreign Secretary:

> I have carefully refrained from asking for any particular mode of reception, but have simply observed that while one of a public character would doubtless be regarded by the Queen and the people of England as a proof of good feeling on the part of the Mikado and Japan I must reserve to His Royal Highness the liberty of making his visit to Japan in a private form if he saw reason to do so, and to myself the right of advising His Royal Highness to decline any proposals in regard to ceremonial that might appear to me to be derogatory to the Prince's rank. The details of the reception still remain to be considered, but looking to the innovations which such an event involves in some of the most deeply cherished ideas of this singularly constituted Court and people, I have much reason to be satisfied with the friendly attention which has been given to the subject and the liberality of sentiment which has apparently guided the decision. At an entertainment given me by the Hosho or Prime Minister [i.e. Iwakura] on the 24th Instant, he assured me that it was the wish of the Mikado and his Government to make such arrangements as should mark their own good feeling towards England and also promote friendship between the two countries.[50]

It gradually became clear that his anxieties were misplaced, and in the end he was extremely satisfied with the reception accorded the duke.

What we would term security was also a concern. It is not directly addressed in the surviving British documents, but Iwakura and others were well aware that there was simmering disquiet in some quarters about the warm reception to be accorded the duke at the palace.[51] Anti-foreign feeling had, after all, been running high in recent memory: in 1867, two British sailors from the sloop HMS *Icarus* had been cut down by Japanese swordsmen. Anti-foreign agitation had by no means abated after the formation of the new government, for in 1868 eleven French sailors were killed in Sakai. By July 1869, Parkes was satisfied that the threat in Yokohama had abated and the foreign guards which had been stationed there since May were withdrawn, but elsewhere the threat persisted. In 1869, Parkes and other Britons had been intimidated by armed men and several Frenchmen had actually been attacked, and throughout the period during which the duke's visit was being discussed by the government, Parkes and the other envoys were constantly pressing the government to take decisive action to safeguard the lives of foreigners in Japan.[52] Towards the end of September, when Parkes was returning, accompanied by armed guards, from the foreign minister's office in Tokyo, a samurai swung his sword at him: this case, he complained, 'furnishes another example of the danger resulting from the custom which permits so large and unreliable a class to carry with them at all times deadly weapons, which they are ready to use at any moment in satisfaction of revenge, animosity, or caprice'.[53]

In the light of all these attacks, and of the duke's recent ordeal in Sydney, it is perhaps remarkable that neither Parkes nor the duke flinched and abandoned the idea of a state visit. An attack would have been an embarrassment that the new government had no need of, so they took appropriate measures. A proclamation was made to the inhabitants of Tokyo that an English prince was coming to Japan and that the government would receive him 'according to the custom observed between friendly countries'. 'Let everyone', the proclamation concluded, 'from the highest to the lowest, bear this in mind, and be careful not to act in an offensive manner.'[54] Security at Hamagoten was tightened by forbidding entrance to anybody without a permit issued by the Foreign Office, and whenever the duke and his party left their quarters at the Enryōkan they were accompanied by thirty-two samurai as well as by twenty-five Royal Marine guards.[55] Perhaps thanks to these precautions, the visit passed off without incident.

Another issue was the question of flags. The Japanese Foreign Ministry was aware that it was the custom on the occasion of foreign visits to put the two flags side by side as a symbol of the friendly relations between the two nations. On this occasion the Royal Standard would be raised at the Enryōkan but, as the Foreign Ministry observed, the Imperial Flag had hitherto been kept secret (a rather delicate way of saying that there had been no such thing as an Imperial Flag before this) so one would have to be made and raised on this occasion. A suitable flag was designed, with a sixteen-petalled chrysanthemum in the centre, for use on such occasions.[56] Thus once again it was European customs that dictated the practice to be followed in Japan.

The *Galatea* reached Yokohama on 29 August and on that very day the Foreign Minister, Date Munenari, came down from Tokyo and 'in the name of His Majesty the Mikado invited His Royal Highness to visit Yedo [Tokyo] as the guest of His Majesty'.[57] The duke landed privately the next day for lunch with Parkes and then for a ride along 'Curio Street' with Vice-Admiral Keppel, where he selected some things to be put aside and purchased later, just like any other globetrotter visiting Japan at the time.[58] He landed in state on 31 August, and 'after the usual salutes, levées, addresses and all the other wearinesses of which loyalty is capable', as Mitford put it, he took lunch in the Legation. These 'wearinesses' included a loyal address signed by around 250 Britons living in Yokohama, which was proclaimed and then presented to the duke: this was roughly half of the British population of Yokohama at the time.[59] The following day he was driven up the Tōkaidō to the Hamagoten in Tokyo in a carriage provided by the imperial household with a mounted escort.

While staying in the Enryōkan, the prince was visited by some of the leading figures of the day, including Prince Sanjō Sanetomi, Iwakura Tomomi and

Ōkubo Toshimichi. He was also greeted by the brother of Tokugawa Akitake: Akitake had been presented to Queen Victoria in 1867 and was now Prince of Mito but was unable to come to Tokyo for some reason. The duke was informed of the gratitude of the Japanese government for the kind reception accorded to Akitake while he was in England. This was a remarkable sign of some of the continuities between the old regime and the new and of the speedy rehabilitation of figures associated with the Bakufu.[60]

Without doubt the high point of the visit was the audience with Emperor Meiji in the palace on 4 September. Charles Beresford (1846–1919), who was serving as a sub-lieutenant on the *Galatea* and was to rise to the rank of admiral, recorded that, 'All along the route the upper windows of the houses were sealed with paper, so that none should look down upon the royal visitor'. Security was tight, too. As Ramsay recorded:

> [Japanese guards] marched in twos by the side of the procession and along the whole length of it. A formidable body altogether and sufficient to guard against any ordinary attack, to say nothing of the revolvers carried by nearly every one of our party.

He recalled that Parkes had said, 'Of course there is not the slightest danger of any attack being made, but you see you never can tell when a small body of fanatics may not rush out from the crowd and do a good deal of mischief in a very short space of time.' Parkes had then added that his party had been attacked before on the way to meet the emperor, 'so you see you never know in this country what the next minute may bring forth'.[61]

When the duke was about to enter the palace grounds, a purification ceremony was conducted. Parkes did not object to this, but the American minister in Japan reported that the ceremony was performed because 'all foreigners, whether of noble lineage or common, are alike impure as animals', and Fukuzawa Yukichi considered that it was a regrettable concession to anti-foreign elements in the government.[62] Once the duke had entered the palace, he first had a formal audience with the emperor: he was attended by Parkes, Vice-Admiral Keppel and Mitford, who was acting as interpreter. This select group were then joined by Beresford and five others. 'I remember', Beresford noted, 'the dim figure of a young man seated behind a screen at the end of the audience chamber'. The *Japan Times* reported that 'The Emperor received the Prince [duke] … on perfectly equal terms' and declared that when Mitford translated the duke's remarks into Japanese it was the first time that Meiji had heard Japanese spoken by a foreigner.[63] As Mitford put it, 'East and West were sharply defined. There were no cocked hats or gold-laced coats among the Japanese of those days. The Emperor and all his court were living pictures out of the dark centuries.'[64]

The informal part of the audience was held in the Waterfall-viewing Pavilion in the Fukiage Gardens. The emperor and the duke sat on either side of a small table and tea was served; Mitford was there to interpret, and Parkes and Keppel were in attendance. The official programme of this part of the visit reads:

> The Commissioners will then conduct His Royal Highness [the duke] to the garden, where he will rest in the maple tea-house.
>
> The Mikado will proceed to the waterfall pavilion.
>
> The Commissioners will conduct His Royal Highness from the maple tea-house to the waterfall pavilion, where the Prime Minister will await His Royal Highness in the verandah.
>
> After the exchange of compliments, His Majesty and His Royal Highness will sit down. Tea and sweetmeats will be served.

The planning was clearly meticulous, and Mitford's detailed account of the proceedings which Parkes sent back to London shows that a great deal of care and thought had been given to this first encounter between a Japanese emperor and a member of a foreign royal family.[65]

According to Mitford's account, possibly based on notes he kept at the time, after initial courtesies had been exchanged, Emperor Meiji said that there were doubtless shortcomings in the reception accorded the duke. In reply, the duke said that 'far from being dissatisfied with the reception, it had exceeded his expectations', which was probably true. The conversation continued as follows:

> It had long been his desire [the duke said] to visit a country of which he had heard so much, and in the realization of this wish he had certainly not been disappointed. It was an additional pleasure to him to have this opportunity of congratulating the Mikado upon the personal resumption of the power which he had inherited from his ancestors. It would be highly gratifying to Her Majesty the Queen to learn that the troubles of last year had been succeeded by the restoration of peace. The Mikado stated that, during the disturbed period through which the country had passed, his Government had received the greatest assistance from the advice and counsels of Sir Harry Parkes, and he was glad to take so important an occasion of acknowledging his debt of gratitude, in order that the expression of his thanks might be conveyed to Her Majesty the Queen. He begged His Highness to deliver this message to Her Majesty.[66]

Before taking his leave, the duke placed in Meiji's hands a diamond-encrusted snuff box as a gift.

Although the conversation was largely conventional, it is significant that Meiji wished to convey a message to the queen and that he expressed his appreciation of the role that Parkes had played in recent events. As Parkes reported later, this first contact between the royal family and the Japanese imperial family had passed off very well and had greater significance than a meeting between two individuals. Ōkubo Toshimichi, one of the leading members of the government, wrote in his diary that the whole business had caused a great deal of anxiety but that he was enormously relieved that all had gone extraordinarily smoothly. There can be no doubt that relations between the British royal family and the imperial family of Japan had got off to a very good start, although all was not to run smoothly in later years.[67]

No photographs were taken of the audience, but the meeting in the Waterfall-viewing Pavilion was at least captured in a watercolour by Nicholas Chevalier (Pl. 4) which shows the waterfall and the setting but does not show the emperor or the duke in any detail. This was presumably because, like most of the other Britons present, he was obliged to keep his distance, but perhaps also because in his paintings he was accustomed to give more prominence to the natural surroundings than to the figures. After the meeting in the Waterfall-viewing Pavilion, there were entertainments inside the palace, including a performance by blind musicians, which was also captured in an oil painting by Chevalier.[68] Nicholas Chevalier (1828–1902) was an artist of mixed Swiss-Russian parentage who had been working in Australia and New Zealand since 1855. In 1869 he was invited by the duke to join the *Galatea* as an artist in Sydney and he remained on board as far as Ceylon (Sri Lanka), producing more than 100 drawings and watercolours, before proceeding independently to England.[69]

John Ramsay, who attended the audience in the Palace, adds a few further details. On arrival at the Palace, the party was conducted into a waiting room and offered tea, but not of a kind he was used to:

> The tea was of a dark olive green colour whipped up till it was all frothy on the top and stronger than any you *could* make in England. The aroma was quite strong several yards off.

Ramsay's comments on the emperor's appearance are unflattering but he seems to have had some sympathy for the restraints under which the emperor lived:

> Riding exercise agrees with the Mikado; he is said to have grown large and muscular and to have enjoyed better health since he took it up. Poor beggar! he *must* have been a wretched object to look at formerly. He is now a youth of 19 or 20

> about my height, tall for a Japanese, ugly, with a pale expressionless parchment face, who looked as if he never could have laughed in his life and never would.[70]

According to Ramsay, when the duke sat down with the emperor in the Waterfall-viewing Pavilion he was the first man ever to have sat in the emperor's presence.

According to the report in *The Times*, the duke 'devoted the rest of his stay to seeing Jeddo', as many continued to refer to Tokyo. As Charles Beresford recalled, 'We were entertained with the most delicate and sumptuous hospitality.' Conjurers, acrobats and sumō wrestlers performed for them at the Enryōkan, and there was also a special performance of Nō and Kyōgen in the residence of the daimyo of Kii in Akasaka. In the palace grounds they saw a display of armed combat, and this hugely impressed John Ramsay:

> There were about 30 couples who performed for our amusement. ... The manner in which they wielded their two-handed weapons [bamboo swords] was quite astonishing, jumping about and yelling defiance like mad creatures ... One thing I am positive of – no European with a European sword would stand a chance in single combat against these Japanese with their long sharp heavy swords wielded with the amazing dexterity which I saw today.

They also went to see 'the tombs of the Tycoons' at the Kan'eiji temple, and had a Japanese dinner, sitting on mats, eating fish with chopsticks and drinking saké.[71]

Just before the duke's departure from Tokyo, Iwakura paid him a visit and gave him a poem composed and written by the emperor in his own hand, which, as Parkes pointed out, was a very rare honour. Meanwhile the *Galatea*, along with two other British warships, had sailed up to Tokyo Bay and on 8 September the duke went on board in the company of the Japanese minister of war and other senior members of the government. The minister of war at the time was Prince Higashi-Fushimi, who was himself to spend several years in Britain in the early 1870s. He spent a couple of hours on board and then disembarked, but Foreign Minister Date Munenari and his deputy stayed on board as the *Galatea* made its way down to Yokohama.[72]

The *Galatea* spent a week in Yokohama, where the British legation became the focus of the duke's social life. The legation had originally been located in the Tōzenji temple in the Takanawa district of Edo, but as a result of several attacks perpetrated by anti-foreign fanatics it was relocated to Yokohama and remained there until the 1870s when the site of the present embassy opposite the palace was purchased. The duke seems to have spent his time in Yokohama shopping and attending formal dinners: the main event was a gala dinner followed by a ball at the British legation, which was attended by Prince Higashi-Fushimi and the foreign minister. It may well be that it was these frequent meetings with the Duke of Edinburgh that encouraged Prince Higashi-Fushimi to think of travelling to Britain, and it was certainly true that his acquaintance with the duke stood him in good stead while he was resident in Britain.

On 13 September, Felice Beato (1832–1909), an experienced photographer who had moved to Japan in 1863, took a group photograph of Prince Higashi-Fushimi, Parkes, Keppel and others who had been at the audience with emperor.[73] Little is known of the duke's other activities in Yokohama, but the *Japan Times* gave a glimpse of his private life there.

> ... according to His Royal Highness' own account, that part of his stay amongst us which he most thoroughly enjoyed was the social intercourse, unrestrained by state trammels or official ceremony, which he was able to hold with some of his old friends in the Navy and his new acquaintances ashore. He seemed to visit the Club, particularly the bowling alley, as often as he possibly could, and in the freedom of that apartment and in the supper room afterwards, showed qualities that must endear him to his private friends, as much as his courtesy and modest dignity make him welcome in public.[74]

This accords to some extent with what we know of how he spent his time in Australia.

On 16 September, the *Galatea* left Yokohama for Hiogo (Kobe), where the duke and his party stayed for two days. On the first they were received by the governor and went for a walk in the country, and on the second they visited Osaka and entertained the governor and the British consul to dinner on the *Galatea*. From Kobe the *Galatea* proceeded to Nagasaki, where the duke had a warm welcome from the Dutch on Deshima as well as from the British community. The foreign settlement was lit up in his honour: 'From Decima [Deshima] downwards ran a perfect sea of lanterns; up hill and down dale there was but one glare of light, bright and coloured according to the hue of the material employed.' The duke did not visit Kyoto: this was probably because sightseeing was not as important a consideration as it was for later British visitors, and perhaps also because the largest British communities were in Kobe/Osaka and Nagasaki, while Kyoto was not yet open to foreign residence. The duke's visit to Japan came to an end on 26 September when he left Nagasaki for China, which he visited in a private capacity.[75]

During the voyage, the duke wrote regularly to his mother and in this way the queen was kept informed of his experiences in Japan. Like many other European visitors, he found Japan 'quaint' and was hard pressed to put his impressions on paper:

> To give you my account of this country I feel quite at a loss. Every thing is so new and so quaint that I am quite bewildered. … the palace I am now living in, which has been filled up in half European half Japanese style, that is to say European furniture and the walls painted 'à la Japonaise'. Unfortunately the whole of yesterday and today as also Tuesday it has been raining hard so that I have not been able to see much. Tomorrow I go to be presented to the Mikado who has only very recently been allowed to see a soul but his personal attendants.[76]

Even after he had left Japan, he was still lost for words except when it came to scenery:

> It would be perfectly impossible for me to describe Yeddo or indeed any other town in Japan in a letter it is too utterly different from anything I have seen before, so I must wait till I get home and explain it all to you with the pictures and photos which I have collected. I remained a week in Yeddo altogether in the charming little palace I was staying at. In the grounds all the different sports and games which the Japanese practise were shown us as well as jugglers and conjurors which they are famous for. … The scenery in the Inland Sea is most beautiful. … Nagasaki is the most picturesque town in Japan that I have seen, a long narrow entrance with a splendid harbour surrounded by high hills up the sides of which the town is built.[77]

It is clear, though, that he appreciated the lengths to which the Japanese court and government had gone to welcome him to Japan:

> My visit to Pekin will be quite a private one as the Chinese I believe have refused to receive me, quite the reverse of the Japanese Govt w[hic]h rec[eive]d me with the greatest civility and attention.[78]

The official British reaction to the duke's reception was highly favourable. At the end of September, Parkes wrote to the Japanese Foreign Minister to express the 'high satisfaction afforded him by the friendly and liberal spirit in which every arrangement connected with the reception of His Royal Highness by the Japanese Government was carried out.' He added that he was 'satisfied that Her Majesty the Queen will hear with gratification of this proof of friendship on the part of His Majesty the Emperor and will earnestly unite in the wish expressed by His Majesty that this visit of the Prince, Her son, may have the effect of promoting a cordial and beneficial intimacy between Great Britain and Japan.'[79] In the eyes of Parkes, the success of the visit clearly held out the prospect of real diplomatic benefits. It should also be mentioned, however, that the costs were entirely met by the Japanese government: these included expenses related to the carriages and horses procured from Hong Kong and Shanghai for the duke's visit, for which Parkes presented a request for repayment of the very considerable sum of $1092 to cover forage and the wages of grooms.[80]

At the same time, Parkes reported to the British foreign secretary that the duke had been 'entirely satisfied with the cordial feeling which was shown towards him'. He was, Parkes was relieved to note, 'received by the Mikado on a footing of entire equality'. The significance of the visit, Parkes considered, lay in the proof it provided not only of the commitment of the new government to abandon the 'long cherished system of isolation' but also of willingness 'to conduct their foreign intercourse according to the rules which obtain among Western Powers', for Emperor Meiji had been brought into 'direct and personal communication with a member of one of the leading Royal families of Europe'.[81] Parkes' satisfaction was complete, but it was based on a sense that British conventions had triumphed. He was satisfied, in other words, that Japan had decided to follow the rules of European diplomacy that he had been constantly pressing Japan to adhere to. This first royal visit demonstrated to him that Japanese compliance now extended to contacts with foreign royal families.[82]

As mentioned earlier, Gladstone reported on the success of the visit to the queen and wrote to his foreign secretary, the Earl of Clarendon, suggesting that a letter of thanks be written. The letter that eventually reached Japan stated that the queen had learnt the full particulars with 'sincere pleasure' and claimed that, 'The Queen earnestly desires that a cordial understanding should exist between Japan and Great Britain, and trusts that it will be promoted by the visit of the Duke of Edinburgh and the gracious manner in which he has been received by The Mikado.'[83]

On the Japanese side, there can be no question that meticulous attention was paid to detail, protocol and ceremonial in order to make a success of the duke's visit. The government must have gone to considerable expense and effort, and all this at a very difficult time with inadequate financial resources and serious unresolved problems. There were domestic considerations involved, too, for the visit publicly demonstrated the new government's acceptance by one of the most powerful countries in the world. The determination to make a success of this visit was, however, undoubtedly also driven by the desire to gain the trust and good will of Britain, and in that respect the visit was a success. In the long run, the duke's visit laid the foundation stone for a closer relationship between Britain and Japan that was to reach its zenith in 1902 with the formation of the Anglo-Japanese Alliance. As the leaders of the new government had evidently realised, in the European world, connections between the sovereigns and their families was a far from negligible part of diplomatic relationships.[84]

What impact did the duke's visit have on the Japanese populace? It came too early in the Meiji period for critical journalism, but there were factual reports in some of the short-lived newspapers published at that time, which were of limited circulation.[85] The only published image is a woodblock print by Ichiryūsai (Hiroshige III) entitled 'Arrival of the English prince' which was published in 1869. This discreetly shows only a corner of the carriage in which the duke is riding on his way to the palace but does show large numbers of mounted and foot soldiers acting as a guard. It thus has less in common with the Yokohama prints of the foreign community than with Edo-period prints showing the processions of ambassadors from Korea, Ryūkyū and Deshima up to Edo to pay their respects to the shogun.[86]

In retrospect, the Duke of Edinburgh's visit to Japan had four lasting consequences. The first and most important was that the new Japanese government accepted the principle of the equality of sovereigns, and thus aligned itself, for better or for worse, with European diplomatic practice. The objective was presumably to align Japan with the 'civilised nations' and thus facilitate the revision of the 'unequal treaties' that had been signed with Western nations by the Bakufu in 1858. If so, success was a long time coming, but it was this decision that made the encounter between the duke and Emperor Meiji possible in the first place.[87] This paved the way for subsequent visits, in both directions. The first beneficiary in Japan was Grand Duke Alexei Aleksandrovich (1850–1908), the fourth son of Tsar Aleksander II and a naval officer, who was received by Emperor Meiji on 5 November 1872. He appears to have been the first visitor to receive a portrait of Meiji, presumably a photograph.[88] Even before this, however, early in 1871 Prince Higashi-Fushimi had already been received by Queen Victoria, as will be described in the following section.

The second consequence was that in 1869 the duke met and made a personal connection with Prince Higashi-Fushimi who was to come to England in 1871 as a student and stay for almost two years. The prince and the duke met on numerous occasions after 1871, including during the official visit that the prince (then called Prince Komatsu) made to Britain in 1887 for Victoria's Golden Jubilee.

The third consequence was that the royal art collection acquired a number of items from Japan. Some of them were given to the duke by Emperor Meiji himself, while others were presented by the government.[89] After his return to England, the objects he had purchased or been given on his voyage were, at his suggestion, put on display at the South Kensington Museum (now the Victoria and Albert Museum) in a special exhibition. The exhibition opened on 25 January 1872 and an illustration in *The Graphic* shows part of his collection with a young boy in Japanese costume described as 'one of the Duke's Japanese pages'. It is not clear who this boy was: it hardly seems possible that the duke would have brought a Japanese boy back with him, so he may have been the son of Japanese residents in London borrowed for the occasion.[90]

The published guide of the Japanese part of the exhibition refers to a number of 'sketches' by Nicholas Chevalier. Two that were executed during the audience on 4 September have already been mentioned. According to the guide, there were also sketches of sumo wrestlers, military exercises and other scenes, but the current whereabouts of these is unknown. In addition, on display at the exhibition was a collection of lacquerware; various bronzes; a number of netsuke; some porcelain; a painting on silk and books of Japanese paintings (possibly meaning *ehon*, illustrated books); and a sloping desk, a *wakizashi* (short sword), and a bronze incense-burner, all presented to the duke by the emperor. Amongst the exhibits was an item described as 'the Mikado's autograph, written in black characters upon a gold-besprinkled piece of cardboard'. This was undoubtedly the poem composed and written by the emperor in his own hand, which Iwakura handed over just before the duke's departure, as mentioned above.[91]

What became of this collection of Japanese art? When the duke moved to Germany in 1893 as the reigning Duke of Saxe-Coburg and Gotha, he took much, but not all, of his collection with him, including forty-four items from his Japanese collection. In 1895 he donated some of them to the Schlossmuseum at Schloss Friedenstein in Thuringia, while other items were given to museums in Gotha. Some of these Japanese artefacts were destroyed during the Second World War but others survive: the most important items that have survived are pieces of seventeenth- and eighteenth-century lacquerware including a decorated *tansu*, lacquered picnic-boxes and ladies' dressing stands.[92] Although most of his collection went with him to Gotha, at least fifteen items from his Japanese collection remain in London as a permanent contribution to the Royal Collections.[93]

The fourth consequence was that the duke was marked for life. I mean this in a literal sense, for he had himself tattooed in Japan. He was not the only one, for Beresford states that he himself acquired some tattoos while they were in Japan, and records that this surprised the Japanese officials in attendance, 'for in Japan none save the common people is tattooed'. In spite of official

Japanese disdain, acquiring a tattoo became one of the goals of male tourists in Japan, and the duke's example was followed by his nephews when they visited Japan in 1881.[94]

PRINCE HIGASHI-FUSHIMI IN ENGLAND

In the years before and after the Meiji Restoration, considerable numbers of Japanese went overseas for periods of study, mostly to Europe and North America. In some cases, they went in pursuit of technical knowledge, while others had less explicit goals, but whichever the case, the hardships they endured abroad for the most part stood them in good stead when they returned to Japan, for many of them became the leading politicians, academics and business leaders of Meiji Japan. What is much less well known is that amongst them were three members of the imperial family. While Japanese were travelling overseas in increasing numbers in the 1860s, the imperial family remained in Kyoto and appeared to have no interest in the world beyond Japan. This was to change rapidly after the Meiji Restoration.

The three members of the imperial family who went abroad in the early Meiji period all belonged to the Fushimi-no-miya family, one of the four cadet branches of the imperial family which were, until the law was changed in 1947, entitled to provide a successor if the main line of the imperial family failed to produce an heir. The Fushimi-no-miya family was founded in the fifteenth century by Prince Yoshihito, who was a son of Emperor Sukō (r. 1348–1351), so by the nineteenth century the head of the family, Prince Fushimi Kuniie, was many generations removed from the main line of the imperial family. Nevertheless, the members of his family enjoyed high status and were considered to be members of the imperial family.

The first member of the imperial family to study abroad was Prince Kachō Hirotsune (1851–1876), who was the twelfth son of Prince Fushimi Kuniie. In 1860, he became the adopted son of Emperor Kōmei, Emperor Meiji's father, so he was Meiji's adopted brother. While in the United States he called himself Azuma Takahiko and it was as Prince Azuma that in 1870 he attended Brooklyn College, probably in order to improve his English; he then entered the Naval Academy at Annapolis in 1873.[95] Unfortunately, he then became unwell, returned to Japan and died in 1876. On the other hand, Prince Kitashirakawa Yoshihisa (1847–1895), who was the ninth son of Prince Fushimi Kuniie, left for Germany in December 1870 and undertook military training and advanced military studies there before returning to Japan in 1877. During his long stay in Germany, he made several brief visits to England, including one on his way to Germany, from late January to mid-February 1871.[96] He was in fact the first member of the Japanese imperial family to visit Britain, but his visit does not seem to have been noticed in Britain, probably because there was no permanent Japanese diplomatic representative in Britain until 1872.[97] On his return to Japan, he rose rapidly in the Imperial Japanese Army; as a lieutenant-general, he participated in the invasion of Taiwan during the Sino-Japanese War of 1894–1895, but he contracted malaria and died there.[98]

The third to study abroad was Prince Higashi-Fushimi Yoshiaki (1846–1903), who was mentioned in the previous section. He was the eighth son of Prince Fushimi Kuniie and thus the brother of both Prince Kachō and Prince Kitashirakawa. He was known by a number of different titles during his lifetime, but it was soon after he was granted the title of Prince Higashi-Fushimi that he went to England, and it was only in 1882 that he took on the title of Prince Komatsu Akihito, the name by which he is now best known. In this section I shall refer to him as Prince Higashi-Fushimi.

Prince Higashi-Fushimi had already in 1868 expressed a keen desire to travel to the West in order to experience Western countries at first hand. His application to do so was unsuccessful, but in 1869 he applied again, this time with the more specific aim of undertaking naval training, probably under the influence of his encounters with the Duke of Edinburgh that year. In 1870, he began the study of English with Mitsukuri Shūhei (1826–1886), a prominent translator for the Bakufu who had already visited Europe and Russia several times. In March, the prince inspected some British warships that were at anchor off Shinagawa, and later that year his application to study in England was approved, with the proviso that he go as a normal student, without any privileges.[99] He spent nearly two years in England, from 1871 to 1872, but he did not undergo any military training or attend any institution, preferring to study with private tutors. Nevertheless, he subsequently had a successful career in the Imperial Japanese Army, rising to the rank of field marshal, and he visited Britain several times in later years.

Prince Higashi-Fushimi left Yokohama towards the end of 1870 with a number of companions including two household retainers and a government appointee, Sannomiya Yoshitane (1844–1905), who had been an anti-foreign activist but had joined the government after 1868, like so many others. William George Aston (1841–1911), an interpreter at the British legation, happened to be travelling back to Britain on the same ship, so the Japanese government undertook to cover his expenses if he would look after the prince on the journey. Before the prince's departure, the foreign ministry wrote to Parkes to point out that the prince, who was twenty-four years old when he left Japan, was to be treated no differently from other Japanese students in Britain.

Parkes, noting that he wanted to travel to England for language study and in order to familiarize himself with the British political system, reminded Terashima of the cordial reception accorded to the Duke of Edinburgh the previous year and stated that the British government and the royal family would wish to reciprocate by welcoming the prince, who had met the Duke of Edinburgh on several occasions during his visit to Japan.[100]

The prince reached Southampton early in 1871 and the day after his arrival travelled by train to London. He settled into the Charing Cross Hotel and then moved to the Alexandra Hotel, where he and his companions began missing Japanese food and especially soy sauce.[101] The foreign secretary called on him promptly, in recognition of his status, and in February 1871 he was presented to Queen Victoria, thus being the first member of the Japanese imperial family to meet her. Alexander von Siebold (1846–1911) was in attendance: Siebold had been employed by the British Legation in Japan but in 1870 he became an employee of the Japanese government and was despatched to England to supervise the work of Japanese students. On this occasion he was presumably acting as interpreter, but since there was as yet no Japanese diplomatic mission in London, he was the only representative of the Japanese government in Britain. The prince's arrival in England was said by the foreign secretary to be a cause of great satisfaction to the British government and he mentioned this to Parkes, who reported all this to the Japanese Foreign Ministry straight away, as well as the news that the prince had already been received by the Queen. The Japanese foreign minister in turn reported this to Emperor Meiji and added that, 'our Government is extremely grateful for these proofs of friendly feeling'.[102]

For his first year in England, from February 1871 to February 1872, the prince resided in Warminster in Wiltshire, about ten miles south-east of Bristol. The *Warminster Herald* not only reported the presence of 'a Prince of the Royal Family of Japan' with his suite but also extended a welcome to 'a number of young Japanese gentlemen' who had taken up residence in the town.[103] According to the 1871 census returns, the prince was described as a student and his suite consisted of an interpreter named Owno (Ōno), and an aide named Igami, and all three were residing at the home of John and Emily Daniell.[104] Who were the Daniells and why did Prince Higashi-Fushimi spend a whole year in Warminster, which is a picturesque, but even now rather small, country town?

John Jeremiah Daniell (1819–1898) was a clergyman from an old Warminster family who became acquainted with five young students from Japan in 1870. The five were all from Tosa in Shikoku and had just arrived in London: amongst them were Baba Tatsui (1850–1888), who later became an advocate of democratic rights, and Kunisawa Shinkurō (1847–1877), who was a pioneer of Western art in Japan. They had travelled to England in the company of John Frederick Lowder (1843–1902), who had gone to Japan as a Foreign Office language student in 1860 and became British consul in Nagasaki in 1869. In 1870, he obtained leave to return to England to study for the bar and was given charge of the five students during their voyage to England. Lowder and his widowed mother had, it seems, been living with the Daniells in 1860 when he took the examination to enter the Japan Consular Service, so he wrote to the Daniells, asking them to look after these five young men when they reached England, hoping that his old benefactor would be able to help them.[105]

Daniell went to the Charing Cross Hotel where the five Tosa students spent their first night in England and he took them straight down to Kington Langley in Wiltshire, where he was a curate. When Daniell moved to Warminster to take up a curacy there in 1871, they moved with him: they were the 'young Japanese gentlemen' welcomed by the *Warminster Herald*. Daniell seems to have taken great interest in Japan, for on 14 October 1871 he gave the inaugural lecture at the Warminster Athenaeum on 'Japan and its people'. This consisted mainly of an account of the history of Japan but he apparently 'spoke in the highest terms of the people – their integrity and high sense of honour – but deplored their abandonment to idolatry', by which he probably meant Buddhism.[106]

In 1871, Daniell resigned his position as curate in Warminster to become Prince Higashi-Fushimi's tutor, but what is not clear is how the prince came to be in Warminster in the first place. The most plausible explanation is that Aston, who was the prince's travelling companion, was aware of the arrangements that his colleague Lowder had made for the Tosa students the previous year and asked that the prince and his party be taken in as well. At any rate, what is certain is that Daniell travelled up to London to meet the prince immediately after his arrival and as a result the prince went down to Warminster. During his residence in Warminster, the prince was presumably concentrating on learning English under the tuition of Daniell, but the local newspapers recorded some of his other activities. Soon after arrival he went on an excursion to Stonehenge, which he had apparently read about before leaving Japan; he donated a prize cup to the Tenth Wiltshire Rifle Volunteers, who were based in Warminster; he attending prize-giving at Lord Weymouth's Grammar School in Warminster, where Baba Tatsui was a pupil; he visited the coal mine at Radstock in Somerset; he presented the Challenge Cup to the winner after the Warminster Rifle Corps shooting competition; and just before leaving Warminster he gave 'a series of entertainments to the aristocracy and gentry of the neighbourhood' and personally distributed cakes and oranges to 1,500 children attending schools in Warminster.[107] By the time he left Warminster in February 1872, after a year's residence, he had evidently become a well-known figure there, for a local photographer described himself in an advertisement as 'photographer to His Imperial Highness Higashi Fushimi no Meya [*sic.*]' and offered for sale photographs of the prince and of the prince with his suite.[108]

Even while the prince was in Warminster he was occasionally attending functions at court in London. He visited the Prince of Wales and the Duke of Edinburgh in June 1871 and presented the duke with a sword from the emperor in remembrance of his visit to Japan in 1869; Mitford and von Siebold were present, presumably as interpreters.[109] After leaving Warminster he remained in England for another six months, but how he spent his time is unclear. He studied geography, grammar, history and mathematics with somebody living at Blackheath Hill and was probably staying with him as a house guest, but it is a mystery how and through whom such arrangements were made.[110] During this time he attended the National Thanksgiving Service at St Paul's for the recovery of the Prince of Wales from typhoid fever, a state ball at Buckingham Palace and a garden party at Chiswick. He was also present at a dinner held by the Royal Geographical Society which was attended by Sir Harry Parkes and his predecessor, Sir Rutherford Alcock, as well as by Higashikuze Michitomi (1834–1912), an aristocrat and member of the government who was visiting Britain as a senior member of the Iwakura Mission to the United States and Europe.[111] In the summer news reached him by telegram that his father, Prince Fushimi Kuniie, had died on 5 August and he therefore brought forward his return to Japan and left from Liverpool on 8 September 1872; he was seen off by his half-brother, Prince Kitashirakawa, who had come over from Germany for this purpose.[112]

At some time during his stay in England, Prince Higashi-Fushimi's portrait was painted by John Edgar Williams (1821–1891), at the time a well-known academic portraitist. This probably came about through the introduction of Kunisawa Shinkurō, one of the five students from Tosa mentioned earlier. He was in fact the first Japanese to study art in the West, and he was later to be famous for opening the Shōgidō, the first Western art school in Japan, in Tokyo in 1874. After moving to London from Warminster, Kunisawa abandoned his plan to study law and became a pupil of Williams.[113] The prince's portrait featured in an exhibition by the Society of British Artists in 1872, and a review of the exhibition referred to it as follows: 'The portrait of Higashi Fushimi No Miya, Prince Imperial of Japan … will attract attention, no less by the refined and tender expression of the countenance, and the merit of the work, than by the curious attire and peculiarly absurd hat his Highness wears.' From this it appears likely that he was painted in traditional Japanese court dress with an *eboshi* hat. The portrait was most likely burnt in the firebombing air-raids of 1945, which destroyed the prince's family home and most of the family possessions.[114]

The Spectator magazine attributed great symbolic significance to the prince's visit:

> A brief notice in the Court Circular of the presentation to the Queen of Higashi-Fushimi-no-Miya, a Japanese Prince, lately come to England for the prosecution of his studies – or, in other words, for an education – is an incident scarcely noticed in the whirl and dissipation of a London season. And yet it marks an epoch in the history of a nation. It is the evidence of a change in the political constitution and ideas of a whole race which is without a parallel for its completeness and suddenness, in either ancient or modern history.[115]

Leaving aside the smug assumption that a British education was the only kind worth having, *The Spectator* was right to suggest that the prince's arrival for a long stay reflected a dramatic change in the Japanese outlook upon the world. What is more, the prince acquired a familiarity with Britain that was to pay dividends in future years. He was on hand when the future King George V visited Japan in 1881, and in later years, now known as Prince Komatsu, he was to visit Britain several more times to take part in great state occasions.

The prince's sojourn in Britain coincided with the visit of the Iwakura Mission from August 1872 to the end of the year. This high-level government mission, which lasted for several years and included several senior members of the government, was expected to negotiate revision of the treaties but made no headway on that front and instead focused on learning as much as possible about Western societies. The mission was led by Iwakura Tomomi and on 3 September, since the queen was at Balmoral in Scotland, they were given a tour of Buckingham Palace. Finally, on 5 December, they were received by the queen at Windsor Castle. The Duke of Edinburgh, who had met Iwakura in Japan, was also present, and Aston was there to interpret. According to Iwakura, whose account refers to the queen as 'empress' (*kōtei*) but does not name her, Victoria asked him if Emperor Meiji was in good health and if his party had found their visit to Britain enjoyable and instructive, and finally she thanked him for the kind treatment of her son while he was in Japan in 1869.[116] The queen's private reaction was unflattering and unsympathetic:

> the Japanese Envoys … have abandoned their fine national dress & came in ugly, European uniforms. They are very small, but intelligent looking. The Address was read in the most extraordinary intonation imaginable.[117]

However, *The Times* was particularly impressed by the visit of the Iwakura Mission, pointing out that, 'We have had Japanese visitors before, but this was a Japanese Embassy', and remarking that 'the Mikado, who has now addressed a letter to our Queen, was, till lately, even in Japan itself, a mysterious and almost unknown personage.' The writer accepted that 'the Japanese Ambassadors know more about us at this moment than we know about them', but suggested that the Japanese 'approach more nearly to the European, or even the English, stamp than any other Oriental people'.[118]

On 26 August 1872 some members of the mission went to observe the autumn army manoeuvres. They were accompanied by Prince Higashi-Fushimi and Prince Kitashirakawa, who had come over from Germany. Prince Kitashirakawa made several trips to England in order to spend time with his brother: during an earlier visit, on 12 April 1871, he and his companions had brought the Japanese population of Warminster up to sixteen.[119]

Prince Higashi-Fushimi's two years in Britain gained him acquaintance with some members of the royal family and some familiarity with life and society in England, and presumably some knowledge of English, too. He was also kept in touch with what was happening in Japan, for regular parcels were sent to him containing, in addition to vital supplies of sencha tea and soy sauce, recent copies of the government gazette, *Dajōkan nisshi*, copies of recently enacted laws and other documents.[120] What impact his experiences in England had on him is difficult to fathom, for no letters or other writings appear to have survived. Although *The Spectator* appreciated the significance of his sojourn in England, visiting royals were hardly uncommon in Victorian Britain, so his visit did not have the level of impact on Britain that the visit of the Duke of Edinburgh had had in Japan.

BRITISH ROYALS IN JAPAN UP TO 1902

After the visit of the Duke of Edinburgh in 1869, the next British royal visit to Japan was that of the two sons of the Prince of Wales, the future King Edward VII, in late 1881. The two boys were Prince Albert Victor (1864–1892), the Duke of Clarence, and Prince George (1865–1936). Prince Albert Victor, who in his lifetime was widely known as Prince Eddy, died of influenza in 1892 at the age of twenty-eight, so it was his younger brother who succeeded their father as King George V in 1910.[121]

The two princes had begun their naval training together in 1877 on HMS *Britannia*, and in 1879 they joined HMS *Bacchante*, an ironclad screw-propelled corvette of 4130 tons, as cadets and later as midshipmen. The *Bacchante*, under the command of Captain (later Admiral) Lord Charles Scott (1839–1911), the fourth son of the fifth Duke of Buccleuch, made several short voyages and then joined the Detached Squadron on a world cruise which lasted until 1882.[122] In fact, the captain, the other officers and the midshipmen were all carefully selected for their suitability to be the princes' mess-mates, and most of them were either of aristocratic birth or destined for high rank. Thus amongst their fellow midshipmen were Rosslyn Wemyss (1864–1933), who had been with the princes on HMS *Britannia* and was later to be First Sea Lord and Admiral of the Fleet; the future Admirals Arthur Limpus (1863–1931) and Arthur H. Christian (1863–1926); Lord Francis Granville Godolphin Osborne (1864–1924), a younger son of the 9th Duke of Leeds; the Hon. George Arthur Hardinge (1864–1901), a younger son of the 2nd Viscount Hardinge; and the Hon. John Charles Montagu Douglas Scott (1864–1935), who was a son of the 6th Duke of Buccleugh and later became the 7th duke. These were clearly no ordinary midshipmen. Finally, serving on HMS *Inconstant*, the flagship of the Detached Squadron, were Midshipman (later Admiral) Charles Lionel Napier (1861–1934) and Lieutenant Prince Louis of Battenberg (1854–1921). The latter enjoyed the patronage of the Queen and the Prince of Wales, and was later to become First Sea Lord, Admiral of the Fleet and Marquess of Milford Haven; he changed his name to Mountbatten in 1917 to demonstrate his commitment to Britain.[123] Of all these fortunate young men it was Christian, Napier, Osborne and the Fleet Surgeon on the *Bacchante*, Dr Alexander Turnbull, who were chosen to accompany the princes on their tours in Japan.

Sea voyages in the nineteenth century were not without their dangers, and several sailors from the *Bacchante* died of illness or as a result of accidents on board. During the passage from South Africa to Australia, the *Bacchante*'s steering gear was damaged and she drifted for several days out of control and out of contact with the other ships in the squadron. While the ship was under repair in Albany, Western Australia, the princes were transferred for several months to the *Inconstant*. They re-joined the *Bacchante* on 2 August and reached Yokohama on 21 October 1881, staying there until 1 November, when the ship left to spend 4–12 November in Kobe before proceeding to China. At the time, Prince Eddy was seventeen and Prince George sixteen, and they were accompanied throughout the voyage by their tutor, Rev. John Neale Dalton (1839–1931). Dalton wrote regular reports to their father and later published an account of the voyage based partly on the princes' diaries.[124]

The Japanese government decided to follow the precedent established in May 1879 when the grandson of the German emperor had visited Japan. The princes would be accommodated in the Enryōkan, which would be guarded throughout their stay; they would have an audience with the emperor and they would be given decorations. By comparison with the arrival of the Duke of Edinburgh in 1869, the government now not only had precedents to draw upon but also the experiences of Prince Higashi-Fushimi in England and information from the minister in London, Mori Arinori, who sent a telegram informing the government that the queen had stated that she did not want the princes to receive too elaborate a reception.[125]

For several days after their arrival in Japan the young princes remained on board receiving calls from the emperor's secretary, the chargé d'affaires at the British Legation and Vice-Admiral George Willes, the commander-in-chief of the China Station. Finally, on 24 October, the princes and their party went ashore. They were met by Prince Higashi-Fushimi and were driven to Yokohama station in two of the emperor's carriages. They travelled up to Tokyo by special train for five days of shore leave. Prince Higashi-Fushimi had already, it seems, met the princes as well as their father while he was in England.[126] After their arrival in Tokyo, they were taken to the Enryōkan and were given lunch. They were pleased with their accommodation, which Dalton described as 'a very comfortable one-storied building in true Japanese style, but fitted up with every European comfort, and standing in a pretty garden and park laid out in native fashion, full of strange trees, with birds and monkeys in cages, and winding fish ponds full of fish'.[127] Ernest Satow was on hand and he accompanied them in the afternoon to Asakusa where they wandered around the Sensōji temple.[128] In the evening several senior members of the government came to dinner, which was accompanied by Japanese court music and followed by fireworks and a display of conjuring and juggling.

On 25 October the princes had an audience with the emperor and empress. During the conversation, Prince Eddy told the emperor that a portrait of the queen had been commissioned and would arrive in due course as a 'token of friendship' and asked the empress to accept two wallabies which they had brought from Australia.

The following day they attended a military review at Hibiya parade ground, with the two princes riding on either side of the emperor, and afterwards used rickshaws to visit the legation (now in Tokyo) and then to go to a craft bazaar where the princes made some purchases. In the evening they attended the palace for dinner with the emperor, at which he engaged both the princes in conversation through an interpreter and then proposed a toast to the health of the queen.

On the 27th the emperor first sent 'four beautiful bronze vases, each three feet high, and worked with silver and gold figures of dragons and flowers on the surface, and four cases containing rolls of silk brocade' as a gift and then visited the princes at the Enryōkan for a short conversation. Once the emperor had left, they visited the Naval College, went to the home of Prince Higashi-Fushimi for lunch and then played Japanese polo (*dakyū*).[129] In the evening, they saw some Nō plays at the residence of a daimyō (English summaries were provided by Satow). This was followed by a dinner described by Ramsay as follows:

> Our feast was also a performance worth remembering. Once in a lifetime one finds oneself seated on a cushion on the floor in a daimio's palace, waited on by numerous gentlemen pages who *knelt* as they performed their menial offices … drinking Saki (a spirit made from rice) with numerous little lacquer dishes in front of you containing upwards of eighty different kinds of eatables. I tasted one or two out of courtesy, but I am bound to say I felt very ill afterwards, and should not like to feast with a Daimio every day.[130]

This was a common pattern: exquisite Japanese meals went unappreciated by English guests.

Later, Satow took the princes in rickshaws up to Atagoyama and the Sengakuji, for they had already read about the forty-seven rōnin in Mitford's *Tales of Old Japan*, which had been published in 1871. The following day they were in the hands of tattooers. 'The man who did most of our party was beautifully tattooed over the whole of his body, and the effect of these Japanese drawings in various colours and curves on his glistening skin was like so much embroidered silk.' Tattoos were evidently popular, for two tattooists took up residence on the *Bacchante* for several days and were busy tattooing officers and men.[131] When the tattooing was done, the princes went shopping in Nihonbashi for netsuke and bronzeware, and then in the afternoon they visited the Fukiage Gardens where they were entertained to a display of mounted combat.[132] In the evening they were entertained to a Japanese dinner, but English visitors were not yet ready to appreciate Japanese cuisine. Dalton commented: 'What we liked best of all the delicacies … was some plain boiled rice'! *The Graphic*, too, reported that, 'They were puzzled by the Japanese delicacies and seem to have fallen back on plain boiled rice.'[133]

On the morning of 29 October, the whole party was photographed in front of the Enryōkan and then returned to the *Bacchante*. The following day the princes made an excursion to Kamakura and Enoshima. The emperor had earlier expressed a wish to visit the *Bacchante* and in the morning of 31 October he went aboard, as Vice-Admiral Willes reported:

> After going around the ship, and inspecting her arrangements with much interest and intelligent attention to details, His Majesty was entertained at luncheon by

> Captain Lord Charles Scott, the two Princes of Wales [*sic.*, i.e. the two princes] being present. Prince Albert Victor, with much grace, proposed the Mikado's health and welcomed him, in appropriate terms on his first visit to a British man of war. I also took the opportunity of expressing my great pleasure in seeing His Majesty on board one of the Queen's ships which I looked upon as a high compliment to the Navy and assured His Majesty that his friendly visit to the sons of the Prince of Wales would tend to cement the cordiality and good will which already existed between Japan and the British Empire.[134]

The emperor spent nearly four hours aboard and was accompanied by Prince Higashi-Fushimi, Prince Kitashirakawa, Prince Fushimi Sadanaru, five government ministers (Tokudaiji Sanetsune, Sanjō Sanetomi, Iwakura Tomomi, Inoue Kaoru and Ōyama Iwao) and two admirals (Kawamura Sumiyoshi and Nire Kagenori).[135] Before lunch there was a demonstration of the use of torpedoes, but Satow overheard the emperor say that he had seen a better performance by the Japanese Navy at Yokosuka.[136]

The following day, Satow came on board and the *Bacchante* left for Kobe. Dalton had a high opinion of Satow: 'He has been not only a most agreeable companion during our stay in Japan, but also of invaluable service to us on account of his special knowledge of everything connected with Japanese history, language, and literature', but this may have been of more interest to Dalton himself than to the two princes.[137]

From Kobe, the princes and Dalton travelled with Satow to Kyoto by train and they were met by Prince Higashi-Fushimi, who had travelled down separately. After seeing something of the city from their carriages, they visited such well-known sights as Tōji, Kiyomizu, Gion, and the Chion'in, and then they went to the quarters that had been prepared for them in the Nishi-Honganji, with European furniture sent from Yokohama to provide some familiar comfort.

After dinner on the night of their arrival there was some unusual entertainment:

> two native artists came and did some painting on paper and also on calico, spread on the floor before them as they sat on their heels. They ask you first to take the brush and make any blot, or draw a triangle, or dash, in any way upon the white surface, and then out of these dots and strokes and blotches they will produce a picture of anything you like to name, an animal, or bird, or flower, with most marvellous skill. When you hand the brush back to them, they look wistfully at the incoherent mess you have made for five or six seconds, and then with firm, clear stroke that never falters or swerves, produce the design they have imagined, generally a humorous one, but always full of life and expression. We were told

> that the extraordinary accuracy of hand and wrist shown by these painters results from the way that from earliest infancy they are taught to use the brush in writing the complicated Chinese characters. Every touch and tail and dot of these has to be most accurately put in without wavering, and without any possibility of rubbing out or erasing a mistake: hence their firmness of touch and accuracy in imitating exactly what they see in bird or flower.

One of these two artists was the young painter Kubota Beisen, who had in 1880 been appointed professor in the Kyoto Prefectural Art School. During the evening Prince George picked up a brush, made some dots on a piece of paper and challenged Kubota to make a painting from them. The result was a picture of a group of fireflies, and Kubota's inscription appended to this painting, which has been acquired by the British Museum, explains how it came into being.[138]

On 6 November they saw the former imperial palace in Kyoto. Satow recorded that there was a performance by a troupe of actors after dinner, but he was unable to pay attention to the plot for 'prince George made me come & sit by him while he had a tiger tattooed on his arm'. On the next day they travelled to Kameoka and, like many other visitors to Kyoto, did the ride down the Hozu river rapids and then had lunch at Arashiyama. On the same day, Dalton recorded, 'one of the Buddhist priests who talked English remarkably well, and had been at Oxford, came and took the princes round the shrines and curiosities of the huge temple they were lodged in'.[139] This was most likely Akamatsu Renjō (1841–1919), who had been sent by the Nishi-Honganji to Europe in 1872 and returned in 1874.

The following day, they made a trip to Uji and saw the Byōdōin. From there they went to Nara and the Tōdaiji and then on to Osaka. It is difficult to imagine a better guide to Kyoto than Satow, and Dalton certainly seems to have appreciated his extensive knowledge of Japan, but Satow's diary makes few mentions of the princes and devotes more space to the booksellers he met and the purchases he made! On 12 November, the *Bacchante* left Kobe for Shimonoseki by way of the Inland Sea. There the ship stayed for several days at anchor in a bay just outside the straits of Shimonoseki before departing for China on 17 November.

Prince George's diary records the details of every day of his stay in Japan, including the tattoos he acquired in Tokyo and Kyoto. A few extracts will show that he enjoyed his visit to Japan and was polite about Japanese food:

> We then had a Japanese dinner which was very curious, we all ate with chop sticks. … I am very sorry to leave Tokio as I have spent a very pleasant time.

> ... Fuji-yama looks very well this evening as it is a very clear night. ... We have spent a very pleasant week on shore up at Nara and Kioto, we saw a great deal in the time, but we were not long enough, it was too hurried. Nearly everybody on board has been tatooed [*sic*.]. I have got a dragon on one arm done at Tokio and a tiger on the other arm done at Kioto.

He punctiliously mentions all the formal dinners and receptions he had to attend, but they clearly made less impression upon him than, for example, the very fast ride in rickshaws from Kyoto to Nara. An entry made on the way to Kobe by sea, 'Went to school in the forenoon. Put some stamps in my book in the afternoon', reminds us that he was still only sixteen and that his education was far from complete. Classes in French, history and gymnastics, together with mathematics and naval sciences were provided for him and Prince Eddy.[140]

Dalton's letters to the Prince of Wales provide some details omitted from the published book which reveal that the princes' tastes were still those of children. In Asakusa, for example, they saw some mechanical dolls (*kara-kuri-ningyō*): 'The Princes were amused by some Japanese wax-works (with moveable heads and arms) and shot at an archery shed in the grounds', and in Kyoto, 'They were much amused by trying their own hand at pottery turning' in the pottery workshops near Kiyomizu; they both 'thoroughly enjoyed' descending the rapids and in Ōtsu Prince George tried on a suit of Japanese armour. Dalton himself, like so many other Britons in Japan, felt that the Japan he was interested in was 'fast disappearing', and his impression of Kyoto is a striking reminder of the changes the city went through after the Meiji Restoration:

> The city is one mass of splendid temples and shrines, now all more or less left to go to ruin. They are all of wood, no stone is used: and the huge wooden pillars are gradually using their colour and gilt, which used to be renewed every few years before the temples were disendowed; but still the wealth of iron and bronze work inside, the carvings and statuary and embroidery are a thing never to forget.

He made it clear to the Prince of Wales back in England how well they had been treated:

> Your Royal Highness will observe that we have seen a great deal of the Emperor. He has certainly come wonderfully to the front during our stay: more so than he has ever done before, and everyone expresses wonder at it. The Princes have certainly been received by him and his government with every kindness and distinction that c[oul]d possibly be shewn to Englishmen.

> I must assure your Royal Highness that nothing could exceed the courteousness and kindness of the Japanese gentlemen who were deputed by the Emperor to manage everything connected with the Princes during their stay on Japanese soil. At the head of these was Prince Higashi Fushimi (whom your Royal Highness must remember in England) – he was always with the Princes, day after day, never sparing himself, getting up early and going to bed late, always agreeable and always cheerful.[141]

In a letter to another correspondent he added his impressions of the emperor:

> [He] is a most strange being to look at. He never smiles. His uncles, who have had an European education are far more presentable. But I believe the Mikado to be struggling fairly well against great disadvantages of up-bringing and undoubtedly he has many able men about him and some corrupt ones. Several who can talk English I have had most interesting conversations with. ... No greater mistake can be made than to suppose they have only taken the exterior manners and dress of Europeans: they have assimilated their knowledge & their spirit & intend to go ahead.[142]

The voyage of the two princes and their visit to Japan were well reported in England. Charles Wirgman, who provided the *Illustrated London News* with sketches from Japan that could be turned into engravings, contributed several pictures. Other sketches were provided by Lieutenant (later Admiral Sir) Percy Scott (1853–1924) of HMS *Inconstant*, the warship which the princes had served on while the *Bacchante* was under repair. It was probably Scott who provided a sketch showing the reception of the two princes by the emperor and empress.[143] *The Graphic*, too, carried a brief account of the princes' visit to Japan, with pictures of them at the Daibutsu in Kamakura and of Prince George being tattooed.

After their return, Dalton prepared a set of photographic albums for the princes' father including one devoted to Japan.[144] Captain Lord Scott also had his own album: this includes a presentation copy of a photograph of Emperor Meiji, which he had requested, and photographs of the two princes on the *Bacchante*.[145]

After their return to England, Prince George continued his naval career. He served on HMS *Canada* on a transatlantic voyage to Canada, attended the Royal Naval College in Greenwich and then joined the Senior Gunnery School at HMS *Excellent*, Portsmouth. In charge of his gunnery work at Portsmouth was the same Percy Scott who had provided some sketches for the *Illustrated London News* and had met the princes when they had temporarily joined his ship, HMS *Inconstant*.[146] Prince George subsequently took command of the gunboat HMS

Thrush and then of the cruiser HMS *Melampus*: he relinquished his command and left the Royal Navy on the death of his elder brother. Years later, when he was the King and when Crown Prince Hirohito was visiting Britain, he is said to have barged into Hirohito's dressing room one morning saying:

> I hope, my boy, that everyone is giving you everything you want while you are here. If there is anything you need, just ask. I'll never forget how your grandfather [Emperor Meiji] treated me and my brother when we were in Yokohama. I've always wanted to repay his kindness. No geishas here, though, I'm afraid. Her Majesty would never allow it.

Just how accurate this reported speech may be is open to question, but what he had to say about his visit to Japan and his reception there probably had a basis in fact, for, later that year, in a speech to a visiting Japanese commercial mission, he said, 'I preserve the happiest recollections of my visit to your beautiful land, alas! more than forty years ago, and I am delighted to think of the approaching visit to Japan of my dear Son, the Prince of Wales [i.e. the future Edward VIII].'[147] At any rate, he was the first British king or queen to have had first-hand experience of Japan, and, apart from Edward VIII, he remained the only one until Queen Elizabeth visited Japan in 1975.

The final visit to Japan by a member of the British royal family in the nineteenth century came in 1890. Prince Arthur Duke of Connaught (1850–1942), who was the third son of Queen Victoria and a lieutenant-general in the army, and the Duchess of Connaught (1860–1917), formerly Princess Luise Margarete of Prussia, had been living in Poona since 1887, after the duke was appointed Lieutenant-Governor of Bombay. At the end of his appointment they returned to England via China, Japan and Canada.[148] They went to Japan with the expectation that they would be able to enjoy the cherry blossoms, but the weather was inclement and most days of their visit were wet and misty.[149] They visited Nagasaki, Kobe and Osaka before arriving in Yokohama on 15 April. They went to the Kabuki theatre and the Third National Exhibition for the Encouragement of Industry (Naikoku kangyō hakurankai) in Ueno, and 'spent so much on curios in both Tokyo and Kyoto that their visit will long be remembered by the curio-dealers'. From Tokyo they visited Kamakura, Nikko, Atami, Miyanoshita and Hakone. As Mary Fraser, the wife of the British minister, noted:

> The Duchess, indeed, is an ardent sightseer, and seems to have only one dread; namely, that she should miss some interesting experience which the ordinary traveller would ferret out for himself. Before the party arrived, word was sent

> that they wished to travel quite unofficially so as to have all possible freedom for sightseeing.

They declined to use the court carriages which were provided for them and instead took public rickshaws, which neither officials nor anybody of status deigned to use.[150]

For most of the period of their visit, Emperor Meiji and the empress were away from Tokyo. They spent some time in Kyoto and then the emperor travelled alone to visit the Kure and Sasebo naval bases. They both returned to Tokyo on 6 May and the following evening entertained the duke and duchess to dinner, the day before they were to depart from Japan. On the morning of their departure Prince Komatsu (formerly Higashi-Fushimi) came to pay a courtesy visit at 8:45 am, but, as Mary Fraser put it, 'neither the Duke nor the Duchess was quite prepared for such an early pleasure.'[151]

The Graphic saw visual appeal in the possibility of enhancing reports on their sightseeing trips with engravings based on sketches made by Arnold Henry Savage Landor (1865–1924), who was visiting Japan at the time.[152] However, *The Times* took a much more critical perspective on the visit. In the view of the Tokyo correspondent, 'It cannot be said that the visit of the Duke and Duchess to Japan has been successful'. This was not so much because of the weather, rather because 'the circumstances of their Royal Highnesses' visit have created a painful impression in the minds of the Japanese'. 'Never before', he noted, 'has Japanese hospitality allowed personages of even comparable distinction to sojourn in the country except as guests of the Government'; consequently, 'no little surprise was caused by the discovery that their Royal Highnesses were to make the British Legation their headquarters, to travel through the country as every-day tourists, and to stop at ordinary hotels in Nikko and Kioto'. As the correspondent pointed out, this was not after all a purely private visit: the duke and duchess stayed in the Legation, received addresses from the British communities in several cities and presided over public ceremonies.[153]

Although *The Times* correspondent gave the impression that the visit was devoted almost entirely and somewhat self-indulgently to sightseeing and the purchase of 'curios', and did nothing to strengthen ties between Britain and Japan, the joint diary of the duke and duchess allows a somewhat different perspective. To be sure, they were thorough in their pursuit of the tourist experience, and as well as describing their travels in great deal, they preserved photographs, maps, cuttings from the English-language press and even menu cards. But they did not completely shun their obligations as guests in Japan. On 22 April, for example, the duchess laid the foundation stone of the hospital at St Hilda's Mission School in Azabu, which is now known as Kōran Jogakkō: present on the occasion were the ministers from the British, French, Austrian and German legations, as well as well-known residents such as Ernest Fenollosa, Erwin Baelz, and James Summers, and the hospital opened the following year. Again, on 6 May the duchess paid a visit to the Peeresses School, which was later to become part of the Gakushūin. She was accompanied by Ada Cavaye, whose husband, Major-General William Cavaye, had been military secretary to the duke in Bombay, and by Alethea Raynor, who was the English wife of Sannomiya Yoshitane, a high-ranking official in the Imperial Household Ministry. The lengthy account she wrote of her visit makes it clear that the duchess took an interest in, and in fact was impressed by, the education provided for privileged young women in Japan.[154]

The visit of the duke and duchess to Japan resulted in an unusual scene at Osborne House the following January. A number of *tableaux vivants* (staged scenes with no movement or speech) were presented, including one by the duke and duchess and their three children pretending to be a Japanese family and wearing clothing brought back from Japan. This gave the queen the confidence to note, when she saw a performance of Gilbert and Sullivan's *The Mikado* later that year, that, 'The Japanese dresses were very correct.'[155] Her judgment was most likely based on the *tableau* she had seen: the queen had not, after all, ever taken much interest in Japan.

JAPANESE VISITS TO BRITAIN UP TO 1902

In the period up to 1902 there were considerably more visits from Japan to Britain than the other way around, and the visits were often of long duration. The first to follow in the footsteps of Prince Higashi-Fushimi was Prince Arisugawa Takehito (1862–1913), whose family was, like the Fushimi-no-miya family, one of the four cadet branches of the imperial family eligible to ascend the throne in the absence of a direct heir; he was the fourth son of the head of the family, Prince Arisugawa Takahito. He started learning English in 1872 and in 1874 he enrolled in the Imperial Japanese Naval Academy at the age of twelve. In 1879, he was permitted to embark on HMS *Iron Duke*, the flagship of the China Station, for naval training, on condition that there was to be no recognition of his status and that he would be accorded no special treatment with regard to discipline or visits.[156] He stayed on the *Iron Duke* for several voyages covering more than a year and when the ship put into Yokohama all the officers down to the midshipmen were invited to a meal at the Shiba Detached Palace. He left the *Iron Duke* upon her departure for England, a move that was perceived as discourteous by the Navy but was excused on account of Japanese ignorance of Navy protocol. After he had served on several Royal Navy warships of the China Station, it was agreed that he would go to England to study at the Royal Naval College in Greenwich to acquire a 'thorough naval education'.[157]

On 11 December 1880, he married Maeda Yasuko, the fourth daughter of the last daimyo of the Kaga domain, and in later years both of them were to travel to England and elsewhere. On this occasion, however, he left Yokohama for England alone, on 9 January 1881, before he had been married a month. On arrival in London, he was greeted by senior representatives of the Foreign Office, the Army and the Navy, and was taken to Westminster Abbey and the Houses of Parliament, but he subsequently stayed for some time in Blackheath working on mathematics and English with private tutors.[158] He had an audience with Queen Victoria at Osborne House in August 1881: in her diary Victoria got his name and age wrong and mistakenly thought he was the son of Emperor Meiji; she seemed surprised that he and his party were in European dress.[159]

In October, he entered the Royal Naval College, and over Christmas visited the naval facilities at Portsmouth, Torquay and Plymouth. In September 1882, he passed the examination for appointment as a midshipman in the Royal Navy and on 1 January 1883 he went to France for several months to improve his French. He returned to London in April and a few days later returned to Japan via the United States. On his return he became an officer in the Imperial Japanese Navy and in the course of a long career he commanded a number of cruisers, including the *Matsushima* during the Sino-Japanese War. He did not take part in the naval actions of the Russo-Japanese War but was promoted to full admiral in 1905.

Prince and Princess Arisugawa made an extensive tour of Europe and America in 1889. They stayed in London for three weeks, but there is no trace of their social engagements or other activities in the pages of *The Times*. In 1897, the prince made a brief visit to London to represent the emperor at Queen Victoria's Diamond Jubilee: this was a purely ceremonial visit and nothing untoward occurred.[160] The prince and princess visited Europe again in 1905, when they represented the Emperor Meiji at the wedding of the German Crown Prince Wilhelm, and on their way back to Japan they visited Great Britain for the last time. This time they stayed for several months and went to Barrow-in-Furness on 4 July for the launch of the battleship *Katori*, which was in 1921 to be the ship that brought Crown Prince Hirohito to Britain. During their stay in Britain, King Edward VII appointed Prince Arisugawa a Knight Grand Cross of the Order of the Bath.

Prince Arisugawa Taruhito (1835–1895) was the eldest son of Prince Arisugawa Takahito and the much older half-brother of Takehito. He commanded the imperial armies in the Boshin War of 1868–1869, which resulted in the military defeat of the Bakufu, and he led the armed forces of the new Meiji government in the suppression of the Satsuma rebellion in 1877. In 1882, he attended the coronation of Tsar Alexander III as the representative of Emperor Meiji, and he returned by way of Europe and the United States. At this stage in his life he was a general and the president of the Genrōin, the national assembly that preceded the Diet, but later, from 1889 to 1895, he was to serve as the chief of staff of the Imperial Japanese Army.

He spent about two weeks in London, staying in the Japanese Legation. He spent several days seeing the sights, including Trafalgar Square, Westminster Abbey, the Houses of Parliament, the Crystal Palace, the Stock Exchange, the offices of *The Times*, the Tower of London, the British Museum, Piccadilly and Bond Street. On 25 November 1882, he travelled to Windsor by train for an audience and lunch with the Queen. She mistakenly referred to him as Takahito, but was evidently impressed:

> The Prince is very small, but a great personage in Japan. He made a speech in a very low voice, & with a little hesitation & grunt, between each word or sentence, as is the Japanese custom. He presented me with 2 beautiful cloisonné enamel vases, & an inkstand.[161]

Although no complaints were made and the prince himself expressed no displeasure in his diary, it appears that the prince was not wholly satisfied with his treatment in Britain. This was apparently because his luggage had been searched by British customs on arrival and because he had to travel on an ordinary train to Windsor: these 'painful incidents', as *The Times* correspondent in Japan later referred to them, were painful because of the contrast with the 'minute courtesy of other European States' that had been extended to him.[162]

Another brief visitor in the 1880s was Prince Fushimi Sadaharu (1858–1903), who was the fourteenth son of Prince Fushimi Kuniie and who succeeded to the headship of the Fushimi no miya family in 1875. By this time, he had entered the Military Academy and was launched on a career in the Imperial Japanese Army. In the 1870s he undertook advanced military studies in France and Germany, and he later took an active part in both the Sino-Japanese and Russo-Japanese wars; he ended his career as a field marshal. In 1885, he was ordered to visit Europe and he spent a year visiting France, Germany, Belgium, Italy, Spain, Austria, Denmark, Sweden and England. He stayed in a London hotel from 2 to 15 July 1886 and then went to Liverpool to return home via the USA. While in London he was entertained at a Buckingham Palace ball and a garden party at Marlborough House, the home of the Prince and Princess of Wales. He was received both by the queen and by the Prince of Wales, and during his brief stay he visited Woolwich Arsenal, the Bank of England, some military barracks and the Houses of Parliament.[163] He visited England again in 1907 and 1910.

The next long-term resident in Britain was Prince Higashi-Fushimi Yorihito (1867–1922), who was the 17th son of Prince Fushimi Kuniie; in 1885, was adopted by Prince Komatsu and the following year by Emperor Meiji as a potential heir.[164] In 1875, he entered the Naval College and was heading for a military career like so many other young members of the imperial family in the late nineteenth century. Having completed his naval education in 1884, he was sent to England, and sailed for San Francisco in the company of a number of other young naval and army officers heading for periods of study in England, France, Germany and the United States. Crossing the United States, he was injured in a railway accident but reached London in June and spent the summer touring Scotland and familiarizing himself with London as well as receiving further treatment for his injuries. His English-language training and his naval education were entrusted to a teacher at Greenwich Naval College, with whom he boarded for more than two years. He then applied to join the Royal Naval College at Dartmouth but was refused because he was much older than the normal age for entry. Consequently, it was decided that he should go instead to the École Navale at Brest, which catered to older boys: he took French lessons and then left England in the summer of 1887 for France, where he was to spend a further four years. During his three years in England, he spent most of his time in Greenwich, but he did travel to the Armstrong Whitworth Shipyard in Newcastle for the launch of the Japanese cruiser *Naniwa* and in 1886 went to Liverpool to see off Prince and Princess Komatsu.[165] By the time he returned to Japan early in 1892 he had spent seven years abroad, longer than any other member of the imperial family before or since.

On his return to Japan, he resumed his career in the Imperial Japanese Navy, serving for a while on the *Naniwa*, but in 1893 he was sent abroad again. Travelling via Vancouver and New York he arrived back in London in October. He stayed in Britain for just over a month, visiting Chatham Dockyards, Woolwich Arsenal, the Armstrong Whitworth Shipyard, Portsmouth, Dartmouth and other places of military interest before going on to France, Belgium, the Netherlands, Denmark, Sweden, Germany, Russia, Turkey, Serbia, Austria, Italy. He had audiences with the sovereigns of each nation he visited, but not in Britain until he returned to London in June 1894 at the end of his long tour of continental Europe. After an audience with Queen Victoria, he met the

Prince and Princess of Wales and the Duke and Duchess of Saxe-Coburg and Gotha (the duke, who had visited Japan as the Duke of Edinburgh in 1869, had become the Duke of Saxe-Coburg and Gotha in 1893) and attended a ball at Buckingham Palace.[166] After less than a month, he left for France and then returned to Japan. Although he once again resumed his naval career on his return to Japan and became an admiral in 1918, this was by no means his last visit to Britain, for he visited again in 1911 for the coronation of King George V and again in 1918–1919. He corresponded with King George and a few months before his death in 1922 he received an unusually warm letter from the King.[167]

Another frequent visitor was Prince Komatsu Akihito, who had first stayed in Britain in the 1870s when he was known as Prince Higashi-Fushimi. His first subsequent visit was in 1886, as part of a European tour that took in France, Germany and Russia as well as Britain. Well before he arrived, Sir Francis Plunkett, who had succeeded Parkes in Tokyo as British minister, made every effort to impress upon the Foreign Office the political importance of the visit, in the hope that he would be treated rather better than Prince Arisugawa Taruhito had been in 1882. On 16 July, shortly before Prince Komatsu's departure, the emperor addressed the following remarks to Plunkett:

> It is highly gratifying to me to know that, by the aid of the Governments of Great Britain and Germany, I may now look forward to the early removal of all those obstacles which have hitherto stood in the way of the establishment of full and cordial intercourse between Japan and the Western Powers. … In order to manifest my sense of obligation to Her Britannic Majesty's Government, I desire to present the Grand Cross of the Imperial Order of the Chrysanthemum to his Royal Highness the Prince of Wales.[168]

It was, as it turned out, a little premature to celebrate the revision of the treaties, but the presentation went ahead none the less.

Prince and Princess Komatsu reached England on 20 November 1886 and were received by the queen two days later at Windsor Castle. As *The Times* was careful to note, they travelled not in an ordinary carriage but in a special saloon attached to the train; at Windsor 'considerable preparations had been made to welcome the party', and they were conveyed to the castle in one of the queen's carriages. The investiture of the Prince of Wales took place on 7 December, and the prince and princess remained in London until early in the following year. The visit achieved its aims, then, but it should be noted that no honour was conferred on the prince on this occasion. It was not until 1890 that any reciprocal decoration was offered, when it was decided, following the

Duke of Connaught's visit to Japan, to make the prince a Knight Grand Cross of the Order of the Bath.[169]

This was predominantly a ceremonial visit, but during their visit they saw *The Mikado* at Savoy Theatre and Prince Komatsu visited various barracks and other military sites in London.[170] During this trip, Prince Komatsu's consort, Yoriko, is said to have lavished money on jewels and clothing: when this came to the ears of Emperor Meiji he was, apparently, furious, and thereafter frowned on members of the imperial family who wished to take their wives with them to Europe.[171]

They left London for Germany in January and remained there until June, when they returned to London for Victoria's Golden Jubilee. They took part in the festivities and were received by the queen again, but they were housed in an ordinary hotel, which contrasted with the treatment accorded to European royalty, and their carriage arrived too late for them to be able to take part in the procession. What was worse, Japan was treated as a minor country alongside Siam, Persia and Hawai'i.[172] Ceremonial visits are of small significance unless they go wrong, and this did go wrong and offended Japanese *amour propre*.

The year 1897 marked Queen Victoria's sixtieth year on the throne, but it also came just two years after Japan's dramatic victory in the Sino-Japanese War which demonstrated that Japan was now the dominant power in East Asia. Consequently, when an invitation was extended to Japan to be represented at the festivities celebrating the Diamond Jubilee, the response was that Japan would only attend if her representatives were treated like those of European powers. The British government agreed to meet this condition and promised that the Japanese representative, Prince Arisugawa Takehito, would be shown 'every courtesy due to his exalted rank'. He was accompanied by Itō Hirobumi, and in addition to taking full part in the festivities he was entertained to lunch by the queen.[173]

The last member of the Japanese imperial family to meet Queen Victoria was Prince Kan'in Kotohito (1865–1945). Prince Kan'in was the sixteenth son of the prolific Prince Fushimi Kuniie, but he was adopted by Emperor Kōmei as a possible heir and was therefore an adoptive brother of Emperor Meiji. He was a career officer in the Imperial Japanese Army and after spending some time in France as a military attaché he served in both the Sino-Japanese and Russo-Japanese wars. In later years, he rose rapidly in the military hierarchy, becoming field marshal in 1919. He accompanied crown prince Hirohito on his trip to Europe in 1921 and was chief of the general staff from 1931 to 1940, but when he visited Britain in 1900 he was still a colonel. Before his arrival, Ernest Satow, who was by then the British minister in Tokyo, had urged that he be treated with particular courtesy to signal Britain's approval of Japan's response to the outbreak of the Boer War, and it seems that his recommendation was followed. Prince Kan'in and the other eight members of his party travelled from Dover to London in a special saloon attached to a regular train, were greeted at Victoria Station and conveyed from there to the Japanese legation in Grosvenor Gardens in carriages provided by Buckingham Palace. He was introduced to the queen at Osborne House on 4 May and he stayed to dinner, and for once Victoria seems to have warmed to a Japanese visitor: she wrote in her journal, 'The Prince, who is very pleasant & intelligent & speaks quite good French, sat on my right.'[174]

Less than a year later, on 22 January 1901, Queen Victoria's long life came to an end. The emperor and the Japanese government had been kept closely informed of her declining health; the emperor ordered twenty-one days of court mourning and instructed Minister Baron Hayashi Tadasu in London to lay a wreath in the emperor's name. The funeral took place at Windsor Castle on 2 February. European royalty was present in force, but there was insufficient time for any member of the Japanese imperial family to travel to England to attend, so Japan was represented by Hayashi, who was temporarily raised to the rank of ambassador for his participation in the funeral. The only other Japanese known to have witnessed the funeral was the novelist Natsume Sōseki, who was living in London and wrote about it in his diary, but doubtless other Japanese in London at the time took the opportunity to witness the funeral that marked the end of Victoria's long reign.[175]

CONCLUSION

By the end of the nineteenth century, several members of the Japanese imperial family and the British royal family had visited each other's countries. Several of the Japanese had spent long periods in Britain, for language study and military training: it was common for male members of European royal families to undergo military training, and Emperor Meiji, explicitly following European practice, made naval or military training a requirement for male members of the imperial family.[176]

Most of the British visits were short, yet we know more about the British impressions of Japan than we do about the Japanese impressions of England. The Duke of Edinburgh's visit in 1869 was important in that it laid the foundations for future relations between the Japanese emperor and foreign sovereigns, but it is probably true to say that none of the British visitors had as much impact on Emperor Meiji as did the former American President Ulysses Grant, who spent several months in Japan in 1879, and none of them were of as high status as the heir to the Russian throne, Nicholas, who visited Japan in 1891 and barely escaped assassination.[177]

The members of the royal family who visited Japan in the nineteenth century formed largely positive impressions, like most British tourists, globe-trotters and long-term residents. They appreciated the scenery, Japanese arts and crafts and the courtesy of the Japanese people they met, but decidedly not Japanese cuisine, and their comments were often marked by a sense of European superiority. In these respects, their response to Japan was conventional for their time. The one lasting contribution that closer ties between the British Royal Family and the Japanese Imperial Family made was to the Royal Collections of art. In addition to the items collected by the Duke of Edinburgh, which have already been mentioned, there was a pair of contemporary bronze vases presented to Queen Victoria by Emperor Meiji in 1882 and a lacquered cabinet presented in 1897 for the Queen's Diamond Jubilee. These were followed by gifts or acquisitions of fine lacquerware in the early decades of the twentieth century.[178]

In spite of the growing personal ties between the two families, the British royal family seems to have attached little importance to Japan and to have given automatic preference to all European sovereigns. In 1884, when the Japanese legation in London received a list of the foreign states to which the queen habitually sent letters notifying recipients of births, marriages and deaths in the royal family, Japan was not on the list but Rumania, Serbia and assorted German duchies were. The legation was later informed that Japan would now be added to the list, but this came about as a result of representations from Japan rather than as a gesture from Britain.[179]

It was inevitable, in the Eurocentric world of the nineteenth century, that Japan buckled under and adopted Western diplomatic practices. This can be understood as realpolitik, a recognition of the might of the Western powers, and there can be no doubt that from the time of the Opium Wars onwards Japan was accustomed to looking upon Britain with fear rather than friendship. There were good reasons for doing so, and even Lord Elgin himself referred to Britain's record of 'violence and fraud, and disregard of right' in East Asia.[180] But Japan was also driven by a fervent desire to revise the treaties that had been concluded by the Bakufu with the Western powers in 1858 and which placed Japan at a disadvantage in terms of tariffs and autonomy. As a Russian diplomat said of Parkes, 'his policy naturally consisted in holding them as strictly as possible to the stipulations of the treaties, which the Japanese felt as a hardship from which their Government naturally desired to liberate itself'.[181] Even after the departure of Parkes in 1883, Britain stood out against revision of the treaties, while other countries began to accept the need for revision.

The unfairness of the treaties was vividly demonstrated by the scandal of the British merchant ship *Normanton* in 1886: when she sank off Japan, the English captain and the European crew members escaped in lifeboats, leaving the Indian and Chinese crewmembers and the Japanese passengers to drown. As a British national, the captain benefited from the extraterritoriality embodied in the treaties and so could not be charged with any offence in Japanese courts. An initial hearing in the British consular court found him innocent of any wrongdoing, but there was an outcry and after government pressure was applied, the captain was found guilty of criminal negligence and imprisoned for three months. The court did not, however, order that any compensation be paid to the relatives of the passengers who drowned.[182]

Two years later, in 1888, Ōkuma Shigenobu, then the foreign minister, reminded Plunkett that Britain exported more to Japan than any other nation and that half of the resident foreign nationals in Japan were British, and he suggested that although Japan remained grateful to Parkes for his help at the time of the Restoration, 'gratitude might turn to hatred if Britain kept blocking treaty reform'.[183] In the end, it was not until 1894 that Britain agreed to renegotiation of the treaties and not until 1899 that extraterritoriality was lifted and resident foreigners became subject to Japanese law. That no lasting damage was done is clear from the formation of the Anglo-Japanese Alliance in 1902, but it is surprising that Britain's intransigence on the issue of treaty reform did not arouse more antipathy in Japan.

In spite, then, of Japan's willingness to play the game by European rules, gaining acceptance in the 'European monarchical club' was a slow process. Religious differences were partly to blame, so were racial considerations, but the harsh fact is that in Britain, Japan was simply not seen as an important world player until its victory in the Sino-Japanese War. And Queen Victoria was anything but encouraging: for her, Japan seems to have remained a distant, if no longer wild, country.[184]

Britain was also much slower than other European nations to bestow honours on Emperor Meiji. In 1879, Prince Heinrich of Prussia, the younger brother of Kaiser Wilhelm II, spent some time in Japan during his trip around the world as a naval cadet and while there he conferred a Prussian decoration on Emperor Meiji. This was the first time that he had been so honoured, and it was followed later the same year by a Russian decoration and by an Italian decoration presented by Prince Tommaso, the Duke of Genoa, during his trip around the world. In 1880, Lord Granville raised the question of an award, after having been sounded out by the Japanese minister in London, Mori Arinori (1847–1889), who was later to serve as Minister of Education. Mori enquired if the Queen would accept the Order of the Chrysanthemum, one of the new Western-style decorations created by the Meiji government.[185] If she were willing to accept it, the decoration would be brought by Prince Arisugawa Takahito, who was soon to come to England for naval training. Mori intimated that a reciprocal award of the Order of the Garter for the emperor would be welcomed; in this way Japan's highest decoration would be exchanged for Britain's highest. Lord Granville, the Foreign Secretary, was unenthusiastic: he wrote to Sir Henry Ponsonby, the queen's private secretary, that 'The Japanese have placed their hopes very high – they expect the Garter for the Mikado!!!' The repeated exclamation marks show that he thought it out of the question, and he wrote to the Prince of Wales that the queen was not prepared to award the Garter. Ponsonby wrote that she found the idea 'preposterous'. Granville did, however, acknowledge that the Garter had already been bestowed upon Sultans Abdul Mecid and Abdul Aziz of the Ottoman Empire and Naser al-Din Shah Qajar of Persia, and that the emperor of Japan had already received the highest Russian, German, Italian, and Belgian orders. Nevertheless, he proposed that the Star of India be conferred on Emperor Meiji, on the grounds that this was a more suitable award for somebody from 'the East'. The queen approved this suggestion and so did the Prince of Wales, but, as Granville later noted, this 'did not satisfy the Japanese, and the matter was dropped.' He reported that Mori had said that 'his sovereign did not like being treated as an Asiatic sovereign'. In the end it was decided to send the emperor a portrait of the Queen instead of conferring any order, but it is difficult to suppose that this episode left no hurt feelings.[186] The correspondent of *The Times* in Japan lamented that while European sovereigns had already offered Emperor Meiji their highest orders, 'Great Britain has never offered to his Majesty any decoration more honourable than the Star of India, which she confers on her tributary princes, and which, as a matter of course, was declined by the Emperor'. It is not entirely clear from the surviving documents but it seems likely that Queen Victoria herself was firmly against the award of the Garter to Emperor Meiji. Whatever the case, it was not until Queen Victoria's son was on the throne as Edward VII that the award of the Order of the Garter was finally made, in 1906, but by then, of course, Britain and Japan were allies.[187]

The views of Emperor Meiji on Britain and the royal family are, like his views on most subjects, entirely beyond our ken. However, when King Kalakaua of Hawai'i visited Japan in 1881, Meiji seems to have expressed agreement with the idea that the countries of Asia needed to stand together to resist the oppressive countries of Europe.[188] Presumably, then, he, like his ministers, understood well the realities of international politics in the late nineteenth century, appreciated the need not to antagonise the great powers and therefore endeavoured to stay on good terms with Britain. Be that as it may, he seems to have been gracious in his reception of all members of the British royal family who visited Japan. However, unlike many members of the imperial family and of the government, Meiji himself never left Japan and so he had no first-hand knowledge of the outside world. Some of those around him looked favourably on the idea of having him travel to Europe, but it is not clear if the suggestion was ever put to him or if he favoured the idea.[189] Consequently, he was not personally known to any of the monarchs of the world with three exceptions: King Kalakaua of Hawai'i, who visited Japan in 1881 and died in 1891; Tsar Nicholas II, who visited Japan in 1891 when tsarevich, was very nearly assassinated there, came to the throne in 1894, and outlived Emperor Meiji; and King George V, who succeeded his father just two years before Meiji died.

The exchange of visits, decorations and correspondence was a familiar routine for European royal families in the nineteenth century. These exchanges, which were monitored by their governments, served to symbolise, underpin and sometimes deepen political relationships within Europe, but extending these courtesies to sovereigns of Asian countries required diplomatic recognition of their equality with European royalty. The first European royal to visit Japan was British, it is true, but the Duke of Edinburgh's visit did not form part of a new policy toward Japan, and Parkes' enthusiasm for the rosy future of Anglo-Japanese relations was not matched in London. In other respects, too, the British royal family was rather slower than other European countries to extend royal relationships to Japan. Yet this perfectly reflected British political unwillingness to take Japan seriously as a modern state until the very end of the century and the conclusion of the Anglo-Japanese Alliance in 1902.

ENDNOTES

* Abbreviations for archival sources: GGS=Gaimushō Gaikō Shiryōkan (Tokyo); KK=Kunai Kōbunshokan (Tokyo); KKB=Kokuritsu Kōbunshokan (Tokyo); NRO=Northamptonshire Record Office (Northampton); RA=Royal Archives (Windsor Castle); TNA=The National Archives (Kew).

1 That this was the tactic of opponents of the Bakufu was made clear when three of the 'Chōshū Five', five young samurai from Chōshū domain who surreptitiously left Japan in 1863 to study in England, were interviewed by Reginald Russell in London in 1864, for they made it quite clear that the sole motive of the attacks had been to embarrass the Bakufu: TNA, FO 46/49, 'Memorandum Japan', Reginald Russell to Foreign Secretary, 1 July 1864.

2 TNA, FO 46/139, Adams to Granville, 12 June 1871, containing a record of Iwakura's conversation with Sir Harry Parkes on 20 May 1871.

3 Donald Keene, *Emperor of Japan: Meiji and his World, 1852–1912* (New York: Columbia University Press, 2002), pp. 18–127; Grace Fox, *Britain and Japan 1858–1883* (Oxford: Clarendon Press, 1969), pp. 105, 137, etc. On earlier British involvement, see William G. Beasley, *Great Britain and the Opening of Japan, 1834–1858* (London: Luzac & Co., 1951).

4 Ernest Satow wrote that he 'was assured by a Japanese well acquainted with what went on beyond the scenes that he had been poisoned': Satow, *A Diplomat in Japan* (New York: Oxford University Press, 1968), pp. 185–6.

5 Keene, *Emperor of Japan*, p.117. This is the translation given in Ernest Satow, *A Diplomat in Japan*, p. 324; the original text in *kanbun* is in *Meiji tennō ki*, 12 vols (Tokyo: Yoshikawa Kōbunkan, 1968–77), vol. 1, p. 595.

6 See John Breen, 'Shintoists in Restoration Japan (1868–1872): towards a Reassessment', *Modern Asian Studies* 24 (1990): 579–602.

7 Antony Best, 'The role of diplomatic practice and court protocol in Anglo-Japanese relations, 1867–1900', in Markus Mosslang and Torsten Riotte (eds), *The Diplomats' World: the Cultural History of Diplomacy, 1815–1914* (Oxford: Oxford University Press, 2008), esp. pp. 37–8; John Breen, 'The Rituals of Anglo-Japanese Diplomacy: Imperial Audiences in Early Meiji Japan', in G. Daniels and C. Tsuzuki, (eds), *The History of Anglo-Japanese Relations 1600–2000*, vol. 5, Social and cultural perspectives (London: Palgrave, 2002), pp. 70–72.

8 Keene, *Emperor of Japan*, pp. 133–6.

9 TNA, FO 262/188, Parkes to Granville, 6 June 1870. On the tours see Takashi Fujitani, *Splendid Monarchy: Power and Pageantry in Modern Japan* (Berkeley: University of California Press, 1996) and Keene, *Emperor of Japan*, pp. 298–302, etc.

10 Keene, *Emperor of Japan*, pp. 143–5. Fox, *Britain and Japan*, pp. 233–4 (the letter of credence signed by Queen Victoria is reproduced as Plate 4).

11 TNA, FO 262/163, Parkes to Clarendon, 13 January 1869.

12 *Meiji tennō ki*, vol. 2, pp. 191–3; Keene, *Emperor of Japan*, pp. 187, 205, 288; Best, 'The role of diplomatic practice and court protocol', p. 242.

13 TNA, FO 262/163, Parkes to Clarendon, 13 January 1869. See 'Mikado', in the *Oxford English Dictionary*.

14 Ben-Ami Shillony, '"Restoration", "Emperor", "Diet", "Prefecture" or: how Japanese Concepts were Mistranslated into Western Languages', in Adriana Boscaro, Franco Gatti & Massimo Raveri (eds), *Rethinking Japan*, vol. 2 (Folkestone: Japan Library, 1990), pp. 300–310; Beasley, *Great Britain and the Opening of Japan*, 206, 215; TNA, FO 46/49, Reginald Russell, 'Memorandum Japan', 1 July 1864; Parkes to Sawa, September 1869, in *Dai Nihon gaikō monjo*, vol. 2 book 2 (Tokyo: Nihon Kokusai Kyōkai, 1938), pp. 544–6.

15 For the decision of 1870, see *Hōki bunrui taizen (dai ippen),* Gaikōmon 3 (Tokyo: Naikaku Kirokukyoku, 1890), p. 101. For Parkes' use of 'tenno', see GGS, 6.4.4.1–3, 'Eikoku Jukku Ettōinburugu shinnō raichō no ken', Parkes to Sawa, 23 November 1869.

16 Best, 'The role of diplomatic practice', pp. 236–7; Breen, 'The rituals of Anglo-Japanese diplomacy: imperial audiences in early Meiji Japan', p. 73. In 1870 the British, French, Dutch, Prussian and Spanish envoys argued that their sovereigns should all be designated as *kōtei* in Japanese and the government accepted this: Hōki *bunrui taizen* (dai ippen), Gaikōmon 3, pp. 8–9.

17 In several documents drafted in connection with the visit to Japan of Prince Alfred, Duke of Edinburgh, in 1869, the first draft uses *joō* but this was then crossed out and replaced with *kōtei*: GGS, 6.4.4.1–3–1, 'Eikoku Jukku Ettōinburugu shinnō raichō no ken'.

18 Online edition of Queen Victoria's journals (http://www.queenvictoriasjournals.org/home.do), entries for 21 September 1858 and 11 June 1862.

19 George Earl Buckle (ed.), *The Letters of Queen Victoria: second series. A Selection from Her Majesty's Correspondence and Journal between the Years 1862 and 1878*, vol. 1 (London: John Murray, 1926), p. 51.

20 RA, VIC/MAIN/Q/15. This file contains the papers placed before the Queen on Japan and China between 1857 and 1879; included is even a photograph of the severed head of the man accused of killing Lieutenant Bird in 1864 (f.56).

21 Online edition of Queen Victoria's journals, 4 December 1867. It seems clear that Akitake was wearing samurai dress for the occasion, but while he was in London he was also photographed wearing Western dress: see Nagai Hiroshi, *Koshashin de miru Bakumatsu Ishin to Tokugawa ichizoku* (Tokyo: Kadokawa, 2018), pp. 203–208.

22 TNA, FO 262/161, Clarendon to Parkes, 17 May 1869, enclosing printed Order in Council of 13 May 1869; Fox *Britain and Japan*, p. 117.

23 TNA, FO 391/24, Gladstone to Edmund Hammond (Permanent Under Secretary of State for Foreign Affairs), 14 September 1869; printed in H. C. G. Matthew (ed.), *The Gladstone Diaries*, vol. 7 (Oxford: Clarendon Press, 1982), p. 128.

24 TNA, FO 262/161, Clarendon to Parkes, 22 April 1869.

25 *Oranda fūsetsugaki shūsei*, 2 vols (Tokyo: Yoshikawa Kōbunkan, 1976–79), vol. 2, p. 197; Matsukata Fukuyo, *Oranda fūsetsugaki to kinsei Nihon* (Tokyo: Tōkyō Daigaku Shuppankai, 2007), p. 154.

26 Fox, *Britain and Japan*, pp. 42–3, 555. The first letter is enclosed in Alcock to Russell, 16 August 1861, printed in 'Correspondence respecting affairs in Japan July to November 1861' (Parliamentary Papers [hereafter PP] 1862, LXIV, pp. 33–5; reprinted in *British Parliamentary Papers Japan*, vol. 1 [Shannon: Irish University Press, 1971], pp. 327–8); Russell to Alcock, 10 May 1862, in 'Correspondence respecting affairs in Japan' (PP 1863, LXXIV, pp. 4–5). Some of the documents cited below are also contained in both of these printed sources, but since *British Parliamentary Papers Japan* simply reprints the original PP, I shall only mention the original PP in subsequent footnotes.

27 *Eikokushi* (Nagato: Onchisha, 1861), p. 1. This was a Japanese translation of a history of England written in Chinese by the missionary William Muirhead and published in Shanghai in 1856.

28 *Fukuzawa Yukichi zenshū* vol. 1 (Tokyo: Iwanami Shoten, 1958), p. 402.

29 TNA, ADM 1/6052, Parkes to Keppel, 29 April 1868, enclosed in Keppel to Admiralty, 2 May 1868; quoted in Fox, *Britain and Japan*, p. 234.

30 TNA, T 1/12969; Hugh Cortazzi, 'Royal Visits to Japan in the Meiji Period, 1868–1912', in Ian Nish (ed.), *Britain and Japan: Biographical Portraits*, vol. 2 (London: Routledge, 1997), p. 6. It appears from Cortazzi's article that the portrait is currently preserved in the imperial palace in Tokyo.

31 Fox, *Britain and Japan*, p. 93. The Queen's presence was reported by one of the students, Kawaji Tarō: Andrew Cobbing, *The Japanese Discovery of Victorian Britain: Early Travel Encounters in the Far West* (Richmond: Japan Library, 1998), p. 82. *The Times*, 9 March 1867, p. 9.

32 Cobbing, *The Japanese Discovery*, p. 96. *The Times*, 9 April 1867, p. 9, 16 April 1867, p. 9, 5 December 1867, p. 9. There was no Japanese minister plenipotentiary in France at this time: the first Japanese envoy, Sameshima Naonobu, was not appointed until 1872.

33 Charles William De la Poer Beresford, *The Memoirs of Admiral Lord Charles Beresford*, vol. 1 (London: Methuen & Co., 1914), p. 98; F. V. Dickins and S. Lane-Poole, *The life of Sir Harry Parkes*, vol. 2 (London: Macmillan, 1894), p. 97; Keppel, *A sailor's life*, vol. 3, p. 190.

34 Earl H. Kinmonth, *The Self-Made Man in Early Japanese Thought: From Samurai to Salaryman* (Berkeley: University of California Press, 1981), p. 22; Cobbing, *The Japanese Discovery*, p. 190. On the impact of *Haiguo tuzhi* on Japan, see Masuda Wataru, *Japan and China: Mutual Representations in the Modern Era*, trans. and ed. Joshua Fogel (Richmond: Curzon Press, 2000), pp. 23–8.

35 Terry Bennett, Hugh Cortazzi and J. E. Hoare (eds)., *Japan and The Graphic: Compete Record of Reported Events, 1870–1899* (Folkestone: Global Oriental, 2011), p. 45 (issue of 13 March 1875). The photograph is said to have been provided by one R. H. Mason. It was the photograph taken in 1873 by Uchida Kuichi for the purpose of presenting to visitors on formal occasions: Keene, *Emperor of Japan*, p. 237. For the extensive coverage of Japan in the *Illustrated London News*, see Terry Bennett (ed.), *Japan and the Illustrated London News: Complete Record of Reported Events, 1853–1899* (Folkestone: Global Oriental, 2006): for the railway inauguration, see the issue of 21 December 1872. On Japan in Victorian journals and writing, see Toshio Yokoyama, *Japan in the Victorian Mind: a Study of Stereotyped Images of a Nation 1850–80* (London: Macmillan, 1987).

36 Breen, 'The Rituals of Anglo-Japanese Diplomacy: Imperial Audiences in Early Meiji Japan', p. 74.

37 TNA, ADM 196/40/3.

38 Steve Harris, *The Prince and the Assassin: Australia's First Royal Tour and Portent of World Terror* (Melbourne: Melbourne Books, 2017), pp. 100–109, 124–5, etc. On the first part of the voyage, see John Milner and Sir Oswald Walters Brierly, *The*

Cruise of HMS Galatea, Captain H.R.H. the Duke of Edinburgh, K.G., in 1867, 1868 (London: W. H. Allen & Co., 1869).

39 For the dates I have relied on the official log of the *Galatea* in the National Archives (ADM 53/9779), and the private log and journal kept by Lt John William Ramsay (1847–1887), who became 13th Earl of Dalhousie in 1880, in Cambridge University Library (MS Add.9279). Details of the crew are contained in William R. Beach, *Visit of His Royal Highness the Duke of Edinburgh, K.G., K.T., G.C.M.G., to Hongkong in 1869* (Hong Kong: Noronha & Sons, 1869). The Duke left Nagasaki for China on 26 September aboard HMS *Salamis*, and the *Galatea* followed a few days later.

40 Dickins and Lane-Poole, *The Life of Sir Harry Parkes*, vol. 2, p. 119.

41 TNA, FO 46/110, Parkes to Clarendon, 26 July 1869; in 'Correspondence respecting affairs in Japan: 1868–70' (PP 1870, LXX, p. 35).

42 TNA, FO 46/111, Parkes to Clarendon, 23 August 1869 (PP 1870, LXX, p. 39). See also the account in John Reddie Black, *Young Japan: Yokohama and Yedo*, vol. 2 (London: Trubner & Co., 1881), pp. 267–8. Black's wording is so close to that of Parkes that it is clear he had access to Parkes' despatches.

43 *Dai Nihon gaikō monjo*, vol. 2 book 2, p. 30; contemporary translation included in TNA, FO 46/110, Parkes to Clarendon, 26 July 1869 (PP 1870, LXX, p. 36).

44 Uchiyama Masakuma, 'Meiji kyūtei gaikō no enkaku: Meiji ninen no eikoku ōji raichō o kiten to shite', *Hōgaku kenkyū* 50.12 (1977), pp. 47–8.

45 Tada Kōmon (ed.), *Iwakura kō jikki*, 3 vols. (Np: Iwakura-kō kyūseki hozonkai, 1927), vol. 2, pp. 768–73. Announcements were also published in the government gazette, *Dajōkan nisshi*: no. 81 (Meiji 2.7.1–10), no. 83 (Meiji 2.7.22–30), no. 100 (Meiji 2.9.18).

46 Documents relating to these visits are contained in several documents entitled 'Hamaten gyōkō' in *Dajō ruiten*, Part I, vol. 52 (available at KKB or digitally on their website).

47 Miyama Jun'ichi, 'Enryōkan no jidai: Meiji Nippon omotenashi kotohajime', Ākaibuzugaku *kenkyū* 26 (2017): 107–109; for the location of the Hamagoten as it was in the 1860s, see the revised edition of Kageyama Muneyasu's *Atagoshita no zu* (Edo: Owariya Seishichi, 1861), in *Edo kiriezu shūsei*, vol. 4 (Tokyo: Chūōkōron-sha, 1982), pp. 88–9. For detailed plans of the Enryōkan, see KK, 38710 & 38711, both entitled 'Enryōkan chiezu'. At one stage the Tokyo Metropolitan Government was planning to rebuild the Enryōkan for the Tokyo Olympics in 2020 and archaeological excavation was carried out to establish the exact location of the original structure, but the plan seems to have been dropped: see http://www.metro.tokyo.jp/INET/OSHIRASE/2016/03/20q3tc00.htm.

48 Lord Redesdale, *Memories* (London: Hutchinson & Co., 1915), vol. 2, p. 495; TNA, FO 46/111, Parkes to Clarendon, 23 August 1869 (PP 1870, LXX, p. 39); Uchiyama, 'Meiji kyūtei gaikō no enkaku', pp. 52–7. For details of the alterations made to the stone building, see 'Hamaten sekishitsu shūshoku', in *Dajō ruiten*,

Part I, vol. 55. On Mitford's role, see Robert Morton, *A. B. Mitford and the Birth of Japan as a Modern State* (Folkestone: Renaissance Books, 2017), pp. 139–47.

49 RA, VIC/ADDA20/660a, copy of letter and journal of J.W.R. [John William Ramsay]. The letter, to his mother, is dated 10 September 1869 on HMS *Galatea* in Yokohama. For the log kept by Ramsay, see note 39.

50 TNA, FO 46/110, Parkes to Clarendon, 26 July 1869 (PP 1870, LXX, p. 35).

51 Oka Yoshitake, *Reimeiki no Meiji Nihon: Nichi-Ei kōshōshi no shikaku ni oite* (Tokyo: Miraisha, 1964), pp. 99, 118; Oka's detailed study of the visit (pp. 99–133) draws extensively on documents in the National Archives. The need for protection is mentioned in Japanese documents: GGS, 6.4.4.1–3, 'Eikoku Jukku Ettōinburugu shinnō raichō no ken', 'Ōji chakufu made no tetsuzuki'.

52 Fox, *Britain and Japan*, pp. 98, 204; Keene, *Emperor of Japan*, pp. 132–3. For a detailed study of post-Restoration violence directed at foreigners and the problems this caused the new government, see Oka, *Reimeiki no Meiji Nihon*, pp. 51–95.

53 TNA, FO 46/112, Parkes to Clarendon, 28 September 1869.

54 *Dai Nihon gaikō monjo*, vol. 2 book 2, pp. 175–6; for translation, TNA, FO 46/111, Parkes to Clarendon, 23 August 1869 (PP 1870, LXX, p. 40). The original contains no references to 'highest and lowest' or to 'offensive' behaviour, so the translation was rather free.

55 Beresford, *Memoirs*, vol. 1 (London: Methuen & Co., 1914), p. 100; Sir Henry Keppel, *A Sailor's Life under Four Sovereigns* (London: Macmillan and Co., 1899), vol. 3, p. 286; 'Eikoku ōji zairyūchū' in *Dajō ruiten*, Part I, vol. 41.

56 *Dai Nihon gaikō monjo*, vol. 2 book 2, pp. 176–8.

57 TNA, FO 46/111, Parkes to Clarendon, 30 August 1869.

58 *The Japan Times Overland Mail*, 4 September 1869, p. 61; Keppel *A Sailor's Life under Four Sovereigns* (London: Macmillan and Co., 1899), vol. 3, pp. 285–6. A day-by-day record of the duke's visit was kept by his Japanese hosts, though it uses the lunar calendar then in use in Japan and it records no details of the time spent in Yokohama: 'Eikoku ōji taizaichū nikki', in *Dajō ruiten*, Part I, vol. 55.

59 TNA, FO 46/112, Parkes to Clarendon, 2 September 1869, enclosure (PP 1870, LXX, p. 40). Redesdale, *Memories*, vol. 2, p. 496. The signed address is preserved in the Thuringer Staatsarchiv in Gotha and is shown in Bernd Schäfer, Uta Wallenstein and Michaela Appel, eds, *Ein Prinz entdeckt die Welt. Die Reisen und Sammlungen Herzog Alfreds von Sachsen-Coburg und Gotha (1844–1910)* (Gotha: Stiftung Schloss Friedenstein, 2008), #41, pp. 102–103. According to a report despatched by Parkes on 29 April 1871, there were then 513 British residents in Yokohama, 134 in Hyōgo (Kōbe) and Osaka, 91 in Nagasaki, 22 in Edo (Tokyo), 16 in Hakodate and 6 in Niigata: 'Commercial reports from Her Majesty's Consuls in Japan 1870–71', p. 123 (*British Parliamentary Papers Japan*, vol. 4 'Embassy and consular commercial reports 1859–71' [Shannon: Irish University Press, 1972], p. 649).

60 Tada, *Iwakura kō jikki*, vol. 2, pp. 767–8; TNA, FO 262/112, Parkes to Clarendon, 30 September 1869.

61 Beresford, *Memoirs*, vol. 1, pp. 100–101; RA, VIC/ADDA20/660a, copy of letter and journal of J.W.R. [John William Ramsay].

62 Keene, *Emperor of Japan*, pp. 184–5; Redesdale, *Memories*, vol. 2, p. 497.

63 'The Duke of Edinburgh in Japan and China', *The Times,* 1 Dec. 1869, p. 4 (this article quotes extensively from the *Japan Times*: see *The Japan Times Overland Mail*, 18 September 1869, p. 77). Oka notes that there were a number of clashes between the British and Japanese sides over the organization of the audience: Oka, *Reimeiki no Meiji Nihon*, pp. 120–2.

64 Redesdale, *Memories*, vol. 2, p. 500.

65 The extract from the translation of the programme for the audience is from an enclosure with Parkes' despatch to the Earl of Clarendon of 4 September 1869 (TNA, FO 46/112; PP 1870, LXX, p. 42). Detailed planning papers are contained in GGS, 6.4.4.1–3, 'Eikoku Jukku Ettōinburugu shinnō raichō no ken', and some are reprinted in Hōki *bunrui taizen* (dai ippen), Gaikōmon 3, pp. 215–39.

66 TNA, FO 46/112, Parkes to Clarendon, 4 September 1869, enclosure, and 30 September 1869, enclosure (PP 1870, LXX, pp. 42–6).

67 TNA, FO 46/112, Parkes to Clarendon, 4 September 1869, enclosure, and 30 September 1869, enclosure (PP 1870, LXX, pp. 42–6); Ōkubo *Toshimichi nikki*, 2 vols (Tokyo: Nihon Shiseki Kyōkai, 1927), vol. 2, pp. 48, 55–7, 61.

68 *A Guide to the Works of Art and Science collected by Captain His Royal Highness The Duke of Edinburgh, K.G., during his Five-years' Cruise round the World in H.M.S. "Galatea" (1867–1871) and lent for exhibition in the South Kensington Museum, February, 1872* (London: John Strangeways, 1872), p. 46. The watercolour is dated 4 September 1869 and is now in the Museum of New Zealand and the oil painting is in the Art Gallery of Western Australia: the latter is signed 'N. Chevalier 1873' so it is clear that he made a sketch of the scene at the time and worked it up into a painting later. A photograph of the same part of the Fukiage Garden taken in 1876 or 1877 survives in the form of an engraving in Isidore Eggermont, *Voyage autour du globe. Japon* (Paris: Delagrave, 1900), p. 47; Eggermont (1844–1923), an accomplished photographer, was a councillor at the Belgian Legation in Japan from 1876 to 1877 and describes, on p. 51, a visit to the garden. A comparison of the watercolour and the engraving suggests that Chevalier exaggerated the height of the waterfall.

69 Marjorie J. Tipping, 'Chevalier, Nicholas (1828–1902)', *Australian Dictionary of Biography*, vol. 3 (Melbourne: Melbourne University Press, 1969), pp. 387–8. The Royal Collection contain some of his sketches from his time on the *Galatea* but apparently none from the visit to Japan: Delia Miller, *The Victorian Watercolours and Drawings in the Collection of Her Majesty The Queen*, vol. 1 (London: Philip Wilson Publishers 1995), pp.189–90.

70 RA, VIC/ADDA20/660a, copy of letter and journal of J.W.R. [John William Ramsay].

71 RA, VIC/ADDA20/660a, copy of letter and journal of J.W.R. [John William Ramsay]; Redesdale, *Memories*, vol. 2, p. 498; Beresford, *Memoirs*, p. 100; Keppel, *A Sailor's Life under Four Sovereigns*, vol. 3, pp. 287–9; *Meiji tennōki*, vol. 2, p. 168. The dinner followed the audience in the palace and was prepared for them at the Enryōkan; this was at the suggestion of the Foreign Minister, who used the term *Nihon ryōri* (Japanese cuisine), perhaps for the first time: *Hōki bunrui taizen (dai ippen)*, Gaikōmon 3, p. 221.

72 *Meiji tennōki*, vol. 2, pp. 167–8; Morton, *A. B. Mitford and the Birth of Japan as a Modern State*, p. 144; TNA, FO 262/112, Parkes to Clarendon, 30 September 1869; Oka, *Reimeiki no Meiji Nihon*, pp. 130–31. Requests for things written in the Emperor's own hand were infrequently granted; the Japanese Foreign Office file (GGS, 6.4.1.14, 'Goshinpitsu kankei zakken') starts with a request made by the Austrian Minister in 1877 in connection with an exhibition of the handwriting of famous people to be held in Prague.

73 Keppel, *A Sailor's Life under Four Sovereigns*, vol. 3, pp. 295–6.

74 *The Japan Times Overland Mail*, 18 September 1869, pp. 78, 84. The Club was the Yokohama United Club. Unfortunately, the *Japan Punch* issues for September and October 1869 do not appear to be extant; the issue for August includes a plea that the Duke be left alone to enjoy himself, pointing out that, 'This is not a British colony and there is no necessity for bodies to affront the Japanese by behaving as if it were': *The Japan Punch* (facsimile edition), vol. 2 (Tokyo: Yūshōdō Shoten, 1975), p. 283.

75 TNA, FO 262/174, Parkes to Clarendon, 8 October 1869, enclosing reports from consuls Gower and Flowers (PP 1870, LXX, pp. 69); *The Times*, 1 December 1869, p. 4, quoting a report in the *North China Herald*. Keppel provides further details in *A Sailor's Life under Four Sovereigns*, vol. 3, pp. 298–301.

76 RA, VIC/ADDA20/1294, Prince Alfred to Queen Victoria, 3 September 1869.

77 RA, VIC/ADDA20/1296, Prince Alfred to Queen Victoria, 3 October 1869.

78 *Ibid.*

79 *Dai Nihon gaikō monjo*, vol. 2 book 2, pp. 544–6; the original is contained in GGS, 6.4.4.1–3.

80 GGS, 6.4.4.1–3, Parkes to Terashima, 15 October 1869.

81 TNA, FO 262/112, Parkes to Clarendon, 30 September 1869 (PP 1870, LXX, p. 43).

82 On the spread of European diplomatic conventions in the nineteenth century beyond Europe, see Best, 'The role of diplomatic practice', p. 231.

83 Uchiyama, 'Meiji kyūtei gaikō no enkaku', pp. 59–60.

84 *Ibid.*, pp. 45–6.

85 See the extracts from *Meiji shinbun*, 12.8.1869, and *Chūgai shinbun*, 16.8.1869, included in *Shinbun shūsei Meiji hennnenshi*, 2nd edition, vol. 1 (Tokyo: Rinsensha,

1936), pp. 303–304, and in *Nihon shoki shinbun zenshū*, vol. 24 (Tokyo: Perikansha, 1990), pp. 140–141, 176, 192, and the extracts included in *Meiji nyūsu jiten*, vol. 1 (Tokyo: Mainichi Komyūnikeeshonzu, 1983), p. 22.

86 The print, 'Eikoku ōji torai', is contained in a book, published in the tenth month of 1869, entitled *Tōkyō hanka ichiran*, which can be found in the International Research Centre for Japanese Studies and Chūōkuritsu Kyōbashi Toshokan in Tokyo.

87 Best, 'The role of diplomatic practice', pp. 244–7.

88 Illustration from *The Graphic* of 25 Jan. 1873 in Bennett, Cortazzi and Hoare, *Japan and The Graphic*, p. 27.

89 *Meiji tennō ki*, vol. 2, pp. 167–8. For the list of gifts, including *makie* lacquerware and ten albums of paintings, to be presented to the Duke and his followers by the government, see *Dai Nihon gaikō monjo*, vol. 2 book 2, 382–5; in the case of the albums, the artists and subjects are identified.

90 *The Times*, 23 January 1872, p. 8; illustration from *The Graphic* of 9 March 1872 in Bennett, Cortazzi and Hoare, *Japan and The Graphic*, p. 15.

91 *A Guide to the Works of Art and Science collected by Captain His Royal Highness The Duke of Edinburgh*, pp. 5–6, 45–56; note that the copy in the British Museum is furnished with photographs of some of the objects, while other copies, bearing the same date, lack the photographs; also, the *Guide* refers to a more detailed catalogue of the exhibits but I have not been able to find a copy of this. In the Print Room at Windsor Castle there is also a scrapbook of the voyage of the *Galatea*, but it unfortunately contains only three items from Japan: a watercolour sketch of a Japanese artist seated on the floor painting a portrait, with the inscription 'Naiamci. artist at Yedo / 72 Years old' (RCIN 928526) and two faint pencil drawings of a man relaxing with a Japanese woman (RCIN 928860, RCIN 928861).

92 On the items preserved in Gotha, see Schäfer, Wallenstein and Appel, *Ein Prinz entdeckt die Welt*, which is a richly-illustrated account of the duke and his travels and includes, on pp. 141–5, illustrations and descriptions of lacquerware and other Japanese artefacts brought back by the duke and preserved in the Schloss Friedenstein. See also Herbert Bräutigam, *Schätze japanischer lackkunst auf Schloß Friedenstein* (Gotha: Schlossmuseum, 1998), which contains detailed descriptions and illustrations of all the Japanese lacquerware preserved in the Schlossmuseum: some of them were acquired in the seventeenth century, but those items donated by the duke in 1895 are identified. The lost items are being documented in the series *Verlustdokumentation. Der Gothaer Kunstsammlungen*, 2 vols (Gotha: Schloß Friedenstein, 1997 and 2011).

93 For descriptions of some items which came from the collection of the Duke of Edinburgh, see John Ayers, *Chinese and Japanese Works of Art in the Collection of Her Majesty The Queen*, 3 vols (London: Royal Collection Trust, 2016), vol. 3, #2202–2207; other items thought by Ayers to have come from other sources have now

been recognised as having come from the Duke's collection: see the entries on the Royal Collections Trust website for items RCIN 29452, 29453, 3484 and 33949 (Ayers, vol. 3, pp. 992–3, 1004, 1006–1007, 1010).

94 Keppel, *A Sailor's Life under Four Sovereigns*, vol. 3, p. 295; Beresford, *Memoirs*, vol. 1, pp. 100–101. On tattooing in Meiji Japan see Noboru Koyama, 'Japanese Tattooists and the British Royal Family during the Meiji Period', in Hugh Cortazzi (ed.), *Britain and Japan: Biographical Portraits*, vol. 6 (Folkestone: Global Oriental 2007), pp. 71–80, and Christine Guth, *Longfellow's Tattoos: Tourism, Collecting, and Japan* (Seattle: University of Washington Press, 2004).

95 Ishizuki Minoru, *Kindai Nihon no kaigai ryūgakushi* (Tokyo: Minerva Shobō, 1972), pp. 149–50; KK, *Kachōnomiya jitsuroku*, vol. 2, report on his travels after his return home (dated August 1873 and extracted from *Kōshinroku*).

96 *Kitashirakawa no miya Yoshihisa shinnō* (1923; facsimile published by Yumani Shobō of Tokyo in 2010), p. 27.

97 On the first Japanese diplomatic representatives in Britain, see Ian Nish (ed.), *Japanese Envoys in Britain, 1862–1964: a Century of Diplomatic Exchange* (Folkestone: Global Oriental, 2007), pp. 17–18, 21–7.

98 KK, *Kitashirakawanomiya Yoshihisa shinnō jitsuroku*, vol. 5, entries for 1871.1.15 & 26 and 1871.2.15 (dates given in this form are in the lunisolar calendar used in Japan before the adoption of the Gregorian calendar on 1 January 1873); Mori Ōgai, 'Yoshihisa shinnō jiseki', in Ōgai *zenshū*, vol. 3 (Tokyo: Iwanami Shoten, 1972), pp. 497–620, especially 556–7. For his visits to England, see the Chronology in this volume.

99 KK, *Komatsu no miya Akihito shinnō jitsuroku*, vol. 4, entries for 1869.12.17 & 20, vol. 5, entries for 1870.1.8, 1870.3.16, 1870.10.8; *Dajōkan nisshi*, no. 43 (Meiji 3.10.4–12); Ishizuki, *Kindai Nihon no kaigai ryūgakushi*, p. 149; 'Higashifushimi no miya gaikoku kingaku', *Dajō ruiten* Part I, vol. 120; *Meiji tennōki*, 2: 309.

100 TNA, FO 46/127, Parkes to Granville, 3 December 1870; FO 262/205, Granville to Parkes, 9 February 1871; *Kōbunroku*, vol. 129, Meiji 3 [1870], 'Imperial household' (available at KKB or digitally on their website); *Dajō ruiten* Part I, vol. 120.

101 KK, *Komatsu no miya Akihito shinnō jitsuroku*, vol. 5, copy of letter written by Prince Higashifushimi's companion, Mori Shigenori, on 8 February 1870.

102 TNA, FO 46/139, Parkes to Sawa and Terashima, 14 April 1871, Sawa to Parkes, 8 May 1871; *The Times*, 22 February 1871, p. 12; 'Higashifushimi no miya chakuei jijō', *Dajō ruiten* Part I, vol. 54.

103 *Warminster Herald*, 4 March 1871. See also Cobbing, *The Japanese Discovery*, pp. 127, 120–1.

104 I am indebted to Mr Danny Howell of Warminster for having furnished copies of documents in his possession, including extracts from the 1871 Census, and for having guided my research on the Prince's sojourn in Warminster. 'Igami' is

probably an error for Igimi, one of the Prince's retainers; why the others were not listed as well is unclear; Ōno did not accompany the Prince from Japan so was presumably already in England.

105 Obituary of Daniell, *The Warminster & Westbury Journal*, 3 December 1898. On Lowder see TNA, FO46/9, #22 and #271, draft of Foreign Office letters to Lowder addressed to him care of Daniell at Kington Langley, 7 June and 25 May 1860; and J. E. Hoare, 'John Frederick Lowder (1843–1902): Consul, Counsel and *o-yatoi*', in Hugh Cortazzi (ed.), *Britain and Japan: Biographical Portraits*, vol. 10 (Folkestone: Renaissance Books, 2016), pp. 300–302. On the Tosa students in England, see Nagakuni Jun'ya, *Tosa-han ryūgakusei ibun* (Kōchi: Tosa Shuppansha, 1989); *Baba Tatsui zenshū*, 4 vols (Tokyo: Iwanami Shoten, 1987–8), vol. 3, pp. 71–3; William Plomer (ed.), *Kilvert's Diary: Selections from the Diary of Francis Kilvert*, vol. 1 (London: Jonathan Cape, 1938) p. 299; and Hagihara Nobutoshi, '*Baba Tatsui zenshū* henshū yoroku', in Ōkubo *Toshikane rekishi chosakushū*, vol. 6 furoku geppō (Yoshikawa Kōbunkan, 1988), pp. 4–6.

106 *Warminster Herald*, 14 October 1871.

107 J. J. Daniell, *The History of Warminster* (London: Simpkin, Marshall & Co., 1879), pp. 83, 148; *Warminster Herald*, 25 November 1871, 23 December 1871, 3 February 1872, 17 February 1872, 24 February 1872; *Western Gazette* 23 February 1872; *Salisbury and Winchester Journal*, 24 February 1872, p. 8; Robert Hope, *A History of the Lord Weymouth School, Warminster* (Warminster: [Lord Weymouth] School Parents' Association, 1970), pp. 97–8; Cobbing, *The Japanese Discovery*, pp. 99, 120–1.

108 *Warminster Herald*, 24 February 1872. Unfortunately, I have so far been unable to find any of these photographs.

109 *The Times*, 16 June 1871, p. 9, 24 June 1871, p. 12, 28 June 1871, p. 8.

110 KK, *Komatsu no miya Akihito shinnō jitsuroku*, vol. 5, extract from his diary containing a report on his return from England dated 14 June 1873. The name of the person he studied with is rendered in *katakana* 'purofessā toryū', i.e. Professor True (or Trew, or possibly Drew), but I have been unable to identify him. There was a schoolmaster named William Martin Trew living at Blackheath Hill in the 1840s, but whether he was still there in the 1870s is unknown: John William Linzee, *The Linzee Family* (Boston, MA: privately printed, 1917), vol. 2, pp. 684–8. Blackheath Hill was the name of a railway station between Greenwich and Lewisham in south London, but it no longer exists. The *jitsuroku* contains no other entries relating to his time in Britain after his arrival in Warminster nor any extracts from letters home.

111 *The Times*, 26 February 1872, p. 10, *The Times*, 28 May 1872, p. 5, 22 June 1872, p. 12, 10 July 1872, p. 5

112 *Kitashirakawa no miya Yoshihisa shinnō*, p. 27.

113 Cobbing, *The Japanese Discovery*, pp. 120–1, 136; Nagakuni, *Tosa-han ryūgakusei ibun*, pp. 126–34; Miwa Hideo, 'Kunisawa Shinkurō no gareki to sakuhin', *Bijutsu kenkyū* 321 (1982): 25–32.

114 *The Examiner*, 13 April 1872, p. 382; *Society of British Artists: the Forty-Ninth Annual Exhibition* (1872), p. 19, #265; most paintings exhibited carry a price in the catalogue, but not the three portraits exhibited by Williams in 1872, presumably because they had been commissioned. I am grateful to Mr Komatsu Kiyohisa, a descendant of the Prince, for the information he provided about the loss of the family possessions in 1945.
115 *The Spectator*, 8 April 1871, p. 11.
116 Kume Kunitake, *The Iwakura Embassy 1871–73*, vol. 2 Britain, trans. Graham Healey (Matsudo: The Japan Documents, 2002), p. 70; the audience is described in Tanaka Akira (ed.), *Tokumei zenken taishi Beiō kairan jikki*, (Tokyo: Iwanami Shoten, 1985), vol. 2, pp. 407–408, in Tada, *Iwakura kō jikki*, vol. 2, pp. 1018–20, and in *The Times*, 6 December 1872, p. 9.
117 Online edition of Queen Victoria's journals, 5 December 1872.
118 *The Times*, 7 December 1872, p. 9.
119 Tanaka, *Tokumei zenken taishi Beio kairan jikki*, vol. 2, pp. 71, 390; in *The Iwakura Embassy 1871–73*, vol. 2 Britain (see note 116), on p. 62, the translation 'Prince and Princess Fushimi' is wrong: the original reads *ryōshinnō* (two princes). *Frome Times* 12 April 1871, p. 3; *Devizes and Wiltshire Gazette*, 30 March 1871, p. 3.
120 KK, 72202, 'Akihito shinnō nenpu shiryō' vol. 12, 'Komatsu no miya nikki shōroku' 4; this volume, which covers 1872, includes a diary of events at his home in Tokyo, details of what was sent to him from Japan and of what he sent back to Japan, including copies of his diary. The diary, which presumably contained details of his life in England, most likely was destroyed in the air raids of 1945: see note 114, above.
121 Andrew Cook, in his *Prince Eddy: The King Britain Never Had* (Stroud: Tempus, 2006), presents a sympathetic account of the Prince's short life and argues that there is no evidence to substantiate any of the rumours that swirled around his name long after his death.
122 TNA, ADM 53/11623, log of HMS *Bacchante*. Lord Scott's private log is on deposit at Northamptonshire Record Office: NRO, Lady Scott archive, Box 17. This was not Scott's first visit to Japan, for he had visited in 1870 while in command of HMS *Icarus* and had visited Kamakura and Nagasaki: NRO, Lady Scott archive, box 30, photograph album of the voyage of HMS *Icarus*. See also Harold Nicolson, *King George V: his Life and Reign* (London: Constable & Co., 1952), vol. 1, pp. 28–9.
123 Cook, *Prince Eddy*, pp. 70–1. For lists of the officers aboard the *Bacchante* and *Inconstant*, see the *Navy List*, 1881.iv (London: John Murray, 1881), pp. 196 and 218.
124 Dalton was strongly against the removal of the princes from the *Bacchante* on the ground that it seriously disrupted their naval and general studies on board:

RA, VIC/MAIN/Z/474/3, 'Memorandum on the removal of Prince Albert Victor and Prince George of Wales from HMS Bacchante', 15 July 1881. Prince George's diary is preserved in the Royal Archives and will be referred to below. Prince Eddy's diary and papers were apparently destroyed by Princess Beatrice after his death: Cook, *Prince Eddy*, p. 77.

125 KKB, *Dajō ruiten,* Part 5, vol. 9, 'Eikoku kōson raisen ni tsuki setsugūhō', 'Eikoku kōson settai shidai', 'Zai Ei Mori kōshi yori wagakuni ni oite Eikoku kōson settai ni tsuki dōkokutei no naitō o hōkoku su' and other documents in the same volume.

126 *The Cruise of Her Majesty's Ship "Bacchante" 1879–1882: compiled from the private journals, letters, and note-books of Prince Albert Victor and Prince George of Wales with additions by John N. Dalton*, 2 vols (London: Macmillan, 1886), vol. 2, p. 19.

127 *The Cruise of Her Majesty's Ship "Bacchante"*, vol. 2, p. 20.

128 Ian Ruxton (ed.), *A Diplomat in Japan part II: the Diaries of Ernest Satow, 1870–1883* (Morrisville NC: Lulu Press, 2009), p. 474. Unless otherwise indicated, the following account of the princes' visit to Japan is based on Satow's diaries, *The Cruise of Her Majesty's Ship "Bacchante"* and Dalton's letters to the Prince of Wales written on 24 and 31 October and 22 November 1881 and contained in RA, VIC/MAIN/Z.

129 The game that is known as *dakyū* in Japan has the same origins as polo but reached Japan via China and Korea in the Heian period. Ramsay provides a detailed description of the game as he witnessed it: RA, VIC/ADDA20/660a, copy of letter and journal of J.W.R. [John William Ramsay]. For a scroll depicting *dakyū* as played in nineteenth-century Japan, see Jonathan A. Hill Catalogue 225, 'Japanese books, manuscripts, and scrolls' (New York, 2018), #59, pp. 123–6.

130 RA, VIC/ADDA20/660a, copy of letter and journal of J.W.R. [John William Ramsay].

131 Bennett (ed.), *Japan and the Illustrated London News*, p. 256; Koyama Noboru, *Nihon no shisei to Eikoku* ōshitsu*: Meijiki kara daiichiji sekai taisen made* (Tokyo: Fujiwara Shoten, 2010).

132 The details are contained in KK, 65140, 'Eikoku kōson raikō ikken', which contains all the palace records relating to the visit; included is a sample of the invitation sent out to selected people to join the princes for the occasion, which specified that frock coats were to be worn.

133 *The Cruise of Her Majesty's Ship "Bacchante"*, vol. 2, pp. 53–4; Bennett, Cortazzi and Hoare (eds)., *Japan and The Graphic*, p. 194 (issue of 8 July 1893).

134 TNA, ADM 1/6576, S.280, Willes to Admiralty, 8 November 1881.

135 NRO, Lady Scott archive, box 24, Album of HMS *Bacchante*; this includes, on the reverse of a letter from the Imperial Household Department dated 21 October 1881, a note made by Captain Lord Scott of those invited to luncheon on

board the *Bacchante* on 31 October 1881. Drumlanrig Castle archives, log of HMS *Bacchante* from 26 January 1881 to 25 August 1881, kept by John Montagu Douglas Scott, entries for 29 & 31 October 1881.

136 Ruxton (ed.), *A diplomat in Japan part II*, p. 475.

137 *The Cruise of Her Majesty's Ship "Bacchante"*, vol. 2, p. 73.

138 *The Cruise of Her Majesty's Ship "Bacchante"*, vol. 2, p. 84; British Museum, Jap.Ptg. Add.1302.

139 RA, VIC/MAIN/Z/474/12, Dalton to Prince of Wales, 22 November 1881.

140 RA, GV/PRIV/GVD/1881, entries for 28–29 October, 3, 8 and 12 November. For the classes on board, see Dalton's letters to the Prince of Wales in RA, VIC/MAIN/Z/474.

141 RA, VIC/MAIN/Z/474/9 (31 October 1881), 474/12 (22 November 1881).

142 RA, VIC/MAIN/Z/474/11, Dalton to Francis Knollys, 31 October 1881.

143 Bennett (ed.), *Japan and the Illustrated London News*, pp. 254, 256; Bennett, Cortazzi and Hoare (eds.), *Japan and The Graphic*, p. 193.

144 Dalton's photograph albums covering the cruise of the *Bacchante* are now preserved in the Photographic Archive at Windsor Castle. The volume devoted to Japan (RCIN 2580920) contains over 200 photographs and the subjects include figures (Buddhist monks, itinerant peddlers of medicines, rickshawmen with lady passengers, archers, the empress's Chamberlain), Yokohama, the tombs of the shoguns in Tokyo, Mt Fuji, the Nishi-Honganji where the party resided in Kyoto, and temples in Kyoto and Nara, and there are many of Nara Buddhist statuary. Some are hand-coloured or have captions printed in the corner, and these were probably bought, but most were evidently taken by a photographer in the party. Some photographs of Nikkō and Miyajima, which were not visited by the princes, are included. The entire set can now be viewed on the website of the Royal Collection Trust (https://www.royalcollection.org.uk/collection/search#/page/1; the catalogue numbers are RCIN 2580921 to RCIN 2581139).

145 NRO, Lady Scott archive, box 22, photographic album of HMS *Bacchante*.

146 Admiral Sir Percy Scott, *Fifty years in the Royal Navy* (London: John Murray, 1919), pp. 39, 59; Nicolson, *King George V*, vol. 1, pp. 32–48.

147 Leonard Mosley, *Hirohito Emperor of Japan* (London: Weidenfield and Nicolson, 1966), p. 57 (adapted; Mosley does not give a source for this anecdote); *The king to his people* (London: Williams and Norgate, 1935), pp. 134–5.

148 Sir George Aston, *His Royal Highness the Duke of Connaught and Strathearn: a Life and Intimate Study* (London: George G. Harrap, 1929) provides details of his years in India, but barely mentions the visit to Japan.

149 *The Times*, 7 June 1890, p. 6.

150 Mary Fraser, *A Diplomatist's Wife in Japan: Sketches at the Turn of the Century*, ed. Hugh Cortazzi (New York: Weatherhill, 1982), pp. 159–63. This account by the wife of the British Minister, Hugh Fraser, provides many details of the visit.

151 Keene, *Emperor of Japan*, 433–4; Fraser, *A Diplomatist's Wife in Japan*, p. 166; for further details of the visit see Cortazzi, 'Royal Visits to Japan in the Meiji Period', pp. 88–91.

152 Bennett, Cortazzi and Hoare (eds)., *Japan and The Graphic*, pp. 140–3 (issues of 7, 14 & 21 June 1890).

153 *The Times*, 7 June 1890, p. 6.

154 RA, VIC/ADDA15/8445, Diary of Duke & Duchess of Connaught, 1 April – 21 June 1890; RA, VIC/ADDA15/5542, Ada Cavaye to the Queen, 30 April 1890. On the marriage between Sannomiya and Raynor, see Noboru Koyama, 'Three Meiji Marriages between Japanese Men and English Women', in Hugh Cortazzi (ed.), *Britain and Japan: Biographical Portraits*, vol. 4 (Abingdon: Routledge, 2002), pp. 383–96.

155 Online edition of Queen Victoria's journals, 1 & 8 January and 4 September 1891.

156 Unless otherwise indicated, the information about Takehito's life and career is based on *Arisugawa Takehito shinnō*, 2 vols (1927; facsimile published by Yumani Shobō of Tokyo in 2010). In vol. 1, facing p. 30 there is a plate showing a drawing of the *Iron Duke* which he made in his diary, and facing p. 32 a plate reproducing a photograph of the young Takehito with Vice-Admiral Robert Coote, the Commander in Chief of the China Station, and Lt. (later Vice-Admiral) Kurooka Tatewaki, who accompanied him to England.

157 TNA, FO 46/246, Parkes to Salisbury, 28 July 1879; FO 46/258, J. G. Kennedy (Chargé d'affaires) to Granville, 13 September 1880 (nos. 153 and 154) and enclosures; FO 262/332, Salisbury to [Parkes], 2 October 1879; Fox, *Britain and Japan*, pp. 269–70.

158 It may be a coincidence, but Prince Higashi-Fushimi also studied with a private tutor in Blackheath in 1872: see note 110.

159 Online edition of Queen Victoria's journals, 20 August 1881. In 1878 he had been adopted by Emperor Meiji as a possible heir, which may explain Victoria's confusion.

160 Bennett, Cortazzi and Hoare (eds)., *Japan and The Graphic*, pp. 113, 116.

161 Online edition of Queen Victoria's journals, 25 Nov 1882; *The Times*, 27 November 1882, p. 10. *Arisugawa Taruhito shinnō*, 2 vols (1929; facsimile published by Yumani Shobō of Tokyo in 2010), vol. 2, pp. 164–7.

162 *The Times*, 9 December 1882, p. 8, 7 June 1890, p. 6; Best, 'The role of diplomatic practice and court protocol', p. 249. However, there is no mention of these incidents or of any dissatisfaction in his diary: *Arisugawa Taruhito shinnō nikki*, vol. 4 (Takamatsu no miya, 1936), pp. 108–15.

163 *Sadanaru shinnō jiseki* (Fushimi no miya, 1931), p. 75. There is no mention of his visit in *The Times*.

164 Keene, *Emperor of Japan*, p. 406.

165 *Yorihito shinnō* (Tokyo: Shun'yōdō, 1927), pp. 32, 37–42.
166 *Yorihito shinnō*, pp. 63, 75–80, 142–3; online edition of Queen Victoria's journals, 25 June 1894.
167 *Yorihito shinnō*, pp. 335, 354–90, 419–44; the letter is reproduced as an unnumbered plate before p. 1.
168 Best, 'Diplomatic Practice and Court Protocol', p. 249; *The Times*, 28 August 1886, p. 4; *Meiji tennōki* 6: 615–6.
169 *The Times*, 23 November 1886, p. 5; 2 July 1890, p. 9; Best, 'Diplomatic Practice and Court Protocol', 248–9.
170 *The Times*, 1 December 1886, p. 6, 8 December, p. 9, 11 December, p. 5; online edition of Queen Victoria's journals, 22 November 1886.
171 Kashima Shigeru, *Miyake no jidai: sepiairo no kōzoku arubamu* (Tokyo: Asahi Shinbunsha, 2006), p. 54; the source of this anecdote is said to be *Meiji tennōki* but I have been unable to find such a passage. The Prince and Yoriko married in 1869 and in 1872, while he was in England, she took English lessons from the wife of Horace Wilson (1843–1927), an American employed by the Japanese government to teach English at the Daigaku Nankō: KK, 72202, 'Akihito shinnō nenpu shiryō' vol. 12, 'Komatsu no miya nikki shōroku' 4.
172 Online edition of Queen Victoria's journals, 20 June 1887; Best, 'Diplomatic Practice and Court Protocol', 249–50; *The Times*, 20 June 1887, p. 6; *Meiji tennōki* 6: 765; Bennett (ed.), *Japan and the Illustrated London News*, p. 261.
173 Best, 'Diplomatic Practice and Court Protocol', p. 250; *The Times*, 1897: 8 May, p. 11, 21 June pp. 14, 17, 28 June, p. 12, 30 June, p. 9, 29 July p. 5; online edition of Queen Victoria's journals, 24 June 1897.
174 Best, 'Diplomatic Practice and Court Protocol', p. 250; online edition of Queen Victoria's journals, 4 May 1900; *The Times*, 2 May 1900, p. 10.
175 GGS, 6.4.7.1–13–1, 'Victoria joō hōgyo no ken'. For Sōseki's diary entry, see *Sōseki zenshū*, vol. 19 (Tokyo: Iwanami Shoten, 1995), p. 52.
176 *Meiji tennō ki* 3: 172.
177 Keene, *Emperor of Japan*, pp. 308–19, 445–53. The English and Japanese records of the conversation between Meiji and Grant are contained in *Guranto shogun to no gotaiwa hikki* (Kokumin Seishin Bunka Kenkyūjo, 1937; facsimile edition published by Honpō Shoseki, 1980).
178 Ayers, *Chinese and Japanese Works of Art*, vol. 3, #2221, 2223–2234, 2237–8. In the same volume, #2221 is described as a lacquered document box presented to the Princess of Wales in 1903 by Prince Sadanoru [sic; Sadanaru] Fushimi and containing his visiting card: if this is correct, it must have been sent, for he did not visit Britain in 1903. He spent two weeks in London in 1885, as mentioned above, and undoubtedly made the acquaintance of the Princess of Wales on that occasion; was this perhaps a delayed coronation present?
179 GGS, 6.4.6.10, 'Nichiei ryōkokukan kōshitsu no kikkyō shinkan nite hōchihō kyōtei ikken'.

180 Beasley, *Great Britain and the Opening of Japan*, 39–42, 91, 111, 156, 163, 177, 180, 187.
181 Baron Roman Rosen, *Forty Years of Diplomacy* (London: George Allen and Unwin, 1922), vol. 1, p. 27. Rosen was Russian vice-consul in Yokohama at the time.
182 Christopher Roberts, *The British Courts and Extra-Territoriality in Japan* (Leiden: Brill, 2014), pp. 186–9.
183 Keene, *Emperor of Japan*, p. 424; *Meiji tennōki* 7: 235–7.
184 Best, 'Diplomatic Practice and Court Protocol', p. 250.
185 On the Japanese decorations and their diplomatic functions, see John Breen, 'Meiji tennō no kunshō gaikō to kyūtei bunka no kokusaisei', *Kikan yūkyū* 153 (2018), pp. 105–16.
186 RA, VIC/MAIN/B/32/19, Granville to the Queen, 14 December 1880; VIC/MAIN/B/32/25, Granville to Ponsonby, 20 December 1880; VIC/MAIN/B/32/30, Granville to Ponsonby, 3 January 1881; VIC/MAIN/T/8/45, Granville to Prince of Wales, 15 May 1881. See also the letters of the Prince of Wales to Dalton in the Royal Archives, GV/PRIV/AA6/255 (16 May 1881) and GV/PRIV/AA6/256 (22 July 1881), and Dalton's letter to the Prince of Wales, VIC/MAIN/Z/473/59 (8 April 1881). Best, 'Diplomatic Role of Diplomatic Practice and Court Protocol', p. 248.
187 Keene, *Emperor of Japan*, p. 321; *The Times*, 7 June 1890, p. 6; Best, 'Diplomatic Role of Diplomatic Practice and Court Protocol', pp. 247–8, 252.
188 Keene, *Emperor of Japan*, p. 348; *Meiji tennō ki* 5: 294.
189 Keene, *Emperor of Japan*, pp. 403–404.

PART TWO

A Royal Alliance: Court Diplomacy, 1902–1941[1]

ANTONY BEST

INTRODUCTION

DURING THE FIRST half of the twentieth century the royal relationship between the British Empire and Imperial Japan played an important part in the link between these two countries. Indeed, after the collapse of the Romanov, the Hohenzollern and Hapsburg empires in 1917–1918, it would not be too far-fetched as to describe it as the most significant royal relationship that remained in existence. To look at why this royal relationship became so important to both powers provides us with a useful way in which to understand the evolution of Anglo-Japanese relations, but it also helps us to comprehend more broadly the special role that royalty continued to play in the twentieth century and the need to take court diplomacy seriously.

As the previous chapter in this volume has demonstrated, the royal relationship between Britain and Japan had provided some useful contacts in the late nineteenth century but it had never become particularly close.[2] The most important symbol of the distance that remained between the two courts was that it had not been possible to achieve a mutual exchange of decorations between the monarchs. This was because the British government was loath from the mid-1870s onwards to bestow the Order of the Garter on non-Christians, while the Japanese were determined not to accept any lower chivalric honour. It is important, though, to put this problem in context by emphasizing that Japan was far from alone in being treated as an inferior. Its position in 1900 was in fact very similar to that of the other non-Christian empires and kingdoms, such as the Ottoman Empire, Persia (Iran), and Siam

(Thailand), which had all tried to adapt to European court diplomacy but still found themselves treated as second-rank monarchies. The only exception to this rule was Qing China which had only avoided similar humiliation because it had done very little to create any ties between the Manchu court and its foreign counterparts.[3]

The patronizing treatment that the Japanese court had received at the hands of Britain meant that by the 1890s the former had developed a great sensitivity where royal relations were concerned. For example, in 1897 the Japanese had only agreed to send a representative to the queen's diamond jubilee once Britain had guaranteed that their prince would be given the same treatment as European royalty.[4] Thus, even before the alliance was signed in January 1902, it was clear that one criteria by which the Japanese government would judge its relations with Britain was how the latter treated Japan's sovereign and his family.

Of course, in some ways this was advantageous for the British in that it meant that Japan might be susceptible to flattery and that stressing royal ties could therefore be a good way in which to cement the political relationship. It also, however, raised potential problems. Most notably, how was it going to be possible to create a satisfactory inter-court relationship when the two countries differed so greatly in terms of culture and religion? Would not the divide prove too great? Moreover, there was the problem that even though the Japanese had come to adopt the rules of European court life, they had done so in a very inflexible manner. Indeed, their predilection for protocol was already in the 1890s beginning to wear down the patience of the European diplomatic corps in Tokyo.[5] Court diplomacy might therefore be firmly on the agenda but it was not going to be easy.

THE ALLIANCE AND THE ELEVATION OF COURT RELATIONS

That the British were fully aware of the importance of using the king as a symbol of its good intentions is evident from the events of 1901. From the start of that year concern had grown both in Britain and Japan that Tsarist Russia intended to turn the three north-east provinces of China known as Manchuria into a protectorate. This prospect had led in July to the opening of talks between the British foreign secretary, Lord Lansdowne, and the Japanese minister to London, Hayashi Tadasu, about the possibility of signing an alliance that would help to contain Russian expansionism.

One problem, however, was that on the Japanese side there was no consensus that an alliance was the best way of dealing with the problem. The leading sceptic was the former prime minister, Itō Hirobumi, who had since the 1880s dominated the politics of Meiji Japan. In the autumn of 1901, Itō, who was now temporarily out of power, went on an overseas tour which included a visit to St Petersburg before he was due to arrive in London in late December. The rumour that reached British circles was that he intended to see if the Russians would be interested in negotiating a mutually advantageous agreement with Japan that would negate the need to proceed with a military compact with Britain.[6]

Accordingly, it was clear that Itō needed to be feted on his arrival in London, even though this would coincide with Christmas and the New Year. Lansdowne therefore decided that it was important to play the royal card and to mobilize the king as a means of winning Itō over. This task, it should be added, was made considerably easier by the fact that Edward VII was already broadly favourable to the idea of an alignment with Japan, having given his blessing to the foreign secretary's initiative as early as August 1901.[7] Lansdowne was thus able to persuade the king into agreeing to invite Itō for an audience in London on 27 December and even to receiving him again at Sandringham on 6 January, although Itō was unable to take up the latter offer.[8] In addition, the king was prevailed upon to bestow on Itō the highest honour that a foreign politician could possibly receive, the Knight Grand Cross of the Order of the Bath (GCB); this also made him the first Japanese politician to be granted any British decoration.[9] As Kimizuka Naotaka has noted, this lavish treatment had a special resonance for Itō as it could not have constituted a greater contrast to his previous visit to London in 1897 for the queen's jubilee when he had only been granted a brief meeting with the prime minister, Lord Salisbury.[10] Itō's visit was thus used as an opportunity to flatter the man himself and to provide through the royal channel a powerful signal that suggested that Britain was now prepared to treat Japan with the respect that the latter believed it deserved.

The Anglo-Japanese Alliance was finally signed on 30 January 1902 and immediately received royal acclamation in Britain when the king noted to the foreign secretary, 'This is most satisfactory & must be a great relief for Ld Lansdowne.'[11] The treaty committed both parties to uphold the status quo in Korea and China and as such was clearly aimed at deterring any further Russian expansion in North-East Asia. It also included a careful set of obligations should deterrence fail and Japan feel obliged to act to defend its interests. It stipulated that if one signatory were to find itself at war with a third party then the other signatory would remain neutral, but that if one signatory were at odds with two powers then the other was committed to come to its aid. In essence, this meant that Japan could launch a war against Russia in the knowledge that the potential for British involvement would deter France from assisting its Russian ally.

In the wake of the alliance's signature, both countries engaged in signalling respect and friendship through their respective royal courts. In March 1902 when HMS *Endymion* became the first Royal Navy ship to visit Japan since the signing of the alliance, the emperor invited its captain to attend an audience while its officers took part in a duck hunt in the grounds of the imperial palace.[12] Later in May that year when Vice-Admiral Sir Cyprian Bridge, the commander-in-chief of the China fleet, came to Tokyo for naval talks with his Japanese counterparts the treatment was even more lavish. Bridge was invited to a lunch and reception at the imperial palace and became the first foreign admiral ever to be asked to sit at the emperor's table.[13]

Meanwhile, the British worked to ensure that the Japanese would be given a warm welcome at that summer's coronation of Edward VII. Knowing that the Japanese representative was to be Prince Komatsu Akihito, who had been aggrieved at his treatment when he had attended Queen Victoria's golden jubilee in 1887, the Foreign Office acted to ensure that his *amour propre* would not be disturbed in any way. Thus, the Japanese royal suite was housed in Claridge's between 12 June and 3 July at the British government's expense, even though this was considerably more expensive than the other hotels in London.[14] In addition, on 23 June, the prince was given the honour of being the only foreign guest to be entertained with a luncheon at the Mansion House in the City of London.[15] It was also noticeable that when the Japanese legation hosted a dinner for the prince many of the British political elite attended in order to demonstrate their support for the alliance.[16] In the end, of course, Komatsu could not attend the coronation as the latter had to be postponed at the last minute due to the king's ill-health. The prince, who was already committed to a tour of the European capitals, could not afford to dally in London and thus left in early July. However, despite this misfortune, the visit clearly contrasted well with Komatsu's previous mission on behalf of the emperor.[17]

A further signal that Japan was now a prized ally came in regard to the naval review that was due to take place at Spithead to mark the coronation. In early 1902 the Imperial Japanese Navy (IJN) requested that it might send two ships to take part in the review. This was out of line with precedent, as the tradition was that foreign countries could only contribute one ship. However, the Admiralty decided to accept the offer on the basis that, 'Japan's position towards us is totally different from that of all other foreign govts and it is just as well to mark it.'[18] In this case, the postponement of the coronation did not make any difference as the Japanese ships stayed on in British waters and were thus able to take part in the review when it was eventually held on 16 August.[19]

Britain's new-found largesse in the royal arena was also evident in the field of chivalric decorations, for in 1902 a number of senior Japanese figures joined Itō in being honoured by the British crown. For example, Prince Arisugawa Takehito, who had attended the queen's jubilee in 1897, was made a GCB, while the veteran politician Matsukata Masayoshi, who visited Britain in 1902, was made a Knight Grand Cross of the Order of St Michael and St George (GCMG). Meanwhile, the military figures that had accompanied Komatsu to London and had used the occasion to take part in joint staff talks with the British armed forces were made Knights Companion of the Order of the Bath (KCB).[20]

It was not, though, all plain sailing. The early years of the alliance were still marred on the British side by its continued ambivalence about what attitude to take towards honouring non-European monarchs. In 1902–1903 a number of officials in the Foreign Office who were closely involved in the day-to-day diplomacy with Japan assumed that the time had now come for the Order of the Garter to be presented to the emperor.[21] Unfortunately, this request could not have come at a worse moment, for the whole issue of whether Britain's most esteemed decoration could be presented to non-Christian monarchs was in the balance in the summer and autumn of 1902.

The reason for this impasse was the infamous 'Shah and Garter' episode, which arose when the British minister to Tehran, without authority, promised the shah that he would receive the Garter if he visited Britain, only to find that King Edward VII was violently opposed to the idea. In the end, this question, which almost led to Lansdowne's resignation in the autumn of 1902, was settled in the shah's favour, but the price that Edward VII demanded for his acquiescence was that no further requests were to be entertained.[22] Thus, despite the fact that Japan was now Britain's ally, the emperor was in 1902 still denied an honour that was regularly given to European sovereigns with whom Britain had no alliance. In its place all he received as a sign of Britain's respect was a diamond-framed miniature portrait of the king.[23]

This slight was not lost on the Japanese. The emperor himself responded by ordering that the wording of the letter of gratitude that he was due to send to the king in regard to Komatsu's welcome should be toned down. His courtiers in the end persuaded him that this was going too far, but the fact that this was his first impulse suggests that the good work that Britain had done in regard to welcoming Komatsu had quickly been compromised.[24] Meanwhile, the Japanese press, on learning of the Garter mission to Tehran, expressed bewilderment on the emperor's behalf and wondered why the shah should be favoured before their own monarch.[25]

The royal relationship created on the signing of the alliance was thus much closer than it had been hitherto, but it still contained elements of inequality. In this it mirrored the nature of the alliance itself in which Britain was quite clearly the senior partner in terms of both the strength of its armed forces and the industrial and financial resources at its disposal. Japan therefore had little choice but to accept Britain's actions and attitudes even if they sometimes grated.

THE RUSSO-JAPANESE WAR

Despite the fact that the king was not disposed to bestow the Garter on the emperor, he remained broadly in favour of the alliance with Japan and kept a watch on its troubled relations with Russia which grew steadily worse during 1903.[26] In March of that year Russia reneged on an agreement that it had made with China twelve months previously in which it had committed itself to a three-stage withdrawal of its occupying army from Manchuria. Meanwhile it increased its activities along the Yalu River leading to Japanese concern that it still harboured the desire to expand into Korea. The Japanese response was to call on Russia to begin negotiations that would lead to a mutually acceptable solution to their rivalry in north-east Asia and uphold the principle of the 'open door' for commercial activity. At the same time, however, the Japanese government was aware that it had to prepare for the worst, in other words if Russia refused to negotiate seriously then it had to contemplate going to war with a European Great Power.

Japan could afford to accept this challenge because in 1903 and early 1904 the rearmament policy that it had followed since 1895 was coming to fruition meaning that the military balance *vis-à-vis* Russia in East Asia had narrowly swung in its favour. However, in the autumn of 1903 a new situation developed that threatened to disturb the narrow lead that Japan possessed in the naval sphere – the sudden availability on the international market of a number of capital ships and cruisers that had originally been commissioned by Chile and Argentina. Initially when these ships were offered to the highest bidder the Japanese had expressed an interest in purchasing them, but by late November 1903 it decided that it could not afford the two most significant vessels, the British-built battleships intended for Chile. This raised the troubling prospect that these vessels might fall into Russian hands instead, thus tilting the naval balance towards the tsar's fleet.

The only sure way of preventing this scenario was for the British state to pre-empt Russia by buying these ships for the Royal Navy, but that raised the question of where the money could be found for this emergency expenditure. Fortunately for Japan, at this point Edward VII entered the picture and again demonstrated his support for the alliance. On learning that the Cabinet was uncertain about how to cover the expenditure, Edward VII wrote to the prime minister, Arthur Balfour, on 28 November recommending that the latter should ask the king's close friend, the financier Sir Ernest Cassell, to extend a short-term loan to the government to cover the necessary funds, which is precisely what the government proceeded to do.[27]

The king's willingness to help Japan in this way does not, though, mean that he actively wanted to see the outbreak of hostilities. At the end of December, he wrote to Balfour confessing his anxiety about Russo-Japanese tensions and his fear that Britain might be dragged into a new conflict against its will only eighteen months after the end of the South African war.[28] Balfour duly responded by noting that Britain was under no obligation to assist Japan unless the alliance terms were invoked by French intervention on Russia's side, thus putting the king's mind at rest.[29]

The Russo-Japanese War began in February 1904 with Japan's launching of a surprise attack on the Russian naval base at Port Arthur. With the Russian fleet pinned back, Japan was quickly able to send an expeditionary force to Korea and then advance into southern Manchuria, thus beginning the land campaign. In line with the alliance, Britain remained a confirmed neutral. Its neutrality meant that the government in London had to watch its words and actions very carefully lest it should give Russia an excuse to accuse it of bad faith, which might in turn have a detrimental effect on German and French opinion. At the same time, this careful policy had the disadvantage that it could trigger Japanese doubts about whether Britain was really willing to live up to the spirit rather than the exact text of the alliance.

In these circumstances the royal channel proved a useful conduit through which reassurance could be signalled to the Japanese government and people in a low-key but effective manner. It was, for example, still possible for the king to send telegrams to the emperor congratulating him on the achievements of his armed forces, safe in the knowledge that this would resonate with Japan's politicians, general and admirals. Indeed, as one British observer with the Imperial Japanese Army (IJA) noted to the king's private secretary, this was a particularly efficacious tool because, 'there is no doubt that the intense loyalty of the Japanese to their own Emperor renders them specially susceptible' to such communications.[30] In addition, the court in Britain proved to be useful in reassuring Japan in other ways. In November 1904 news reached Lansdowne that members of the Japanese legation were feeling left out of 'high society' and feared that their Russian counterparts had better access to the British elite.[31] The most logical way of correcting this imbalance was for the king to step in and ask Hayashi to attend an audience, and this was duly arranged in the following month.[32]

An even more important opportunity arrived in the summer of 1905 with the visit to London of Prince and Princess Arisugawa Takehito, who had come to Europe having been appointed as the emperor's representatives to the wedding of the German crown prince.[33] The royal couple arrived in Britain on 26 June and stayed until 11 July. As is the custom, in the first part of their stay they were official guests of the king. They were thus welcomed at Victoria Station on 26 June by the Prince of Wales and the Duke of Connaught and then taken on to Buckingham Palace where they met the king before being escorted to St James's Palace where they resided for the first part of their ten-day stay before moving on to York House.[34] On 27 June, a dinner was held in their honour at Buckingham Palace at which the prince, who had already in 1902 been made a GCB in its civil division, was now, in his capacity as a Japanese admiral, awarded a military GCB.[35] In addition, as their visit coincided with the king's birthday the prince and princess were invited to attend the Trooping of the Colour on 30 June. It was also arranged, following the precedent set for Komatsu three years previously, that the prince and his consort should be honoured with a formal lunch reception at the Mansion House.[36] Aside from the above, they were also made guests of the Prince of Wales, the Duke of Connaught, the Marquess of Salisbury and the Marquess of Lansdowne, and attended the Royal Agricultural Show, a tea party organized by the Japan Society in Regent's Park and a dinner at the Savoy Hotel where part of the premises were adapted to mimic a Japanese garden.

The clear implication of this warm welcome was that Britain's sympathies were with Japan in its war against Russia, but two events made this sentiment more overt. First, on 29 June, Princess Arisugawa met with a delegation of British and Japanese women who had put together a committee to provide knitted woollens to protect Japanese soldiers from the Manchurian winter. Second, in early July, the royal couple made a brief trip outside of the capital to travel to the Vickers shipyard at Barrow-in-Furness where the princess had the honour of launching Japan's latest battleship, *Katori*.[37]

The visit by Prince and Princess Arisugawa was a success that produced just the right note in Anglo-Japanese relations. There had been some murmurings in Japan in early 1905 that Britain was sticking too rigidly to the terms of the alliance and not showing sufficient appreciation of the Japanese war effort, which, after all, stood to benefit British interests as much as anyone else's.[38] The warm welcome given to the royal couple helped to negate this impression by demonstrating, even while the war was still in progress, that the British crown was happy to proclaim its friendship towards Japan. It was the most successful visit to date and set a template for those to come in the future.

However, the sheer scale of Japan's achievement in defeating Russia raised the difficult question of what more Britain could do to congratulate its ally and celebrate the alliance. As early as January 1905, when the fall of the naval base at Port Arthur marked the greatest victory that Japan had yet seen, the issue of what could be in the diplomatic and royal spheres was raised by the parliamentary under-secretary at the Foreign Office, Earl Percy. In a letter to Balfour he suggested that Britain could signal its goodwill and profound respect in three ways; it could offer to renew the alliance, raise its diplomatic representation in Tokyo to the ambassadorial level (thus signalling that it saw Japan as a Great Power), and finally confer the Garter upon the emperor.[39] At this point Balfour and Lansdowne were only prepared to move ahead tentatively with the alliance talks and thus approved the other two ideas in principle alone. In particular, the idea of reviving the Garter controversy had little appeal to Lansdowne who had been scarred by his experience regarding the shah two years previously.[40]

The successful renewal of the alliance did, however, provide a further opportunity in itself to marshal royal largesse. Negotiations for a new treaty of alliance began in April 1905 and reached their conclusion in August. The new terms extended the alliance beyond East Asia to include India and, in order to deter any Russian war of revenge, stipulated that, from this point on, any attack by a third power on one signatory would lead the other to come to its aid.[41] To mark the signing of the alliance and Japan's successes in the war to date, the king duly agreed to bestow the GCB on the Japanese Prime Minister, Katsura Tarō, and a GCMG on the Foreign Minister, Komura Jutarō.[42]

THE FIRST GARTER MISSION, 1906

Once the Russo-Japanese War ended in September 1905, and with the new alliance just signed, a decision on Percy's two outstanding suggestions could no longer be delayed. Accordingly Lansdowne reluctantly arranged what he feared might be a fateful meeting with the king.[43] Much to his surprise and relief, Edward VII proved more amenable than hitherto. The latter agreed both to the elevation of the legation to embassy status and to the Garter being awarded to the emperor. Moreover he proposed that the Garter mission to Japan should be led by his nephew, Prince Arthur of Connaught, and, on his own initiative, suggested that the military version of the newly created Order of Merit (OM) should be presented to Japan's two outstanding wartime leaders, Admiral Tōgō Heihachirō and General Ōyama Iwao.[44]

Over the next few months assiduous attention was paid in Britain to ensuring that the Garter mission took place without a hitch. Edward VII decided that Prince Arthur's suite should consist of Lord Redesdale (the former Algernon Mitford who had served as a diplomat in Japan between 1866 and 1869), Admiral of the Fleet Sir Edward Seymour (who had been commander-in-chief on the China station at the time of the Boxer rebellion), as the representative of the Royal Navy, and one of the king's favourites, General Sir Thomas Kenny-Kelly for the army.[45]

The mission duly set off in early 1906 and reached Japan on 19 February, arriving in Yokohama on board the cruiser HMS *Diadem* and with a squadron of IJN ships accompanying it into the harbour.[46] This proved to be the grandest occasion yet in the history of the alliance. For its part, the Japanese state spared no expense in the welcome given to Prince Arthur, treating him almost as if he were a visiting monarch. At Yokohama the prince was greeted by two heroes of the recent war, Admiral Tōgō and General Kuroki Tamemoto, as well as by hordes of cheering schoolchildren. He then went by train up to Tokyo where, in a break from precedence, the emperor specially came from the imperial palace to Shinbashi station to meet him on his arrival in the city.[47] The prince then proceeded to the Kasumigaseki Palace and in the evening was given a formal dinner by Prince and Princess Arisugawa.

The investiture took place the next day at the Imperial Palace. In the account of the Garter Mission that Lord Redesdale published later in the year, this event was discussed in a sombre tone with emphasis placed on the silence of the room, the slow precision of the ceremony and the dignified majesty of the emperor.[48] Much of this no doubt was true, but it also provided, unsurprisingly, a positive gloss on events. One of the things that Redesdale neglected to mention was that the solemnity of the occasion was punctured quite literally when the young and rather nervous Prince Arthur managed accidently to prick his finger with one of the pins used to attach the Garter to the royal calf.[49] He also failed to note that on the way to Japan, the members of the suite had discovered to their horror that the Garter itself was too big to fit any human leg and that elastic had had to be added to make sure that it would fit.[50]

In addition to smoothing over the difficulties arising from the ceremony itself, it is worth noting that Redesdale's description of the emperor was one that was designed entirely for public consumption. In one of his first references to the emperor, Redesdale reflected on all that had happened in his long reign, his devotion to public service and observed that 'the strength which is written in his face is his great characteristic'. Here then was an august sovereign who epitomized his proud and noble people and who by inference was a monarch whose word was his bond. In creating this image, Redesdale was describing a symbol rather than the man himself. Most Britons who met with the emperor throughout his life were underwhelmed by his demeanour and this impression only got worse as the sovereign's health deteriorated in the 1900s.[51]

The disconnection between image and reality is also evident from the Japanese side of the equation. Donald Keene has noted in his biography of the Meiji emperor that the reception given to Prince Arthur owed little to the inclinations of the emperor himself who had grown to dislike the ceremony involved in welcoming foreign guests. He had even, to the horror, of his own advisers said in January that he had scant interest in accepting the Garter and had suggested that the mission be cancelled. Moreover, it seems that on the day he was bemused by the investiture ceremony and could hardly contain his amusement at its pomposity.[52]

The Garter, of course, was not the only honour to be awarded, for the suite carried with it with a wide array of decorations for Japan's military, naval and political elite. These included, among many others, the OMs for Ōyama, Tōgō and the 'father' of the IJA, Yamagata Aritomo, as well as GCBs for the two service ministers, Admiral Saitō Makoto and General Terauchi Masatake.[53] Meanwhile, the British representatives were themselves festooned with decorations; the prince receiving the Order of the Chrysanthemum and the others the appropriate class of the Order of the Rising Sun.[54]

Following the investiture, the formal part of the visit continued for six more days. This time was spent in Tokyo, except for a day trip to the naval base and arsenal at Yokosuka, at which the prince and his suite saw four captured Russian ships which were being converted for IJN use.[55] Aside from the usual formal lunches and dinners, the highlights included an Anglo-Japanese 'entertainment' at the Kabuki-za organized under the auspices of the Tokyo business community and the, by now, obligatory duck hunt. On 27 February the prince left Tokyo to tour the country. He first travelled down to Kyushu by train via Shizuoka and Kyoto. In Kyushu he was taken to the Sasebo naval base, where he saw more captured Russian ships as well as Tōgō's now stricken flagship, the *Mikasa.* He then went on to Kagoshima in which Mitford records the streets as being lined by a million people. This was, of course, an apt destination because in 1863 Kagoshima had been the scene of a confrontation between the British fleet of Admiral Kuper and the forces of Satsuma. The prince's visit was thus used as a symbolic representation of the great arc that Anglo-Japanese relations had travelled over the last fifty or so years. Interestingly his stay in the city included a visit to the grave of Saigō Takamori, one of the heroes of the

Meiji Restoration of 1868 who had later turned against the regime in 1877 by leading the abortive Satsuma rebellion. After this, the prince returned by HMS *Diadem* to Honshu. Over the next few days, he visited Miyajima, Etajima, Kure, Hiroshima (where he witnessed some IJA manoeuvres), Kobe, Kyoto, Nara and Nagoya before finding himself back in Tokyo on 13 March. The following two days were spent on a trip in Nikko and then finally on 17 March the members of the Garter mission travelled down to Yokohama, boarded ship and headed off into the Pacific Ocean for their homeward voyage via North America.

The mission's members and the staff of the embassy in Tokyo were pleased with what had been achieved and were convinced that the visit had been an unqualified success. On a personal level, two letters that Prince Arthur sent to his mother capture his positive impressions of the welcome he received from what he called 'the charming people of this delightful country'. In particular, he felt gratitude for the care and attention shown to him by Kuroki and Tōgō. Indeed, he records that at one party he played musical chairs with the admiral, which hardly fits the usual shy image given to the great man.[56]

However, the aspect of the visit that most impressed the royal suite and the British embassy was the enthusiasm of the Japanese people for their visitors. As the report written by Miles Lampson, a junior official in the Foreign Office who acted as the secretary to the mission, noted, 'The ebullition of popular feeling in favour of the alliance was both overwhelming and universal from all classes … Everywhere throughout the length and breadth of the land the spirit of the alliance appeared to have permeated.'[57] Of course, much of this welcome was officially encouraged and people are, in any case, naturally drawn to participate in such ceremonial occasions, but it seems clear that the individual members of the suite were genuinely impressed by the warm reception that they received. Lampson himself noted in a private letter to the head of the Treaty Department of the Foreign Office, 'I hope that people in England realise how lavishly we were entertained and how enthusiastic they are about the alliance.'[58] Captain William Wyndham, the prince's attaché, concurred, observing to a member of the British court, 'What strikes me most is the extraordinary enthusiasm all through the country even in the villages …. All the people are drawn up, as we pass through, shouting Banzai for all they are worth.'[59]

In regard to the political impact of the tour, the embassy sent back to the Foreign Office summaries of what had been written in the Japanese press, which amply attested to Britain's popularity and highlighted the fact that the people felt a debt of honour for the way in which the British had supported

Japan in its life and death struggle with Russia and had then sent a royal prince half way around the world to congratulate it on its achievement.[60] Fortified by this great outpouring of friendship, the British ambassador in Tokyo, Sir Claude MacDonald, in his telegram announcing the prince's departure, was moved to observe that the mission 'has undoubtedly greatly strengthened the ties already existing between Japan and England'.[61]

To seal the moment one further initiative was necessary. During the mission, Redesdale had kept a diary purportedly for the benefit of his wife. On his return he decided to publish this journal. He duly brought his manuscript to the Foreign Office for vetting, which led to Sir Edward Grey, the foreign secretary, to press only for a few excisions and to ask whether the Japanese might not object to his frequent references to the 'perpetual rain'.[62] The book was published later that year and is, as noted earlier, a bland read; its greatest interest lies in the author's reflections on how much Japan had changed since he left it as a young man in 1870 rather than anything it has to say about royalty.[63] As an uncontroversial and amiable account of the prince's visit, though, it probably had some worth, not least as a corrective to the unwise reflections that the late military attaché to Japan, General Sir Ian Hamilton, had recently made about the IJA during the Russo-Japanese War in his *A Staff Officer's Scrapbook during the Russo-Japanese War*.[64]

THE FUSHIMI MISSION TO BRITAIN, 1907

With the success of Prince Arthur's mission the royal relationship between the two countries entered a new stage, for it began a tradition of high-ranking official visits that was to continue well into the inter-war period. The result was that, although the two royal houses did not share any dynastic links or even the same religion, a special bond began to develop that was not present in the British court's ties with any other non-European dynasty, or for Japan in its links with the sovereigns of Europe and elsewhere.

That is not to say that the relationship evolved smoothly avoiding all difficulties, for there clearly was a wide geographical and cultural divide that had to be bridged. Geography was important because the most obvious type of state visit, one by a reigning monarch, could not be contemplated due to the distances involved and in Japan's case the lack of any precedent, thus all missions had to be carried out by princes representing the sovereign. This created problems because the royal houses of Europe had developed very particular codes of conduct and precedence in their dealings with each other. How a royal prince was to be treated when on an official visit to another country was seen as entirely dependent on his status within his own court, thus an heir apparent was seen as clearly worthy of better treatment than a mere prince of the blood. These gradations of ceremony were sometimes lost on the Japanese and this led to a number of difficult incidents.

This problem first manifested itself during Prince Arthur's visit to Japan in 1906, when the Japanese court decided to assign the country's most senior military figures to his suite as a sign of their respect for their ally. As Prince Arthur was only the king's nephew this was in fact inappropriate for someone of his standing, but no complaint or correction was made at the time, for fear that this might appear ungrateful. Another *faux pas* was made later that year when the outgoing British minister to China, Sir Ernest Satow, who had served in Japan as Macdonald's predecessor, travelled back home via Tokyo. To mark this occasion the Japanese government decided to bestow upon him the Order of the Rising Sun First Class but did not bother to consult with the Foreign Office beforehand. This was contrary to British rules and so, although Satow was allowed to accept this decoration, the Japanese authorities had to be told that 'we cannot depart from the regulations again'.[65]

The difficulty of dealing with Japan at the royal level became fully evident for the British authorities in 1907 when Prince Fushimi Sadanaru, came on an official visit to London to express the emperor's gratitude at receiving the Garter. When the king was initially consulted in March 1907 by the Foreign Office about how this visit should be handled, he ordered that it should be line with the welcome given to Prince Arisugawa two years previously, with the only difference being that, as his state visit was for five days, it might be possible to add Woolwich Arsenal and Aldershot to his itinerary.[66] However, by early April a note of panic began to reverberate among the British officials responsible for organizing the visit due to the battery of questions that were emanating from the Japanese embassy. Such was the level of Japanese attention to the detail of the state visit that Lampson in the Foreign Office who had the duty of liaising with the court, wrote to his opposite number at Buckingham Palace, Colonel Arthur Davidson, that 'I cannot help feeling that the Japanese are looking out for anything in which they can consider their Prince is being treated less well than Prince Arthur! Nothing definite has been said to me, but I merely infer from general observation.'[67]

Accordingly, and on the basis that Prince Fushimi, in contrast to Arisugawa, was coming as the emperor's representative, the officials sought ways to create a more favourable impression. One aspect of this was that, based on the precedent in Tokyo for Prince Arthur, they argued that it was imperative for Britain to break with European tradition and to attach its highest-ranked military and naval officials, Field Marshal Lord Roberts and Admiral of the

Fleet Sir Edward Seymour, to Fushimi's suite, lest the Japanese otherwise take offence.[68] In addition, a variation from normal practice was suggested for the prince's ceremonial visit to the City of London, which would allow him to call at the Guildhall as well as the Mansion House, which was a privilege traditionally reserved for crowned heads.[69]

The officials had, though, been reckoning without Edward VII who was both a stickler for protocol and a man prone to spectacular explosions of rage. In mid-April, the king let it be known from his spring sojourn in Naples that Fushimi's visit had become 'distasteful' to him, that he resented being 'forced into Japanese methods' and that if things continued as they were then Britain might as well adopt Tibetan customs.[70] Thus, the officials were forced into the unenviable task of charting a course between a suspicious Japan and a disgruntled king.

Moreover, fear of Japan's sensitivity also led to other difficulties. Shortly before the prince's arrival, officials at the Japanese embassy in London learnt that a new D'Oyly Carte production of the Gilbert and Sullivan comic opera, *The Mikado*, was about to open. Briefed on the offence that this would give, the British Lord Chamberlain's Office promptly moved to suspend the production. The D'Oyly Carte Company was duly told that, although the opera had been licensed twenty years previously, times had now changed and that:

> ... the position of the Japanese Empire has altered to such an extent that, on political grounds, it was of the greatest importance to avoid doing anything prejudicial to the good feeling now existing between England and Japan – more especially at the present moment, on the eve of a visit of the Representative of the Japanese Emperor to this country as an honoured guest of the King.[71]

This rushed gesture created an unpleasant backlash with even questions in Parliament being asked about this arbitrary use of power.[72] Meanwhile, further panic ensued in the Lord Chamberlain's Office when it was realised that the conductors of military bands may well think that music from *The Mikado* would provide an appropriate welcome to the Japanese prince. A hint to the contrary was therefore supplied to the Services, and most notably to the band that would first greet the prince at Dover.[73] As an exasperated Lampson noted at one fraught moment, 'Our worries are endless ...'[74] The final irony in this aspect of the story was that it was later reported in a London newspaper that the familiar air of 'A wandering minstrel I' had been heard emanating from the IJN ship *Tsukuba* which was docked at Chatham throughout the prince's visit.[75]

In the end, thankfully, the king calmed down and Fushimi's visit passed without any major problems. The prince arrived in Britain on 6 May on a steamer from France and then travelled by train from Dover to Victoria Station in London. Here he was greeted by the Prince of Wales who escorted him to Buckingham Palace where he took tea with the king before going on to York House, his residence for the duration of the official visit.[76] The following day was marked by a series of receptions, during which the king bestowed a GCB on the prince, and culminated in a formal state banquet in the evening. On 8 May, the prince made a visit to inspect the Royal Artillery at Woolwich and the day after was supposed to attend a military review in Aldershot with the king. The latter, though, had to be cancelled due to the weather.[77] On 10 May came the visit to the City in which the prince first went to the Guildhall to receive an address of welcome from the lord mayor before proceeding to the Mansion House for lunch. The official visit came to an end on 13 May. The prince then, after spending a few more days in London, left the capital to tour the country. His first port of call on 16 May was Newcastle where he paid a visit to the Elswick works, which had produced so many ships for the IJN, and stayed overnight at the home of Sir Andrew Noble, the then head of the Armstrong Whitworth company.[78] He then paid a short visit to Scotland where he was given tours of Edinburgh and Glasgow and stayed with the Duke of Montrose, before heading south again on 21 May to inspect another major producer of arms for Japan, the Vickers shipyard at Barrow-in-Furness.[79] He then returned to London via Liverpool, had a further visit to Portsmouth to see the Royal Navy dockyard and on 28 May was finally able to observe military manoeuvres in Aldershot with the king.[80] He finally left Britain on 31 May and sailed over to Canada where he was also afforded an official visit.

During this almost four-week stay in Britain, there was no sign from the Japanese suite or the embassy that they thought anything was amiss. Indeed, they expressed their delight at the reception that the crowds gave to the prince on his visit to the City of London and it seems that he was also warmly welcomed when he toured the country after the state visit had come to an end.[81] Moreover, the press in Japan enthused about the visit, noting once again that it demonstrated the strength of the bond between the two allies.[82] At a more personal level, though, the visit proved something of a trial as the prince and his retinue proved to be unprepossessing guests. One American journalist gleaned from a British officer who had been attached to the prince's suite that the mutual inability to engage in conversation allied to the prince's stolid personality had made the visit heavy-going for the British court.[83] The cultural divide was therefore still acting as an obstacle to the creation of anything closer than a formal and proper relationship.

TWO FUNERALS AND TWO CORONATIONS, 1910–1915

As can be seen from the above example, maintaining the royal relationship involved a great deal of attention and patience on the part of British officials as it was so easy to cause offence. The effort was, though, worthwhile, for Japan needed to be cultivated and appreciated evidence that it was seen as an equal. This was particularly important in the light of developments in the political field where in the late 1900s and early 1910s, some difficult issues arose between Britain and Japan over, for example, the negotiating of a new commercial treaty, Japanese emigration to the self-governing colonies of Canada, Australia and New Zealand, trade rivalry in China and Japan's annexation of Korea.[84] Against this background, having a means of signalling continued respect and favour was undoubtedly useful in helping to ameliorate tensions and keeping the wider benefits of the alliance in mind.

This process was aided by circumstance, for the relatively difficult period between 1908 and 1911 roughly coincided with the deaths of the two monarchs. The relatively short space of time that elapsed between the death of Edward VII in 1910 and that of the Emperor Meiji in 1912 created in the form of funerals and coronations a number of ceremonial occasions in which the British and Japanese courts could come together.[85] The frequency and grandeur of these events meant that more than ever the royal relationship came to be seen as the personification of the close ties that existed between the two countries.

The momentum in Anglo-Japanese court relations was sustained after Prince Fushimi's departure by the fortuitous presence of three young Japanese princes in Europe between 1908 and 1910. Prince Fushimi Hiroyasu, the son of Prince Fushimi Sadanaru, arrived in Britain in 1908 to study naval affairs, while his cousins, Prince Kuni Kuniyoshi and Prince Nashimoto Morimasa, were undergoing military training in Germany and France.[86] This allowed the British court to cultivate relations by providing receptions for the princes. Thus, in May 1908, Prince Fushimi Hiroyasu briefly met with the king at Buckingham Palace, while in the summer of 1909 the princes studying on the continent made separate incognito visits to Britain in June and July respectively.[87] During this period, all three princes received the same decoration, the Knight Grand Cross of the Victorian Order (GCVO), an honour that the king could bestow as a personal gift.

The next major royal occasion, planned for the summer of 1910, was that Prince Fushimi Sadanaru was to come to London as one of the two royal patrons, along with Prince Arthur of Connaught, of the Japan-British Exhibition that was planned to be held at the newly opened White City stadium in London.[88] However, on 6 May 1910, only four days before his arrival in London, the nature of his mission was changed dramatically by the death of the British king. As Prince Fushimi Sadanaru was already in Europe, he naturally was appointed to represent the emperor at the funeral. This avoided the necessity of nominating the Japanese ambassador, which the issues of distance and time would otherwise have dictated, and fortuitously meant that, because of the prince's senior status, Japan was able to take the high-profile role at the ceremony that its position as an ally warranted. Naturally, on such an occasion, with so many royal guests paying their respects, no great fuss could be made of the emperor's representative, but the prince did meet individually with King George V and Queen Mary on 25 May shortly before his departure for Japan.[89] Meanwhile, in Tokyo, a memorial service for the late king was arranged at which the emperor was represented by the crown prince and which saw virtually all of Japan's political elite in attendance. Moreover, on the day of the funeral in London, all of the banks in Japan and most of the businesses remained closed as a mark of respect.[90]

More important, though, in celebrating the alliance was the question of what position Japan would be able to take up at the following year's coronation for the new king. It was clear from early January 1911 that the Japanese government was determined to use the occasion for the maximum advantage. This was evident from the fact that it decided that the emperor's representative, Prince Higashi-Fushimi Yorihito, would be accompanied by two of Japan's most illustrious heroes from the war with Russia, General Nogi Maresuke and Admiral Tōgō.[91] This decision reflected the uncertain times. Britain had recently begun to make noises about the need to renegotiate the terms of the Anglo-Japanese Alliance as it had become concerned about the tensions that had developed over the past few years between Japan and the United States. Clearly Britain had no desire to be forced to take Japan's side should these two countries come to blows. Against this background it was imperative that Japan showed how much it valued the alliance and it therefore made sense to use the coronation as a means of communicating this message.[92]

The prince's suite arrived in Britain on 7 June and spent time in the country before coming to London for the pre-coronation reception on 20 June. Prince Higashi-Fushimi marked his arrival in the capital by investing the new king with the Order of the Chrysanthemum, before attending that evening an official banquet for the royal guests who were attending the coronation.[93] On the day after the coronation, which took place on 22 June, Japan's special status as an ally was marked by the fact that Tōgō and Nogi were invited to join Prince Higashi-Fushimi at the foreign secretary's coronation banquet, they being the only second-ranked figures from any delegation invited to do so.[94] Furthermore, they were given favourable treatment at the coronation naval review that took place at Spithead on 24 June where they were allowed to view proceedings from HMS *Enchantress*. The IJN again sent two ships to the review, but on this occasion the Admiralty only allowed one, *Kurama*, to take part in the formal proceedings.[95]

Furthermore in Tokyo on the day of the coronation, the Japanese political and military elite once again attended *en masse*, this time at a reception held at the British embassy. The most astonishing event, however, was that a Tokyo newspaper, the *Chūō Shimbun*, invited the people of the city to join in a lantern procession to parade past the embassy that evening. Afterwards it was estimated that 15,000 people had participated which resulted in the parade taking two hours to complete.[96] As a senior official in the Foreign Office noted, 'This shows more than anything I have seen the great value attached by the Japanese people to the British alliance.'[97]

In the following year it was sadly Britain's turn to pay its respects. At the end of July, after a reign of forty-five years, the emperor passed away. On learning this news, the Lord Chamberlain's Office in Britain ordered three weeks of court mourning and appropriate messages of condolence were sent by the king, the government and both houses in Parliament. This still left, though, the difficult question of who should represent the king at the funeral, considering that Tokyo was so far away.[98] The British court and the Foreign Office soon found that a decision had more or less been taken for them, for in early August it became apparent that Germany intended to send the kaiser's younger brother, Prince Heinrich.[99] Clearly in these circumstances Britain could not afford to have its representative out-ranked by its German rival. Accordingly, the king decided that Prince Arthur of Connaught should once again pack his bags and this time be accompanied by Field Marshal Lord Methuen, Admiral Sir Edmund Poe, and once again Miles Lampson.[100]

Even then, however, a new problem soon loomed into sight, for rumours began to circulate that the kaiser intended Prince Heinrich to take this opportunity to award Germany's highest honour, the Order of the Black Eagle, to the new emperor. Here again, Britain could not afford to be outbid and thus it was quickly decided that the German initiative should be trumped by arranging for Prince Arthur to bestow the Order of the Garter on Emperor Yoshihito (known posthumously as Taishō).[101]

Prince Arthur, therefore, duly arrived in Japan in early September with the dual mission of representing the king at Meiji's funeral and investing the new emperor with the Garter. He was supported in his efforts not just by his suite but also by three ships from the China station, HMS *Minotaur*, HMS *Monmouth* and HMS *Kent* and 500 marines, the latter acting as the British contingent in the late emperor's funeral procession.[102] The funeral on 13 September 1912 proved to be a singular affair, for while Japan had adopted Western ways in so many aspects of its life, including its court protocol, the rites for the late emperor remained largely traditional. Thus the funeral took place at night between 8.30pm and 1.30am. The Japanese and British troops in their modern ceremonial uniforms were interspersed with dignitaries dressed in ritual court costumes, while at the centre of the two-mile long procession the late emperor's body was carried on a slow-moving cart drawn by oxen. In the background were, what MacDonald described in his official despatch as, 'musicians piping an ancient dirge, weird and wonderful beyond description'.[103] As one British observer noted, 'It was very "creepy" and incomprehensible.'[104]

Stranger still was the news the next morning that after the funeral, General Nogi, the head of the Peer's School and a member of the Japanese suite attached to Prince Arthur, had returned to his home and committed ritual suicide. This was a shocking act for the British guests as, on the evening before the funeral, Nogi had personally entertained the prince and his companions and had presented Methuen with two books of maps of Port Arthur.[105] His suicide, thus, underlined the fact, as already hinted at in the funeral itself, that Japan was a hybrid of modernity and tradition and that it possessed cultural traits that had no resonance within Britain.[106]

Following the funeral, the British party repaired to Nikko for a brief rest from the solemnity in Tokyo and the summer heat. It also had the distinct advantage that it provided a breathing space between the two very different aspects of their mission. On 18 September, Prince Arthur duly returned to Tokyo for the investiture ceremony which took place at the Imperial Palace. Fortunately the event this time passed without any mishap. The party then travelled to Kyoto, thus repeating the visit that the prince had made six years previously. This time the crowds that greeted him were not as great as they had been in 1906, but this was probably due to the nature of his mission and the existence of an official period of mourning rather than its being any reflection on the popularity of the Anglo-Japanese relationship.[107] Meanwhile, it is worth noting that at home the Lord Chamberlain Office's once again bravely came to the rescue of Anglo-Japanese relations by banning a performance of 'The Mikado' that was due to take place on the day of the emperor's funeral.[108]

This visit proved to be the last flourish of royal relations in the pre-war period for, in contrast to 1906–1907, the Japanese were this time loath to send another royal mission to London. This was again not a reflection on the condition of Anglo-Japanese relations, but rather an insight into the perilous state of the national finances. Caught between the services' demands for higher expenditure and the need to pay off its war debts, the government in

Tokyo was keen to cut back on unnecessary expenditure. Meanwhile on the British side, there was a sense that the royal relationship was now in good fettle and that it did not need the constant attention that had been required in the alliance's first years. Thus, when, in June 1913, the Japanese embassy in London asked in trepidation whether a repeat of the thank-you mission of 1907 was required, the Foreign Office was pleased to put its mind at rest.[109] Following this, in December 1913, came the further news from Japan that the government did not think it would be possible to invite royal representatives to Emperor Yoshihito's enthronement in Kyoto, as the city had no capacity for foreign guests on that scale and in any case the ceremony itself involved little in the way of pageantry.[110] Accordingly, the Foreign Office indicated that it was happy simply to appoint the new ambassador to Japan, Sir William Conyngham Greene, as the king's representative.[111]

The enthronement was planned for 1914 but eventually took place in November 1915, having been delayed for a year due to the death of the empress dowager. The fact that by this stage the First World War had broken out confirmed that it would remain a low-key affair and that Britain would only be represented by its ambassador. To an extent, this was a relief as the royal relationship had undoubtedly proved to be time-consuming and occasionally irritating. However, at the same time, the sudden cessation of the confidence-building measures that had punctuated the period since 1905 was a problem, because it allowed the everyday tensions in Anglo-Japanese relations to fester. Indeed, by 1916 it was apparent that the alliance was in poor shape as Britain and Japan squabbled over a number of issues, including most notably the latter's assertion of greater influence over China. Moreover, in Japan itself there appeared to be doubt over whether it had backed the right side in the European War which became a matter of open speculation in the Japanese press.[112]

THE FIELD MARSHAL'S BATON AND SWORD MISSIONS, 1918

By the autumn of 1917, things had come to such a pass in Anglo-Japanese relations that one of the former British army language officers in Japan, Major F.S.G. Piggott, was so concerned that he proposed revitalizing the court link through the expedient of awarding a British field marshal's baton to Emperor Yoshihito, which would be the first time that a non-European had been honoured in such a manner.[113] By a circuitous route, this idea found its way through to Arthur Balfour, who by this point had become the foreign secretary in the wartime coalition led by David Lloyd George.[114] Piggott's proposal arrived at a crucial point during the war. By the end of 1917 Britain, despite its disappointment at the relative lack of Japanese assistance up to this point and its irritation with the latter's scheming in Asia, hoped that Japan could be persuaded to send forces to bring stability to post-revolution Siberia, thus denying the area to either German or Bolshevik influence. Accordingly, Piggott's idea became caught up in still larger issues.

Britain made an official announcement that the emperor had been awarded a field marshal's baton in early January 1918.[115] However, there was then a division of opinion between Cabinet ministers as to the nature of the baton mission which was to deliver this honour. Lord Beaverbrook, who was the minister of information with responsibility for propaganda in allied countries, was keen that the mission should have an overtly political dimension, but this was opposed by Lord Derby, the secretary of state for war, and by the Foreign Office once it had consulted with the Japanese ambassador, Chinda Sutemi.[116] After a long debate, it was decided to rely on a military mission alone, and the king was prevailed upon to agree that it should again be led by Prince Arthur.[117] Very deliberately, all of the officers chosen for the mission, including the prince himself, had served on the Western Front and during the visit, in order to emphasise this point, they wore khaki rather than ceremonial dress.[118]

The prince and his suite arrived in Japan on 18 June and, again, he was paid the honour of the emperor coming personally to Tokyo station to greet him. The following day the ceremony in which the emperor received the British field marshal's baton was held at the Imperial Palace. Over the next few days, before going on to rest at Nikko and Kyoto, the prince and his suite engaged in a number of functions which had, unsurprisingly, a martial theme, for example, visiting a school for military cadets.[119] Most noticeably, however, Prince Arthur paid his respects at the grave of his former host in Japan, General Nogi, which as well as being a personal tribute had clear symbolic value and was, accordingly, widely reported in the Japanese press.[120] In addition to these ceremonial events, the prince and his suite also engaged in a number of press interviews which were designed, in propaganda terms, to reinforce Anglo-Japanese friendship and to disseminate the British perspective on the war in Europe. Most notably, General Sir William Pulteney talked to the Japanese press of the German use of poison gas, of the fine quality of the IJA troops who had lined the streets of Tokyo, and lastly stated how much Britain appreciated the work being done by the IJN destroyer squadron that was currently serving on convoy duty in the Mediterranean.[121] The prince departed on 11 July travelling to Victoria in British Columbia on the Japanese battle-cruiser *Kirishima*.

The effect that the mission had was profound as far as the British onlookers could gauge. Immediately after its departure, the British ambassador in Tokyo, reported to the Foreign Office that:

> … it seems to me that the Prince's visit has been the very best kind of propaganda, because it made people think well of Britain, and yet made them do so unconsciously … it has … given British and Japanese alike an opportunity of drawing closer together, and of thus re-forging links which the wear and tear of warfare had perhaps tended to impair.[122]

This impression was confirmed by an interested onlooker, the chaplain to the British embassy, Lionel Chomondeley, who felt that the mission, as if by 'a touch of magic', had brought the alliance back to life.[123] Perhaps, most importantly, however, the visit was useful because it forced the Japanese government into the position of once again praising relations with Britain. Most notably on the eve of the visit, this involved the prime minister, General Terauchi Masatake, who in a recent indiscretion had talked of the potential for a post-war Japanese-German alignment, giving an interview to the Japanese press in which he had no choice but to speak in laudatory terms of the alliance.[124]

Japan too now felt the need to play the royal card. In May 1918, it decided to reciprocate the British gesture by sending one of its own princes to London to make the king a field marshal in the IJA and at the same time to bestow the Order of the Chrysanthemum on the Prince of Wales. The British, in the midst of the war, were not overjoyed at the prospect of welcoming a Japanese mission to London, but clearly could hardly afford to rebuff the emperor's largesse.[125] Once again the Japanese mission was led by Prince Higashi-Fushimi Yorihito. As it was still wartime the prince, despite the fact that he was on an official mission, could clearly not travel under his own name, lest the enemy find out. He therefore travelled under the pseudonym of Count Mishima and in order to ensure his security HMS *Orvieto* was assigned to provide him with safe passage in his journeys across the Atlantic.[126] Moreover, to simplify the arrangements in Britain it was decided that the prince should stay for the official part of his visit at Buckingham Palace.[127]

The British government and court duly gave the prince as good a welcome as the wartime circumstances allowed. He was met at Paddington Station on 28 October by the king and was then given the distinction of having the only state banquet held during the First World War being laid on in his honour, with the gold plate being brought up from Windsor especially for the occasion.[128] Also following the precedent that had been set in 1907, during his visit to the City of London on 1 November he was given the privilege of receiving an address at the Guildhall before taking lunch at the Mansion House.[129] The prince then went with the king to a 'northern port' to inspect the Grand Fleet before ending his official visit on 6 November.[130] His next port of call was France where on 11 November he was a witness to the start of the armistice.

CROWN PRINCE HIROHITO'S VISIT TO BRITAIN, 1921

The fact that the respective field marshal missions seemed to revive Anglo-Japanese relations, at least in the eyes of contemporary beholders, demonstrates that the royal relationship continued to be seen as a significant element in maintaining the health of the alliance and on the face of it this appeared to augur well for the future. However, the problems within the alliance were mounting. The lingering suspicions of Japanese behaviour during the war meant that many of Britain's experts on the region believed that the alliance had run its course. Meanwhile, Japan's attitude towards Britain was adversely affected by events at the Paris peace conference in 1919, when the British Empire delegation played the major role in defeating the Japanese attempt to have a racial equality clause added to the Covenant of the League of Nations.[131] The situation was therefore not dissimilar to that which had existed between 1909 and 1911, but just as royal relations had maintained their momentum in those years, so they continued to develop as the 1920s opened.

The next initiative in court relations came in early 1921 when the Japanese court and government decided, after a prolonged and sometimes bitter debate, to send the young Crown Prince Hirohito on a European tour with Britain as his main port of call. The Japanese decision to send the young prince abroad was in large part for educational purposes in that it was believed that he would benefit from engaging in close observation of how other monarchs handled their political roles. This was particularly important because his father was in poor health and it was not known how long the latter would continue to be able to rule. The idea behind the visit also, though, reflected tensions within the Japanese elite about the prince's upbringing to date, his proposed choice of bride and the need to reform the court both in terms of personnel and outlook. In other words, even though it took place at a delicate moment when the Anglo-Japanese Alliance was coming up either for renewal or abrogation, it was largely brought about by domestic concerns rather than any focus on the international impact of the prince's tour.[132] Indeed, such was the intensity of the debate within the court that, shortly before the crown prince's departure, members of the court explicitly asked the new British ambassador to Japan, Sir Charles Eliot, whether it would be possible for the British to provide lessons on the popularity of the House of Windsor.[133]

According to Eliot, the anachronistic practices of the Japanese court were manifold. The activities of the royal princes appeared to be entirely restricted to appearing at court functions and military reviews. There were no public outings to the theatre or other forms of public amusement. At state banquets it was common for there to be four tables; one for the emperor or the crown prince as host, two for the royal princes, and one for the diplomatic corps, which hardly provided a suitable environment for developing any sense of rapport.[134]

The Foreign Office was aware of some of these issues, but naturally, with the future of the alliance in the air, the temptation within its walls was to interpret the prince's visit mainly in terms of its effect on Anglo-Japanese relations.[135] Indeed, the short notice it received of the Japanese government's intention that the prince should visit only underlined this conclusion.[136] As such, the prince's tour of Britain clearly had to be handled carefully. On the one hand, he had to be honoured with all the pomp appropriate to a visiting heir to the throne, but on the other hand it was important that the political atmosphere surrounding the visit should be determinedly neutral in regard to the future. Another worrying aspect of the visit was uncertainty about the character and health of the crown prince. Eliot had reported in June 1920 his concern that the prince 'does not leave an impression of energy and spirit' and on the eve of the latter's departure for Europe was still not reassured.[137]

In terms of protocol, it was clear that Britain was still hemmed in by the breaks from precedence that had been taken place during Prince Fushimi's visit in 1907 and that the crown prince's welcome had to be equally grand. As had happened before, the king chaffed at what he saw as this excessive treatment, but in response the foreign secretary, Lord Curzon, explained that it was difficult to escape from details such as attaching a field marshal and an admiral to the crown prince's suite and observed stoically, 'As we are to receive the Prince we may as well do it well.'[138] Accordingly it was arranged that the king would meet the prince on his arrival in London and that the latter would then stay as a royal guest at Buckingham Palace for three nights. In addition, it was agreed that as the heir to the throne he was entitled to a reception at the Guildhall in the City of London. In regard to honours, it was decided that he should receive a GCB and be made a general in the British army.[139]

Meanwhile, on the political front the Foreign Office worked assiduously to ensure that no hostages to fortune were made during the crown prince's stay. For example, it insisted on vetting all of the official speeches of welcome. Thus, the speech that Curzon drafted for the king to deliver at the state banquet on 9 May dwelt on past comradeship and the good that Anglo-Japanese friendship had brought to the world, but it studiously avoided any mention of the future.[140] Meanwhile the lord mayor of London was permitted in his speech at the Guildhall on 10 May to acknowledge Japanese assistance during the war, but the Foreign Office insisted that he delete a sentence in which he had intended to refer to the hope that the visit 'may more closely cement the alliance now existing between us'.[141] This policing of municipal addresses to the prince even extended to the provinces; in mid-May the mayor of Dunfermline found himself barred by the Foreign Office from mentioning the alliance and was instead restricted to vague verbiage about the strong ties of friendship.[142]

The Crown Prince, who was chaperoned by his uncle Prince Kan'in Kotohito, took the sea route to Europe travelling on board the Vickers-built battleship *Katori*, accompanied by its sister-ship *Kashima*, and stopping briefly in Hong Kong, Singapore, Ceylon [Sri Lanka], Egypt, Malta and Gibraltar, where he was greeted on each occasion by the local governor (or in the Egyptian case, high commissioner).[143] The visit to Britain duly began on 9 May 1921 with the prince's arrival at Portsmouth where he was welcomed by his fellow young heir to the throne, the Prince of Wales. He then travelled by train to London and was greeted at Victoria Station by the king, the Duke of York and the Duke of Connaught before taking the usual carriage ride to Buckingham Palace where the ceremony took place to invest him with his honours. In the afternoon of that day he engaged in a new aspect of court ceremonial that was soon to become customary, namely paying his respects at the Cenotaph in Whitehall and at the Tomb of the Unknown Soldier in Westminster Abbey.

That evening, the king held a state banquet in the prince's honour and, as might be anticipated, made a speech in which he reminisced about his own visit to Japan forty years ago.[144] In addition, though, he discussed in frank terms the political problems that Britain faced in the aftermath of the war. This included a reference to the coal strike that was at that moment bringing chaos to the country. This strike had a few days previously led the king to consider asking the crown prince to delay his arrival by waiting in Gibraltar. However, on the advice of Curzon it had been decided to make a virtue of the dispute and to refer to it as an example of the problems inherent in managing a democratic, pluralist political system.[145] In other words, it was used to demonstrate the modernity of Britain's politics and its willingness to be open and honest with its ally.

The official period of the crown prince's stay occupied the next nine days and was naturally centred upon London, although it also took in day visits to Windsor, Oxford and Aldershot. The most significant function took place on 11 May when the prince made his visit to the City for his reception at the Guildhall, at which, for the first time in his life, he had to make a public address. This was then followed by lunch at the Mansion House.[146] On 18 May, with the official part of the visit now over, the crown prince left London to travel north. His first stop was Cambridge where he was given a lecture in British constitutional politics by Professor John Tanner and received an honorary doctorate in law.[147] He then went by train to Scotland, where, after visiting Edinburgh and the naval base at Rosyth, he become a guest for the long weekend of 21–23 May of the 8th Duke of Atholl at Blair Castle in Perthshire. Here he was introduced by the duke, who had deliberately not created a packed programme for the young prince, to the leisurely pastime of fly fishing and landed a large salmon.[148] His next stop was Manchester, where he visited the works of Metropolitan Vickers and Armstrong Whitworth. He then returned to the south for a number of functions in London before on 30 May departing for the continental European leg of his tour.[149]

The impression that the prince made during his visit was fortunately not as poor as Eliot had feared beforehand. Hirohito was undoubtedly shy and constrained by his lack of English, but he appeared in the words of the king to be 'quite nice', while another witness referred to him as being 'courteous and appreciative'.[150] More warmly still, the brother of the Duke of Atholl observed to his sister, Evelyn Murray, that 'we found our visitors most delightful people to entertain, cheery and simple folk, yet intelligent and up to date and possessing a great sense of humour.'[151] On the Japanese side too, those in his suite and at the Japanese embassy in London were pleased with his performance.[152]

For Hirohito himself, despite the political winds that buffeted his progress, his visit to Britain seems to have had an important effect. Until the end of his life he would observe that he treasured the experience of observing the workings of a true constitutional monarchy at close quarters. Moreover, he would record that he had gained much from a number of informal conversations about politics that he had had with King George V, who had taken a paternalistic interest in his guest. These had included discussions of the king's role in British political life and the advice that in his subsequent European tour the crown prince should be certain to visit the battlefield of Ypres in order to understand the scale of Britain's sacrifice in the Great War.[153] In addition, in later years he referred many times, in a mood of pleasant nostalgia, to the comparative freedom that he had felt while on his tour of Britain, especially during his time as a guest at Blair Castle.[154] Some might cast doubt on these reminiscences and argue that his record as Japan's war leader suggests that he was a far more calculating figure and that these were merely convenient sentiments.[155] The consistency with which the emperor made such remarks, both before and after 1941, might, though, suggest that it is possible to take cynicism too far.

In regard to the impact of the visit, its consequences were felt largely on the Japanese side. Most notably, it appears to have emboldened the remaining genrō and those within the Japanese court who supported reform to push for the retirement of some of their conservative opponents and to deliberate on what could be done to bring the monarchy and people closer together.[156]

This did not mean adopting the British constitutional arrangement wholesale, but rather trying to understand how the latter contributed to bringing society together and applying those lessons that appeared relevant.

A first tentative step was taken when the crown prince returned to his homeland in late June. Prior to this occasion, Japanese crowds had been told always to show obeisance to their rulers by maintaining a sombre silence in their presence. This time, however, the order was countermanded at the last moment and the people were told to cheer the prince instead, which led, at least in Kyoto, to a chaotic welcome.[157] At the same time, further personnel changes were made at the court, although Eliot felt it was too early to say that the conservatives had been routed.[158] Meanwhile, the urgency of the court's investigations was made all the greater by the ever-worsening physical and mental health of Emperor Yoshihito. Indeed, in December 1921, shortly following his return to Japan, Hirohito was forced to step up to the role of prince regent in order to rule in his father's place.[159]

In contrast to its effect on court politics in Japan, the visit did not make any difference to the debate about whether to extend the Anglo-Japanese Alliance. In large part, this was because the Japanese side had the good sense to avoid using the prince's visit to engage in any overt political lobbying or make predictions for the future in his speeches that would later come to be regretted. Such a tactic could, after all, have backfired and in doing so only compromised the authority of the heir to the throne. It might, of course, have been that there was some hope on the Japanese side that his mere presence might help to rejuvenate the alliance, but if this wish existed there is little evidence that the visit had any such effect.

EDWARD, PRINCE OF WALES, AND JAPAN, 1922

As is well known, after a period of intense debate between Britain and the Dominions, it was reluctantly decided at the Washington conference which began in November 1921 that the Anglo-Japanese Alliance should be terminated. This is often represented as a short-sighted British betrayal of Japan brought about at the behest of the United States. This, though, is a dangerous simplification of the position. The reality was that the Japanese government itself recognized that the alliance was losing its *raison d'être* and that it could not continue in its present form in the face of American opposition.[160] As such, the decision to replace the alliance with a Four-Power Pact (Britain, Japan, the United States and France) to uphold the status quo in the Pacific was seen as a logical and uncontroversial solution that was acceptable to all parties. In other words, the end of the alliance was not an abrupt parting of the ways due to any profound differences over policy.

Accordingly, in the aftermath of the conference, both of the former allies were keen to emphasize that they remained friendly powers and that the 'spirit' of the alliance would linger long into the future. This duly set the scene for the royal relationship to continue to flourish, for it clearly provided the most suitable arena for the mutual exchange of signals of respect and cordiality. Most notably, the post-alliance era began with as positive a signal as could be made – a reciprocal visit to Japan by the Prince of Wales.

The visit by the Prince of Wales to Japan in April 1922 was an interesting affair because he brought with him a new image of what royalty could be. The young energetic prince had already shown a gift for resonating with the population at large through his ability to engage in good-humoured informality. This provided a warm contrast with his stiff forebears and was accepted, within certain limits, by British court officials as it was seen as helping to humanize the royal family in the new democratic age. This, after all, was not an unimportant task when one recalls that most of the major royal houses in Europe had been extinguished at the end of the First World War.

The idea that the prince might usefully visit Japan had first been mooted by the Foreign Office in 1920 as an adjunct to the idea that he should make a tour of India.[161] Both George V and the Japanese government had agreed to this proposal at the time, but in the end it had been postponed due to the prince's ill health.[162] The plan was revived in July 1921 when the Japanese emperor formally issued an invitation to the prince having learnt that the latter was due to visit India in early 1922. This idea quickly met with the blessing of both the king and Curzon.[163] From the outset, it was clear that this was likely to be a highly political event and the outcome of the Washington conference only enhanced its significance. Therefore, in preparation for the tour, the prince was provided with advice on good books to read about the country and a series of political reports was drawn up for his benefit by the British embassy in Japan.[164]

Setting the itinerary proved a challenge. As the prince was tired from his exertions in India and Burma, the Japanese authorities were requested to refrain from over-packing his schedule with official lunches, dinners and receptions. Moreover, arranging the first week of his stay was complicated by the fact that it coincided with Easter. Eliot therefore had to make clear to the Japanese that the prince could not take on functions on certain days as this would outrage Christian opinion at home, although the ambassador himself, to the fury of the king, managed to make the faux pas of planning a ball at the embassy on Easter Saturday.[165]

The Japanese leg of the prince's Asian tour began on 12 April when he arrived on board the battlecruiser HMS *Renown* in Yokohama, where he was greeted by the impressive sight of thirty IJN ships providing him with a twenty-one gun salute. One observer of the scene was the prince's young cousin, Lord Louis Mountbatten, then a lieutenant in the Royal Navy. Mountbatten recorded in his diary:

> Next to our service I have never seen such fine ships; any one of them could have taken us on on equal terms. They were spotlessly clean, the men who were manning the ships stood rigidly still and somehow I received an impression that here was a power to be reckoned with in a way in which no one who has not been here and seen for himself can possibly conceive.[166]

Mountbatten was, of course, to have the chance to reflect on these words in his later life when in 1943 he was made the head of South-Eastern Asian Command in India.

After being welcomed onshore in Yokohama, the Prince of Wales then travelled by train to Tokyo where the prince regent, other princes of the blood and Japan's political elite were awaiting him. This warm welcome was, though, outdone by the response of the general public. As Sir Herbert Russell, a Reuters correspondent who accompanied the prince throughout his tour and later wrote a book about it, recalled, the railway journey from Yokohama to Tokyo had been notable for the 'practically unbroken multitudes' who had lined every inch of the track and for the 'thousands of Japanese throats' who roared their approval at Tokyo station. According to Russell, the Japanese court officials, who had only just got used to the idea of cheering, watched on in a state of shock.[167]

The tour lasted for the next three weeks. The first of these, which was spent in Tokyo, comprised the official state visit. The most important ceremony held during this period came when the prince was made a full general in the IJA. This was then followed on 15 April by his wearing his Japanese uniform at a review of IJA units at Yoyogi parade ground. On this occasion, Mountbatten was less complimentary, noting that the army training had submerged each soldier's individuality to 'a degree hitherto only attained by Germany' and observing, as Western figures often did, that the Japanese cavalry were of indifferent quality.[168]

Aside from that, the prince had to engage in an endless series of functions which were regulated by what another journalist, Sir Percival Phillips, described as the 'rigid etiquette' of the Japanese court.[169] Among the events that the prince attended there were performances of both noh and kabuki drama, a sumō tournament, as well as a surfeit of lunches and dinners. In addition, he was the main guest, among 9,000 others, at an imperial garden party which was held to admire that year's display of cherry blossom. This occasion proved unfortunate on two fronts; first, heavy rain had already brought an end to the best of the blossom, and, second, the party was disturbed partway through by clouds of smoke wafting over from the Imperial Hotel which had caught fire. The latter proved to be of great inconvenience as many of the prince's suite and the officers from the *Renown* were staying at the hotel and lost all their possessions in the conflagration.[170] In terms of sporting relief from these 'entertainments', the major event was the game of golf that the prince had with the prince regent. This was memorable, because, although it was Hirohito who suggested the idea, it was clear that he had very little if any experience of the sport. The Prince of Wales accordingly decided that etiquette called upon him to slice his own shots. Hirohito, however, proved a dab hand at another pursuit, the ever popular duck hunt.[171]

Once the formal part of the tour had ended, the prince and his suite travelled to Nikko and Lake Chuzenji. Relatively free from the clutches of the Japanese court, Prince Edward was now able to enjoy himself more and on one notable occasion insisted on pulling a rickshaw for the senior member of his suite, Rear-Admiral Lionel Halsey, which ended with the unfortunate passenger being deposited in a ditch when the prince misjudged his descent down a steep hill.[172] The prince then returned to Tokyo for one further function, a party held in his honour by Baron Mitsui, before proceeding to Yokohama. Here, he performed the solemn task of unveiling the Allied War Memorial Gates at the general cemetery, thus honouring the sixty-two Britons, fifteen French and seven Americans from the Yokohama community who had lost their lives in the war.[173] The formal part of the visit ended at this point.

On leaving Yokohama, the prince went to the Hakone area for four days, but this did not mean that he was now free of protocol, for the prince regent had come up from Tokyo to stay at the Detached Palace at Miyanoshita and this led a series of other functions. After this, the prince and his British and Japanese suites travelled to the Kansai region, spending time in Kyoto, Nara and Lake Biwa. Among his hosts in Kyoto was one interesting figure, Count Ōtani Kōzui of the Nishi Honganji Buddhist sect, who only recently had been a target of British intelligence in India.[174] Such matters were now, of course, forgotten.

The prince and his suite then had a brief visit to Osaka, where his welcome was the most raucous to date; Percival described it as being akin to the noise made by 'an English football crowd'.[175] From there, they went on to Kobe where they boarded a Japanese steamer to take them through the Inland Sea, stopping at Takamatsu and Miyajima. They then transferred to the new IJN cruiser *Kiso* which brought them to the Japanese naval academy at Etajima where the prince regent's younger brother, Prince Takamatsu, was studying as a cadet. After inspecting the academy, Prince Edward and his entourage went on to the nearby naval base at Kure, where HMS *Renown* was waiting for them to re-embark. This short visit proved interesting for the evidence it provided that Japan was living up to its obligations under the Five-Power Treaty signed at the Washington conference to limit its naval armaments. The proof lay in the form of the gun turrets that had been removed from the former battleship *Kaga*, which was now being converted into an aircraft carrier.[176] This, though, was not their last stop, for it had been suggested by Eliot that *Renown* should travel to Kagoshima before leaving Japan.[177] Fittingly the prince was entertained here by the descendant of the man who once had been Britain's enemy, Prince Shimazu. With this final engagement completed, on 9 May the prince left Japanese waters and headed for the next stop on his gruelling tour, the Philippines.

On the face of it, it would appear that the visit that the Prince of Wales made to Japan was a considerable success. Much of this was down to the personality of the prince himself who appeared to impress the Japanese public with his vigour and frank manner and who gave good copy to the media.[178] This included his skilful handling of a press conference, which took place after the media had complained that the Japanese authorities were hampering their access to the royal visitor, and which had threatened the visit's success.[179] The most notable episode, however, took place when the prince and some of his suite were photographed riding bicycles in front of an adoring crowd.[180] As Sir Herbert Russell put it in his book, the prince resonated with the crowd because:

> They [the Japanese] beheld, at first with astonishment, but very soon with affection, a young man of thoroughly human temperament, full of humour and sporting instinct, and able to do the things of everyday life without ever the faintest suggestion of a sacrifice of dignity.[181]

In other words, the prince, as Russell succinctly described it in another passage of his account, represented 'royal democracy'.[182] The result, to quote Percival Phillips was that, 'the prince was carried across Japan on a torrent of cheers.'[183]

It is evident that even the Japanese court responded favourably to the prince's charisma. Eliot observed in a report to the king that even the empress and other members of the royal house, who were normally 'extremely stiff' seemed to mellow in the young prince's presence.[184] Some in the court saw the potential for developing such an image for their own young heir to the throne. It is this that had led Hirohito, who was seven years younger than the Prince of Wales, to be encouraged to join in a game of golf with the British visitors.[185] This desire to learn the secret of Prince Edward's appeal raised, as one British newspaper put it, the prospect of Britain's acquiring a new responsibility in its relations with Japan, namely teaching the Japanese court how to act as a constitutional monarchy, which was surely a fitting role in this democratic post-alliance era.[186]

In addition, the Prince of Wales made a number of telling speeches, largely written by the embassy, which caught the mood of the time. Most notably, he did not avoid the issue of the passing of alliance, but rather expressed the belief in an address at Tokyo Imperial University that it had now been 'merged into a broader instrument' and that there was no reason why the 'ancient friendship' between the two former allies could not deepen further.[187] He also made reference to the Regent's recent visit to Britain and invoked 'the friendship' that had developed between the two heirs to the throne as 'a symbol of the ties of sympathy which bind our two countries together'.[188] The feeling of the embassy in Tokyo was that the prince's presence and the sentiments that he had expressed could not have come at a better time, as it quietened Japan's concerns following the Washington Conference.[189]

The reality of the tour was unfortunately somewhat different. In truth, the Japanese did not comply with the request to keep the itinerary light and the Prince of Wales came increasingly to resent the never-ending formalities and the inflexibility of the programme that had been set for him. Moreover, the fact that, even after the state visit had ended, the prince was still accompanied by a suite of ten Japanese functionaries did not help matters. Indeed, Rear-Admiral Halsey noted in a letter to his parents that the official functions in Tokyo had been 'very, very boring' and that even after that first week '... Japs have no intention whatever that we shall have any time to ourselves – it is really almost killing by kindness ...'[190]

A greater problem was the nature of the prince himself. His long trip to India, followed by the painfully formal ways of the Japanese court, had led him to become disenchanted with his role in life and prone to black moods. Despite all of the work that had been done to prepare him for visit, the prince, according to Eliot, showed little interest in the political aspects of the programme or in Japan as a whole.[191] Nor could it be said that he warmed to his royal hosts. He affirmed that Hirohito, whose golfing skills were negligible, was 'dippy', thus making it clear that if any warmth existed in the relationship between the two heirs to the throne it was entirely one-sided. Worse still, he averred to Eliot at one point that he could only wonder why the Japanese tolerated such 'a queer set of creatures' as a royal family and assumed that their role was simply to act as national mascots.[192] The prince was not the only person to lose his patience; Mountbatten observed on leaving Japan that he felt that he had regained his 'freedom of speech'. However, the unhappy prince was much blunter. According to one source, his last words on departure were, 'Thank God that's the last of the bloody Japanese!'[193] This outburst should, though, be read as the words of a troubled young man rather than as a lasting comment on Anglo-Japanese relations. It is worth noting here that two years before his death, the then Duke of Windsor, having abdicated in 1936 and now living in exile in Paris, would meet again with Hirohito during the latter's 1971 tour of Western Europe. It was, according to all accounts, a touching occasion.[194]

ROYAL RELATIONS AND THE 'SPIRIT OF THE ALLIANCE'

The problem with the creation of an image of cordiality between the two heirs to the throne was, of course, that once it had been invented it had to be perpetuated. The difficulty here was that, with the alliance now a thing of the past, both Prince Edward and King George V proved to be less amenable than before to inconveniencing themselves for the sake of Anglo-Japanese relations. For example, in 1924 Hirohito's long-delayed wedding finally took place. In accordance with the previous stress on the importance of the royal relationship, Eliot recommended from Tokyo that a royal prince should attend, but George V promptly vetoed the idea. Then, to Eliot's consternation, the king even proved grudging on the question of whether he and the Prince of Wales should send presents.[195]

Nor did it help that the Japanese court's attempt to 'democratize' itself soon began to flounder. In December 1922 Eliot reported that the regent had recently attended a sports event, but that any attempt to reach out to the public had been hindered by his being forced to sit alone on a platform and that, rather than taking the lead himself, a courtier had presented the winning cup for him.[196] The circumstances surrounding the regent's wedding in 1924 were no better, for it consisted of a low-key Shinto ceremony to which the Japanese government had no intention of inviting foreign royalty.[197] Thus even if the Prince of Wales had agreed to go, his offer might have been rebuffed. As the king's private secretary, Lord Stamfordham, noted in response to Eliot, the wedding demonstrated the substantial degree to which Japan remained 'separated … from the West in her mode of life, natural, social, religious and domestic.'[198] Even more restricting was that, in December 1923, Hirohito was the target of an unsuccessful assassination attempt, the Toranomon incident, when a communist fired a gun at him while he was travelling in a horse-drawn carriage near the Akasaka Palace in Tokyo. Following this, security around the regent was heightened and thus his ability to be 'on-show' to the people became ever more constrained.[199]

Despite the inability of the regent through both personality and circumstance to emulate the Prince of Wales, there were still some signs in the first half of the 1920s that the progressives in the court remained active. The most important manifestation of this came in a scheme dreamt up by a former Oxford graduate who had risen to become a courtier, Matsudaira Keimin, who proposed in 1923 that the regent's more outgoing younger brother, Prince Chichibu, who was next in line to the throne, should come to England to complete his education. This plan had to be temporarily postponed due to the Yokohama earthquake, but was then revived in the summer of 1924.

From the first, the Foreign Office was keen to encourage this idea, for it raised the prospect that at the end of his time in Britain the prince might return to Japan as a confirmed Anglophile; moreover, there was even a chance that the regent's weak physical condition might mean that one day Chichibu would accede to the throne.[200] When the news of the prince's impending arrival was confirmed in July 1924 there was therefore much satisfaction that useful groundwork could now be laid for the future of Anglo-Japanese relations. At the same time, the decision was also welcomed because it was known to have taken place in the face of pressure from the IJA to send the prince to France for military training instead and it was thus seen as demonstrating the continuing depth of Anglophilia within the Japanese court despite the abrogation of the alliance.[201] Moreover, it was not just the Foreign Office that expressed its contentment; King George V was also pleased, observing that, 'I think it an excellent idea.'[202]

Another advantage of the proposal was that it coincided and thus could be used to blunt the effect of an important strategic move by Britain that had the potential to strain relations with Japan, namely the construction of a naval base at Singapore. In January 1925, the new Conservative government led by Stanley Baldwin decided that the base, which had been cancelled by its Labour predecessor, should go ahead.[203] It was clear to all observers that this initiative was aimed at Japan, but it was hoped that a public announcement that the king was happy to accept Prince Chichibu as a guest would help to a small degree to dampen its impact. Linked to this, the king also advised the government to ensure that when it announced the decision to proceed with the base it should simultaneously make a public affirmation in the House of Commons of Britain's continuing friendly sentiments towards Japan. An explicit statement on these lines was duly made by Baldwin in February 1925.[204]

Prince Chichibu finally arrived in Britain in July 1925 for what was intended to be a stay of two years. His host was Katherine Drummond, the wife of Major-General Lawrence Drummond, and the prince stayed most of the time at their London residence, Kenry House, in Kingston Hill. One of his first engagements in the country was to be invited to lunch at Buckingham Palace, where he made a good impression on the king, who noted that he 'seems quite intelligent and is learning English'.[205] Over the next few months he spent some time in Scotland for the shooting season, stayed at the homes of a number of the leading aristocratic families and visited some prominent British institutions such as the Old Bailey, Cambridge University and the headquarters of the Salvation Army, as well as occasionally attending functions that returned him into the orbit of the royal family.[206]

The prince's presence in Britain was in the summer of 1925 a welcome development because, by this stage, the need to emphasize Britain's continuing friendship towards Japan had become more urgent than ever. In May 1925, Chinese nationalism, which had been gaining pace since 1919, boiled over in the shape of the May Thirtieth movement into a nationwide boycott and strike aimed against British goods and companies. Such was the effect that this febrile atmosphere quickly brought the economy of Hong Kong to a standstill.[207] Faced with these circumstances, Britain was desperate to form a united front with its fellow treaty powers, Japan and the United States, in order to put pressure on the Guomindang (Chinese Nationalist Party), which was leading the movement, to bring the demonstrations to a halt. The warm welcome given to Chichibu thus had ulterior motives.

At the same time, the British government added another string to its bow by agreeing with the king that the youngest of the king's sons, Prince George, who was at that point serving as a naval officer on the China station, should use this opportunity to visit Japan. Thus, at the height of the difficulties on the Chinese coast, the Commander-in-Chief China, Admiral Sir Edwyn Alexander-Sinclair, was ordered, to his consternation, to take his flagship HMS *Hawkins* and the prince to Japan.[208] Despite the unfortunate timing, this visit did prove worthwhile because, even though it was an unofficial trip, the prince got the chance to make a public appearance when he arrived in Tokyo and managed to meet with members of the Japanese royal family.[209] The king was pleased at this news and let it be known to Eliot that, 'It will be everything if we can work in friendly conjunction with Japan in settling the rather serious difficulties with which, thanks to the Bolsheviks, we are confronted in China.'[210]

In order to encourage such cooperation, further friendly gestures were made in the royal sphere in 1926. Most notably, the Foreign Office began to make preparations for Prince Chichibu to study at the University of Oxford. The plan was for him to take a one-year course at the undergraduate level at Magdalen College, which was the alma mater of the Prince of Wales. In January 1926 the permanent under-secretary at the Foreign Office, Sir William Tyrrell, duly wrote to the president of Magdalen, Sir Herbert Warren, asking if this would be possible. At first Warren demurred. This led Tyrrell to make it clear in no uncertain terms that, against the background of the crisis in China, the college's cooperation was essential, observing:

> I cannot disguise that a refusal to receive the Prince would have really grave political dangers ... If it were to get abroad that the heir to the Japanese throne ... had been refused at Oxford the political consequences would be very serious. This is no exaggeration.[211]

Cowed by this outburst, Warren duly toed the line. As a result, in October 1926, the prince took up a place at Magdalen studying a curriculum of history and politics courses, while at the same time indulging his passion for sport (he was one of the team that won the College Fours in rowing) and making a number of lifelong friends such as the future Conservative politician Duncan Sandys. According to Warren, he proved to be a good, diligent student who showed himself to be 'generally agreeable, good natured and unaffected'.[212]

Further bolstering Anglo-Japanese relations, the same year saw the Admiralty agree to a request relayed through the Japanese embassy in London that Prince Takamatsu should be allowed to serve on board a Royal Navy ship for a year.[213] Meanwhile, a further plan was made in regard to the heir to the Korean throne, Prince Yi Un (known in Japanese as Ri Gin), who now lived in Tokyo under the protection of the Japanese. This involved the prince, who was a captain in the IJA, coming to Britain for a year and being attached to a British army regiment, although this visit had to be delayed in the spring of 1926 due to the ill-health and subsequent death of his elder brother (the former Emperor Sunjong).[214]

Lastly, the king continued to take an interest in Chichibu. In May 1926 the king invited the young prince for lunch and bestowed upon him his personal decoration, the GCVO. Afterwards the king noted in his diary that 'He speaks English fairly well now.'[215] By the end of 1926, it therefore appeared that royal relations were in a healthy state. In regard to the Japanese court, it seemed as if the Anglophile, progressive element was now in the ascendancy, while in Britain the king was keen to use the powers at his disposal to encourage this sympathetic tendency.

THE SHŌWA EMPEROR AND THE GARTER

In December 1926 this calm was disturbed by a momentous event, the death of the Taishō Emperor and Hirohito's ascendancy to the throne. This affected the momentum of royal relations in a number of ways. Most obviously, it raised the question of how Britain should mark this sad occasion. This threatened to be a complicated issue because the situation had obviously changed since the last state funeral when the two countries had been allies. Fortunately for the Foreign Office, the Japanese took the lead over the funeral arrangements and helped to cut short British deliberations by announcing that they did not want any special envoys to attend the ceremony and that it was not necessary for the China station to send any ships.[216] Britain was thus able to show its respect by simply holding a memorial service at Westminster Abbey, flying flags at half-mast on the day of the funeral and arranging for both houses of Parliament to offer their condolences.[217]

The next and more knotty problem was how the British court should mark the elevation of Hirohito to the imperial throne. Here too, the precedent set by 1912 had to be taken into consideration. At that time, with the alliance still in existence, the Garter had been very quickly bestowed on the new sovereign. The question in early 1927 was, therefore, whether the 1912 precedent was pertinent or did the termination of the alliance now mean that Britain was released from this obligation. In regard to this issue, the consensus in the court and political elite was that the awarding of the Garter to Meiji and Taishō had been out of line with the decoration's statutes and had only come about because of the existence of the alliance.[218] This meant that Britain was now free to act as it so desired; it could continue making an exception for Japan or it could return to the traditional position of only bestowing the Garter on Christian monarchs. Nor was it believed that there was any immediate requirement to promote Hirohito to the rank of field marshal in the British army as the gesture made to his father in 1918 had been entirely based on the then political context.[219]

Deliberations on this issue began in earnest after the Taishō Emperor's funeral in early February. On 17 February, the foreign secretary, Sir Austen Chamberlain, sent a telegram to the ambassador in Japan, Sir John Tilley, asking for his opinion about whether the Garter should be awarded and if so when a mission should be despatched. In this communication he indicated his preference by noting:

> … I am anxious to mark in every suitable way the close and friendly relations of this country to Japan and to do all that is possible to remove the soreness left

> by the termination of the alliance. The King approves this effort and is willing to do whatever he can to promote it.[220]

Tilley duly reported back his approval of this policy and indicated that the best time to send such a mission would be after Japanese court mourning came to an end in January 1928.[221] It therefore looked as if a decision to honour the emperor had been taken, but in mid-April Chamberlain abruptly reversed himself. In a letter to Tilley he reported that the king had decided that, as the alliance had lapsed, there was no longer any need to bestow the Garter on a non-Christian.[222]

The major reason for this change of heart was that the king and Chamberlain were forced by events in China in the spring of 1927 to conclude that Britain's benevolence in the royal sphere over the past two years had not led to any positive benefits in terms of Japanese foreign policy.[223] This perception had been growing for some time but reached its peak in 1927 as the full force of Chinese nationalism ranged itself against British interests. At the start of the year the British concession at Hankou was seized by a Chinese mob and it was feared that the next event might be an attempt by the Nationalist army under Jiang Jieshi to occupy the International Settlement at Shanghai. In desperation, Britain had turned to the United States and Japan in the hope that they might form a common front. In particular, Chamberlain had placed his faith in Britain's former ally, noting to the king on 16 January that 'Everything depends on Japan, as they alone can get to China quickly.'[224] However, no support arrived and then in late March the same sorry story repeated itself in regard to an incident at Nanjing in which Guomindang troops attacked foreign civilians and property.[225] Britain had thus called for united action but was met with silence. Thus in his letter to Tilley, Chamberlain explained that the king believed that 'there is nothing peculiarly friendly or helpful to us in Japanese policy at the present time', and that he personally concurred with this judgement.[226]

This, though, was perhaps not the only reason for the shift in the king's attitude, for there is also evidence to suggest that he was displeased at this point with the activities of the Japanese court. The death of the Taishō Emperor had meant that Prince Chichibu had to break off his studies at Oxford University to return home and that the forthcoming visits to Britain of Princes Takamatsu and Yi were postponed. This was, of course, to be expected, but by early February 1927 it appeared that a conservative revival at the Japanese court was going to curtail any revival of the exchanges that had flourished in 1925–26. In particular, it was apparent that there was a great deal of opposition to the idea of Chichibu returning to Britain to renew his studies.

The official reason for this was that the prince could not leave Japan as long as the period of national mourning was in progress, but the subtext was that the conservatives felt that he should not be exposed to foreign influence.[227] The king, who had liked the prince, and had made clear in a telegram to the new emperor that he would welcome Chichibu's return, felt that this showed ingratitude and a lack of faith in Britain.[228] His gruff response to the news was to note, 'I quite understand & I am sure that Prince Chichibu will not be allowed to return to England which I regret.'[229] In addition, the status of Takamatsu's planned attachment to the Royal Navy was put in abeyance while court mourning was in place and by the end of the year had been dropped entirely.[230] Thus the only exchange that did take place was the least significant, the arrival of Prince Yi.

Unsurprisingly, Tilley was deeply disturbed by the king's decision not to bestow the Garter on the emperor, for he feared that the Japanese court and government would interpret this as a deliberate insult and that it would cause a further worsening of relations. In particular, he pointed out the flaw in the argument that Britain had been released from its obligation due to the alliance having been terminated. This, he observed, was hardly consistent with the propaganda line that the British elite had followed ever since 1921 of arguing that, although the formal ties had been sundered, the 'spirit of the alliance' remained.[231]

The king was not greatly impressed by this argument, but rather than dismissing the matter completely, he decided to postpone it for later consideration.[232] Nor was his mood so dark that royal diplomacy as a whole was left in abeyance. In September 1927, the king agreed to accept a proposal from the Foreign Office that Prince Yi should be given a decoration during his stay in Britain. He thus arranged for his third son, Prince Henry, to present a Grand Cross of the British Empire to the Korean prince, with the order that 'as much should be made out of the compliment as possible'.[233]

The issue of the Garter lay dormant until March 1928 when, as was almost inevitable, the Japanese began to make enquiries about it.[234] As a result, Chamberlain decided that the time had come to tackle the king's reluctance. He therefore, in his own words, 'begged' the king to meet with Tilley, who was on home leave, so that the latter could fully set out the implications of any decision not to make the award. Tilley duly performed his magic with the outcome that the king agreed that a Garter mission should be despatched in the following year and decided that it should be led by Prince Henry.[235] This news was relayed to the Japanese shortly before the emperor's coronation. The latter event, as in 1915, was designed primarily for Japanese consumption and required no more than Tilley being appointed as a special ambassador.[236]

In order to prepare for the mission, the court decided that it needed to consult with the then junior diplomat who had accompanied Prince Arthur to Japan in 1906, Miles Lampson. The latter was now British minister to China and in February 1929 he wrote back with advice on the need for the mission to arm itself with expensive presents and decorations and always to keep in mind Japanese sensitivities. He warned, 'They are apt to think that all foreigners look down on them instinctively.'[237] If this were not forbidding enough, the mission were also informed from other sources that it would be necessary for them to wear the single most unpopular item of formal wear, the dreaded frock coat, 'an article to which the Japanese attach the highest importance'.[238]

The Garter mission reached Yokohama on HMS *Suffolk* on 2 May 1929. Prince Henry (who by then had become the Duke of Gloucester) was accompanied by the Earl of Airlie, Rear-Admiral Sir Herbert Meade, who had commanded HMS *Renown* during the visit by the Prince of Wales in 1922, and Major-General Sir Hugh Elles. As on previous occasions, the mission proceeded without any great mishap. The duke was greeted on his arrival by Prince Chichibu, who then accompanied him on the train to Tokyo station, where the emperor was present to welcome him. The investiture took place on 3 May with 'great solemnity' and in the view of Tilley made a favourable impression on the court.[239] On the next day the duke had a chance to underline British friendship to Japan when he went to Tokyo Imperial University to be shown the books that Britain had donated to replenish the stocks of the library, which had suffered grievously in the earthquake of 1923.[240] On 9 May, the final day of the official section of his stay, he attended an evening production at the Kabuki-za where his entry into his box was met with a reception of spontaneous and warm applause from the Japanese public; an act that convinced Tilley that the visit had been worthwhile.[241] After this, the duke set out on the usual tour of the great sights of Japan and finally left the country on 23 May. In his formal report of the visit, Tilley noted how both the press and the public had been very warm in the welcome and opined that, 'No ill-feeling and only regret is now evident at the termination of the Anglo-Japanese Alliance.'

As on prior occasions an act of generosity on one side had to be reciprocated by the other. Japan therefore announced in the autumn of 1929 that Prince and Princess Takamatsu would visit Britain in the summer of the following year in order to show the emperor's appreciation to the king. The Foreign Office was aware that this mission was intended, as with Gloucester's visit, to have an overtly political dimension, for an intercepted diplomatic telegram to the Gaimushō from Matsudaira Tsuneo, the ambassador in London, made this abundantly clear.[242] Accordingly, the Foreign Office believed that it was important to lavish pomp and attention on the royal guest in order to create a positive impression. In cooperation with the Lord Chamberlain, the Treaty Department at the Foreign Office therefore pushed for the ceremonial to be in keeping with that provided for Prince Fushimi in 1907.[243] Furthermore, the Foreign Office insisted to the Treasury that after the end of the state visit, the British government should pay for the newly-married prince and princess to stay for one extra week in London. In making this proposal, it noted that 'Japanese friendliness and co-operation' were particularly important at this time due to the need to form a united front against Chinese demands for treaty reform and to negate any disappointment that Japan felt following the recent London naval conference when it had been forced to accept a compromise on the numbers of cruisers it possessed. More broadly, the Foreign Office pointed out that the passing of the alliance had left Japan uncertain about British friendship and that it was necessary to use royal diplomacy to provide a sense of reassurance, observing 'The Japanese have in the last two years expressed a great desire for our co-operation, and it is not always easy to respond since our interests are not always identical, so that courtesy is valuable to fill any gap.'[244]

This need to inculcate a spirit of friendship also led to serious attention being given to the need to provide further honours to the Japanese. In regard to Takamatsu himself, he was given the Royal Victorian Chain (RVC). This decoration was higher than the GCVO and was considered more appropriate because the prince was on an official mission.[245] The most important question, though, was whether now was the time for Britain to play another card in order to honour the emperor, namely by promoting him to the rank of field marshal in the British army. This matter had been under discussion since 1927, but had taken a backseat to the issue of the Garter, which was clearly more prestigious. In 1930, it was revived by the outgoing military attaché in Tokyo, and immediately appealed to the Foreign Office, the War Office and the king, with the result that it was decided that Takamatsu should be presented with a field marshal's baton to take back to his brother.[246]

The Prince and Princess Takamatsu duly arrived in Dover on 26 June 1930 where they were greeted by the Duke of Gloucester. They then travelled to London, were welcomed at Victoria Station by the Duke of York and had the usual procession by carriage to the palace where the king was awaiting their arrival. Once at the palace the prince delivered the emperor's formal message of gratitude and this ceremony was followed in the evening by a state dinner. Meanwhile, to coincide with the prince's arrival, the king sent a telegram to the emperor informing him of his promotion to the rank of field marshal.[247] On 27 June, the prince and princess followed in the steps of their predecessors in London in being entertained by the City of London. On this occasion, however, the ceremony was not quite as inflated as it had been in the past for there was, this time, no visit to the Guildhall; the guests thus received the ceremonial appropriate to their status rather than following, as the Foreign Office had wanted, the precedent that had been created for Prince Fushimi.[248] The royal couple stayed on in Britain until 12 July when they departed for a long tour of Europe. They returned briefly in September and then made a final visit in March 1931 before returning to Japan.[249]

ROYAL RELATIONS BECALMED, 1931–1935

Takamatsu's visit proved to be the end of an era. By the summer of 1930 the world recession was already beginning to bite and over the next few years its malign effects would bring the relative peace that had marked international politics in the 1920s to a rapid conclusion. In its place, political and commercial tensions rose in Europe and Asia. Japan was particularly badly hit for its banking system was not robust and its exports were overvalued in world markets once the yen returned to the gold standard in January 1930. As a result, Japanese unemployment soared and faith in representative democracy began to fray. On the side-lines, the army was poised to step into the political vacuum with its own sweeping solutions to modern dilemmas.

In this febrile atmosphere, Japanese attention turned to Manchuria, the vast north-eastern region of China whose economic potential remained relatively untapped. Japan had treaty rights in the south of the region dating from its victory over Russia in 1905 but these were now under threat from the Chinese nationalist regime in Nanjing. Meanwhile, the IJA watched nervously as the Red Army began to reassert strong Soviet control over Eastern Siberia and to project its power into north Manchuria. By the summer of 1931 Manchuria was a potential fire merely waiting for a match to strike. On 18 September, the cataclysm began when the Japanese army in the region staged an incident for the purpose of justifying a full-scale military campaign to seize the three provinces. All China could do, aware of its own domestic weakness, was to appeal to the League of Nations for assistance in the hope that Japan might be forced to negotiate. Britain, as a leading member of the League of Nations Council, was thus forced to confront a problem which presented it with a choice between two unpalatable options, offending Japan or undermining the effectiveness of collective security.

In these circumstances there was little use for royal diplomacy as it was ill-suited to periods of crisis. The problem in this regard was that the only tactic one could use in such a situation was for one monarch to send a communication to the other calling upon him to act as a peacemaker. This clearly was a blunt and risky gambit, for it could only be done once and contained the danger that it might well worsen relations if such an overture were ignored. Moreover, there were obvious dangers within a constitutional monarchy in utilizing the sovereign in such a manner.

A case in point came when the fighting in Manchuria spread to Shanghai in late January 1932. On 30 January the American secretary of state, Henry Stimson, mentioned in a telephone conversation with the British prime minister, Ramsay MacDonald, that President Herbert Hoover was thinking of sending a telegram directly to Emperor Hirohito asking for a cessation of hostilities and asked if the king could take parallel action. MacDonald, after a day's deliberation responded in the negative, noting 'that proposal re King constitutionally, & for other reasons, impossible'.[250] Further to this, when on 15 February the foreign secretary, Sir John Simon, briefed George V on events in China, the king responded by suggesting that 'as he had always maintained friendly relations with the Emperor and … was on intimate terms with the Emperor's brother, Prince Chichibu, who had stayed at Buckingham Palace', he could perhaps make a personal initiative in the hope that this would lead to a de-escalation of tensions.[251] But again, this offer was not taken up.

In the end Britain had no choice but to back the League over the Manchurian crisis as too much emotional capital had been invested in collective security. As a result, Anglo-Japanese relations began to deteriorate. This situation was then exacerbated by the rise of commercial tensions between the two countries as British industry (especially cotton textiles) reacted furiously to what it saw as unfair trade competition in British colonial markets.[252] A sign of the increasing distance came in 1934 when Prince and Princess Kaya Tsunenori came to Britain in the spring of 1934 on a three-week private visit in which they were the honoured guests at a Japan Society dinner.[253] On this occasion the Japanese embassy indicated to the Foreign Office that that there was no need to arrange any meeting with the royal family.[254]

It is clear that the gulf developing between the two former allies was a matter of some regret for the king, especially as he, unsurprisingly considering his age, preferred the age-old certainties of traditional diplomacy to the trend for internationalism. It is noticeable, for example, that Sir Alexander Cadogan, the new minister to Peking, noted in his diary after meeting with the king just prior to departing for China, that His Majesty 'held forth for about 20 minutes on the Far East. Not very enlightening. Rather obvious views of the Lindley kind.'[255] (This refers to the British ambassador to Japan, Sir Francis Lindley, who had argued during the Manchurian crisis that Britain should not sacrifice its good relations with Japan for the sake of the League.[256])

Acting on these sentiments, in the late summer of 1934 both the king and the Prince of Wales acted behind the scenes to try to instil new life into Anglo-Japanese relations. Most notably, they both let it be known that they supported the idea of sending an unofficial mission organized under the auspices of the Federation of British Industry (FBI) to visit Japan and Manchukuo in order to assess the potential market for British business.[257] Around the same time a courtier, in response to rumours of a desire within the British government for a rapprochement with Tokyo, observed to a leading figure in the Foreign Office that, 'I think that His Majesty was rather pleased to hear that we were beginning to flirt with Japan, who will probably be a better ally to us than Uncle Sam.'[258] Then in the following year when the prominent Treasury official Sir Frederick Leith-Ross was charged with the mission of seeking to develop trilateral economic co-operation between Britain, Japan and China, the king decided to take advantage of this opportunity to ask Leith-Ross to deliver a friendly personal message to the emperor.[259]

The king's interest in seeing better Anglo-Japanese relations was reciprocated by the Japanese court. It too sought out ways to signal its continued friendship. For example, in September 1934, having learnt of the king's support for the FBI initiative, the court arranged for this unofficial mission to receive an audience with the emperor.[260] In addition, it is notable that the Japanese court was enthusiastic about celebrating King George V's silver jubilee in 1935, which provided a ready-made opportunity for it to communicate its continued respect. In his reports back to London, the ambassador in Tokyo, Sir Robert Clive, noted in May 1935 that Prince and Princess Chichibu along with a number of government ministers had attended the church service to celebrate the king's jubilee and that the church had, in fact, proved too small to accommodate all those who wished to attend. He also indicated that the Japanese press had displayed great interest in the festivities in London.[261]

PRINCE CHICHIBU AND THE CORONATION OF KING GEORGE V, 1936–1937

The most important royal overture of the 1930s also arose from an opportunity. On 20 January 1936 King George V died. This gave both the Japanese court and state a chance to use two events, the funeral and the crowning of the new king, as a means, if it desired, of signalling to Britain its interest in establishing better relations. The way in which Japan handled these matters in 1936–1937 certainly suggests that it was keen to use this channel as a means of communicating its wish for closer friendship. In order to understand why this was the case, it is important to recognize that the court had become one of the last bastions of pro-British sentiment in Japan. This was due not just to the emperor himself, but also to the nature of the figures appointed to senior positions in the court. The most prominent of these was the pro-Western former foreign minister, Makino Nobuaki, who had been Japan's leading diplomat at the Paris peace conference of 1919. He had acted as the lord keeper of the privy seal between 1925 and 1935 but retained considerable influence in the court even after his retirement. Moreover, he had privileged access in regard to policy towards Britain because his like-minded son-in-law, Yoshida Shigeru, was appointed as the Japanese ambassador to Britain in 1936. Meanwhile, another important Anglophile was Yoshida's predecessor in London, Matsudaira Tsuneo, who in 1936 became the minister of the imperial household. He too was able to exert influence beyond his formal position, in his case because his daughter, Setsuko, was the wife of Prince Chichibu.

From the moment of King George V's death, it was evident that the Japanese state and court intended to mark the occasion with a great deal of pomp and ceremony. Sir Robert Clive reported back to the Foreign Office on 22 January 1936 that the prime minister, foreign minister and finance minister had all personally come to the embassy to pay their respects and that messages of condolence had been received from the IJA and IJN.[262] Moreover, the foreign minister, Hirota Kōki, informed Clive that all IJN ships would fly their flags at half-mast for two days, which was a day longer than was normal for a head of state, and forwarded an offer from the armed forces to provide 1,000 men to act as a guard of honour to line the streets at the time of the memorial service in Tokyo; Clive had to decline the latter on the grounds that the streets approaching St Andrew's Church were too narrow for this to be practical.[263] At the memorial service on 31 January the emperor was represented by Prince Takamatsu with most of the Cabinet also in attendance.[264]

It then took less for a month for the Japanese to begin to make enquiries about the forthcoming coronation of Edward VIII. On 22 February Clive informed London that he had been approached by the prominent Anglophile, Count Soejima Michimasa, who said that Japan would greatly appreciate receiving an invitation to send a prince to the coronation. In so doing, he played on the commonalities between the two countries, noting, 'the British and Japanese monarchies were unique in their stability and in the devotion they inspired.'[265] This was then followed by strong intimations to Clive that should an invitation transpire then Prince Chichibu was the most likely member of the royal family to be given this important mission.[266] This decision was confirmed in October 1936 when it was formally announced that Chichibu would represent his brother.[267]

The road to the coronation was not, though, all smooth sailing. Aside from the abdication crisis in Britain and the problems continually generated by Japanese foreign policy, which included in November 1936 its signing of the Anti-Comintern Pact with Germany, Japan's heavy handling of its own domestic security raised difficulties. In December 1936 an incident took place at Keelung in Taiwan in which Japanese police assaulted three British sailors. This proved embarrassing because it influenced the question of whether the IJN should be invited to send a ship to the coronation naval review. The result was that in February 1937 the British Cabinet only agreed to invite the IJN to take part on the condition that the Keelung incident be concluded satisfactorily, which fortunately turned out to provide the necessary impetus.[268]

While Japan's initial sloth over settling Keelung suggested that Anglo-Japanese relations were still in the doldrums and that its actions to date over the king's death could be taken as token gestures, the way that the court in Tokyo acted in the early months of 1937 suggested that something more significant was taking place. Moreover, this manoeuvring had support within the newly-formed government of General Hayashi Senjūrō . Indeed, the minister of communications, Kodama Hideo, speculated, in a measure that recalls the British debate about the field marshal's baton mission in 1918, whether Chichibu should be accompanied in his visit to Britain by a leading political figure 'for the promotion of Anglo-Japanese goodwill'. In the end, this proposal was turned down as it was felt to be premature, but the fact that it was even made is telling.[269]

In early January, Yoshida informed the Foreign Office that Prince Chichibu intended during his visit to present George VI with the Order of the Chrysanthemum. Typically this kind of practice was not allowed at the time of coronations, but on this occasion the Foreign Office indicated to Buckingham Palace that 'on political grounds' this offer should not be declined as long as the ceremony took place once the formal coronation period had ended.[270] This was then followed by another interesting initiative, the news that after fulfilling a number of engagements in Europe in the summer of 1937, the prince intended to return to Britain in September 'in the hope ... of establishing more friendly feelings between our two countries'.[271]

The most singular event, however, was the lunch that the emperor hosted at the imperial palace on 22 February to mark the departure of Prince and Princess Chichibu to London. This occasion was remarkable in part because of those who were invited, which included the staff of the British embassy, all of the princes and princesses and Prime Minister Hayashi.[272] Even more interesting, though, was that the emperor made a point of talking to the Britons present and that he reminisced at length about his own visit to Britain in 1921. In his report to the king on this episode, Clive noted that, 'it was a very unusual party. It was far more like an Anglo-Japanese demonstration.'[273] Drawing on this experience, the ambassador observed in a private letter to the Foreign Office that, 'It is no doubt genuinely hoped that something will come out of the Chichibu visit in the way of more intimate relations. What exactly the Japanese hope I don't know and I dare say they don't know themselves.'[274]

Given the range of problems that Britain faced in 1937 and in light of the fact that the Japanese overture did not appear to contain any untoward conditions, it clearly made sense for the British state to reciprocate. This was particularly the case as events in Japanese domestic politics seemed to suggest that a thaw was under way. Most noticeably, for the first time since late 1931, a known moderate, Satō Naotake, was appointed in March 1937 as foreign minister, which Clive and others saw as an encouraging development.[275] Accordingly, the Foreign Office was determined that Prince and Princess Chichibu should be treated with due care and deference. It was, for example, arranged that a representative of the royal family would be present to greet them on their arrival in Britain.[276] Moreover, the prince was favoured by the order of precedence for foreign guests at the coronation. With the Italian royal house having absented itself due to the fact that Britain had invited Emperor Haile Selassie of Ethiopia to send a representative, Prince Chichibu was the only figure present who was a member of a foreign monarchical Great Power and thus outranked all of the other coronation missions. The Dutch government sought to take advantage of the situation by arguing that the order of precedence should be based on blood ties rather than status, but this was categorically rejected by the foreign secretary, Anthony Eden, who made it clear that he would be 'very strongly opposed to any change which would involve degrading Prince Chichibu'.[277]

Prince and Princess Chichibu duly arrived at Southampton on board the liner *Queen Mary* on 13 April 1937. The royal couple then made a brief visit to London where they met with the Duke of Gloucester before moving down to Hove which they made their home for the interval leading up to the coronation on 13 May.[278] At the time of the great event itself they came up to London to attend a flurry of balls, dinners and other functions. The most important occasion, however, came on 19 May when the prince came to the palace to bestow the Order of the Chrysanthemum upon the king. In return, he received the RVC, following the precedent created during his younger brother's visit in 1930.[279]

The response in Japan to these events seemed to confirm that relations were moving in a more positive direction. On 20 May, Clive reported to the Foreign

Office that on the day of the coronation an official service was held in Tokyo that was attended by Prince and Princess Takamatsu, Prime Minister Hayashi and many Cabinet ministers, and that afterwards these dignitaries had visited the afternoon garden party at the British embassy. He also reported that NHK had relayed a full account of the proceedings in London, that the annual sumo tournament in the capital had been interrupted for the unfurling of the Japanese and British flags and that Japanese fishing vessels flying Union Jacks had sailed up the Sumida River.[280] He was also able to report that, in his valedictory audience with the emperor, the latter had expressed his satisfaction with the warm welcome his brother had received. Further positive noises from Hirohito followed in late June when in a telegram sent directly to the king he expressed the hope that Prince Chichibu's visit 'will do much to cement more firmly than ever the amicable relations between our respective houses and empires'.[281]

This optimism was, of course, ill-placed. On 7 July the Marco Polo Bridge incident broke out to the south-west of Beijing marking the start of the Sino-Japanese War. The beginning of that conflict quickly forced the cancellation of the long-planned talks between Britain and Japan in London, and also inevitably overshadowed Prince Chichibu's return to Britain in September, following a tour of Europe, for what was intended to be a further wooing of British opinion. By the time Chichibu reappeared on 16 September, British relations with Japan had deteriorated to their worst point to date. British public opinion was appalled at what it saw as Japan's indiscriminate bombing of civilian targets in China and even worse some Japanese aviators in late August had shot and wounded the British ambassador to Nanjing, Sir Hughe Knatchbull-Hugessen.[282]

In these circumstances, all Chichibu could do was to send a farewell letter to King George VI in which he expressed his regret about the shooting incident and his continuing desire for better relations, noting:

> It is my firm conviction (and I know that of my brother the Emperor) that our respective Empires should stand together as in many ways the welfare of our peoples may be maintained by collaboration as the past has shown.
>
> It is most unfortunate that the Alliance which our forebears were wise enough to conclude no longer exists.[283]

Although this message was seen as sincere, the king clearly could not in the present situation respond in the same vein. The Foreign Office therefore wrote a reply for him that presented a far gloomier picture, stressing that no talks could take place between Britain and Japan until peace had returned to China.[284] On 18 September the prince left Britain for home for the final time.

THE DEEP FREEZE

From this point on, royal relations withered on the vine. From the British perspective, it was clear that Japan was the aggressor in the East and that nothing could be done to improve relations until the government in Tokyo indicated that it was prepared to retreat from its expansionist policies. On the Japanese side of the equation, hostility grew towards Britain in the belief that it was encouraging Chinese resistance. Accordingly, in the autumn of 1937 an anti-British campaign began in the press and manifested itself on the streets of Tokyo and Osaka in the form of demonstrations and other protests. This antipathy towards Britain had a direct effect on royal relations, for it provided radicals with a means of attack against the liberal courtiers who advised the emperor. It thus became more difficult than ever for figures such as Makino and Matsudaira to suggest using the royal link as a means of ameliorating tensions with Britain.[285]

There were occasional proposals to reactivate this channel of communication and respect, but these were all quickly rejected as inappropriate. For example, when the king's private secretary, Sir Alec Hardinge, in December 1937 picked up upon a suggestion that the Duke of Gloucester might write to Chichibu, Eden dismissed the idea out of hand.[286] Another potential opportunity presented itself in August 1939 when the sudden conclusion of the Nazi-Soviet Pact left Japan unexpectedly isolated on the world stage. Accordingly, Hardinge wondered whether this might be the right occasion for the king to reach out to the emperor. However, the foreign secretary, Lord Halifax, rejected the idea on the grounds that there was no reason to think that a positive response might be expected.[287] Ironically, at exactly the same time, the Japanese emperor was himself insisting that the Japanese government 'must follow the line of friendship with England and America', which begs the question of whether Hardinge's initiative might have had a positive effect.[288]

The last such idea was aired in the autumn of 1941 during the descent into outright confrontation. In late November an unnamed Japanese intermediary, who claimed to be in touch with the lord keeper of the privy seal, Kido Kōichi, revealed to the British ambassador in Tokyo, Sir Robert Craigie, that the emperor was nervous about the possibility of war breaking out. At the same time, however, Hirohito was concerned that he could only attempt to veto any further Japanese advance if it were clear that this would lead to an open and immediate clash with Britain and the United States. Accordingly, the intermediary suggested that if a strong warning were sent to Hirohito that even a move into Thailand might provoke a general war, this might give the emperor the weapon he needed.[289]

This proposal did not, though, meet with a positive reception in the Foreign Office, for there were severe doubts about whether the emperor had the constitutional power to act in this manner. Moreover, it was argued that if any such message should be sent it could not directly come from the king, as that too raised constitutional issues. The only person who could act in that fashion was the president of the United States who had the benefit of being both the head of state and chief executive.[290] In fact, in the last days of peace the American president, Franklin Roosevelt, did, indeed, toy with the idea of communicating directly with the emperor, but in the end his letter arrived too late.[291]

The royal card was thus not played and on 8 December 1941 the Japanese invasion of Hong Kong and Malaya began the opening of hostilities. With this move, there was only one sorry final task for the British court to complete. On 10 December, Hardinge initiated the process to strip the emperor of the Order of the Garter. The latter's banner was duly taken down from St George's Chapel at Windsor Castle on 20 December and news of the removal of his decoration was formally announced in the *London Gazette* in the following month.[292] At the same time arrangements were made for all other Japanese nationals to receive the same treatment. Royal relations were at an end for the war's duration.

CONCLUSION

As can be seen from the above, court diplomacy during the first four decades of the twentieth century played an important role in Anglo-Japanese relations. In 1902, the link between the two monarchies began with the signing of the alliance to blossom as never before, although it is important to note that it still did not reach a state of something akin to equality until Japan's victory over Russia in 1905. After this date, the royal relationship prospered and it soon came to constitute one of the most significant foundations of the alliance. Indeed, such was its centrality that in 1918 it provided the most logical channel – in the form of the field marshal's baton mission – for reviving a relationship that had become badly strained during the war against Germany. Moreover, so integral was the inter-relationship between the alliance and the ties between the two courts that even once the formal treaty partnership was abrogated in 1922, it made sense to continue exchanges in the royal sphere in order to add ballast to the argument that the 'spirit of the alliance' lived on. And even when relations came under severe pressure in the 1930s, it is significant that overtures for a rapprochement came in this forum.

Thus for both countries the interaction between the two royal houses provided a vital channel for signalling their goodwill and, as is clear from the historical record, much time and effort was spent on ensuring that the right messages were sent and received. The members of the respective royal families were not merely the pawns of their advisers in this process. Some of them did take an active interest in promoting mutual ties. In the 1900s, King Edward VII consistently supported the alliance and used his powers of patronage to reward those who worked to improve relations between the two countries. It also seems clear that the princely visits made to each other's countries did create some sentimental attachment. This is most clearly the case with Emperor Hirohito and Prince Chichibu, but it is noticeable that even the idiosyncratic Prince Edward in 1934 gave his support to the FBI mission. Clearly, though, there were limits to how far this relationship could be taken. Both religion and race meant that there was no chance of intermarriage, while the stolid character of the Japanese royal house and its stiff attitude towards protocol had a stifling effect. However, within the bounds of what could be achieved this was a reasonably effective relationship which contributed in a positive vein to the ties between the two countries. How it could be reconstructed after a vicious and debilitating war was, though, a different matter.

ENDNOTES

1 This chapter is a much expanded version of my essay, 'A Royal Alliance: Court Diplomacy and Anglo-Japanese Relations, 1900–41' in Hugh Cortazzi (ed.), *Britain and Japan: Biographical Portraits* vol.VI, (Folkestone: Global Oriental, 2007) pp.63–70.

2 Aside from the chapter in this volume by Peter Kornicki, the evolution of Anglo-Japanese court relations in the second half of the nineteenth century can be studied in Hugh Cortazzi, 'Royal Visits to Japan in the Meiji Period, 1868–1912', in Ian Nish (ed.), *Britain and Japan: Biographical Portraits* vol.2 (Richmond: Japan Library, 1997) pp.79–93, Michio Yoshimura, 'Nichi-Ei kyūtei kōryu shi no ichimen: sono seijiteki seikaku to hiseijiteki seikaku' [One Face of Anglo-Japanese Imperial Court Relations: Their Political and Non-Political Character], in Yoichi Kibata, Ian Nish, Chihiro Hosoya and Takahiko Tanaka (eds), *Nichi-Ei kōryu shi, vol.1, Seiji-Gaikō* [The History of Anglo-Japanese Relations: Politics and Diplomacy] (Tokyo: Tokyo University Press, 2000) pp.309–14, and Antony Best, 'The Role of Diplomatic Practice and Court Protocol in Anglo-Japanese Relations, 1867–1900', in Markus Mosslang and Torsten Riotte (eds), *The Diplomats' World: The Cultural History of Diplomacy, 1815–1914* (Oxford: Oxford University Press, 2008) pp.231–53.

3 The best source for comparing the British approach to Japan with its treatment of other non-Christian countries is Naotaka Kimizuka, *Joō Heika no Buru Ribon: Gātā Kunshō to Igirisu Gaikō* [Her Majesty's Blue Ribbon: the Order of the Garter and British Diplomacy], Tokyo: NTT Shuppen, 2004), pp.88–95.
4 TNA FO83/1567 Salisbury to Satow (Tokyo) 2 April 1897 (tel.).
5 D'Athenan (Tokyo) to de Méroda 2 January 1894, in George A. Lensen (ed.), *The D'Athenan Despatches from Japan, 1894–1910* (Tallahassee: Diplomatic Press, 1967) p.7.
6 Ian Nish, *The Anglo-Japanese Alliance: The Diplomacy of Two Island Empires, 1894–1907* (London: Athlone 1966) pp.187–92, and Naotaka Kimizuka, 'Itō Hirobumi no Roshia homon to Nichi-Ei domei: Igirisu seifu shunōbu no taiō o chushin ni' [Itō Hirobumi's Visit to Russia and the Anglo-Japanese Alliance: Concentrating on the Response of the British Government], *Kanagawa-ken ritsu gaigo tanki daigaku kiyo*, 23 (2000) 33–44.
7 Royal Archives (RA) Windsor, VIC/MAIN/W/42/29 MacDonnell to Ponsonby (BP) 26 August 1901, and Lansdowne papers, British Library (BL), Add. Ms.88906/17/4, Knollys (KPS) to Lansdowne 6 November 1901. I have to acknowledge the gracious permission of Her Majesty Queen Elizabeth II to use quotations from the Royal Archives.
8 Kimizuka, 'Itō Hirobumi', p.40.
9 The GCB is the decoration normally given to foreign presidents and prime ministers.
10 Kimizuka, 'Itō Hirobumi', pp.38–42.
11 Lansdowne papers, BL, Add.Ms.88906/18/10 Edward VII to Lansdowne 30 January 1902.
12 TNA FO46/563 MacDonald (Tokyo) to Lansdowne 10 April 1902 no.42.
13 TNA FO46/552 MacDonald to Lansdowne 22 May 1902 no.61.
14 TNA FO83/1982 Synge (Treaty Dept) minute 23 January 1902.
15 *The Times*, 24 June 1902, p.8.
16 Kimizuka, *Joō Heika no Buru Ribon*, p.123.
17 Ibid.
18 TNA ADM116/132 Thomas minute 28 May 1902.
19 TNA FO83/1900 Maycock (Treaty Dept) minute 7 August 1902, and *The Times*, 16 August 1902, p.7.
20 TNA FO46/559 Hayashi to Lansdowne 8 November 1902 and Lansdowne papers, FO800/134 MacDonald to Barrington (FO) 5 November 1902. Kimizuka claims in *Joō Heika no Buru Ribon* p.123 that Komatsu received the GCB at this point, but this had in fact already been bestowed upon him in 1890.

21 Lansdowne papers, TNA, FO800/134 MacDonald to Barrington 9 April 1902, RA VIC/MAIN/W/42/105 Bertie (FO) to Knollys 24 August 1902, and Satow (Peking) diary entry 17 June 1903, in Ian Ruxton (ed.), *The Diaries of Sir Ernest Satow: British Envoy in Peking (1900–1905)* vol.1 (Morrisville NC: Lulu Press, 2006) p.346.
22 For the 'Shah and Garter' episode, see Simon Kerry, *Lansdowne: The Last Great Whig* (London: Unicorn, 2017) pp.161–2 and Kimizuka, *Joō Heika no Buru Ribon*, pp.111–26.
23 TNA FO46/565 MacDonald to Lansdowne 21 January 1903 no.5.
24 Yoshimura, op. cit., p.315, and Kimizuka, *Joō Heika no Buru Ribon*, pp.126–7.
25 TNA FO46/565 MacDonald to Lansdowne 21 January 1903 no.5.
26 See, for example, the king's undated note on FO46/568 MacDonald to Lansdowne 22 October 1903 tel.107.
27 Balfour Papers, BL, Add.Ms.49863 Edward VII to Balfour 28 November 1903, f.228, and TNA CAB41/28/24 Balfour to Edward VII 30 November 1903. The most detailed study of this episode is Hiraki Yabuki, 'Britain and the Resale of Argentine Cruisers to Japan before the Russo-Japanese War', *War in History*, 16/4 (2009), 425–46.
28 Balfour Papers, BL, Add.Ms.49863 Edward VII to Balfour 25 December 1903 ff.242–5.
29 Balfour Papers, BL, Add.Ms.49863 Balfour to Edward VII 28 December 1903 ff.254–8, and Knollys to Balfour 30 December 1903 f.259.
30 RA VIC/MAIN/W/67/18 Hamilton to Knollys 20 November 1904.
31 Lansdowne papers, BL, Add.Ms.88906/20/11 Buckle to Landowne 29 November 1904. See also Kimizuka Naotaka, 'Nicho-Ro sensō to Nichi-Ei oshitsu gaikō: Meiji Tenno e no gata kunshō juyo o megutte' [The Russo-Japanese war and Anglo-Japanese court diplomacy: concerning the conferment of the Order of the Garter on the Meiji Emperor], *Gunji Shigaku*, 40 (2004) p.119.
32 Lansdowne papers, BL, Add.Ms.88906/17/4 Knollys to Lansdowne 11 December 1904.
33 Lansdowne papers, BL, Add.Ms.88906/17/4 Lansdowne to Knollys 12 July 1905.
34 *The Times*, 27 June 1905, p.10.
35 *The Times* 28 June 1905 p.9, and *The Times*, 30 June 1905 p.11.
36 Sir Paul Newall, *Japan and the City of London* (London: Athlone, 1996) p.11.
37 *The Times*, 30 June 1905, p.10.
38 For a reference to this uncertainty, see TNA FO46/873 MacDonald to Lansdowne 15 February 1905 no.40.
39 Balfour papers, BL, Add.Ms. 49747, Percy to Balfour 13 January 1905 ff.145–6.

40 Balfour papers, BL, Add.Ms. 49729, Lansdowne to Balfour 16 January 1905 ff.55–6.
41 For the negotiation of the second alliance, see Nish, op. cit., pp.298–344.
42 TNA FO46/598 Lansdowne to MacDonald 9 August 1905 no.41 (Treaty) and Lansdowne to MacDonald 6 September 1905 no.47 (Treaty).
43 Balfour papers, BL, Add.Ms. 49729, Lansdowne to Balfour 29 September 1905 f.171. See also Kimizuka, 'Nicho-Ro sensō to Nichi-Ei oshitsu gaikō', p.130.
44 Balfour papers, BL, Add.Ms. 49729, Lansdowne to Balfour 8 October 1905 ff.184–5.
45 RA VIC/MAIN/W/47/323 Edward VII note n.d. [October 1905]?
46 Lord Redesdale, *The Garter Mission to Japan* (London: Macmillan, 1906) p.2. This book is also reproduced in Hugh Cortazzi, *Mitford's Japan: The Memoirs and Recollections 1866–1906 of Algernon Bertram Mitford the first Lord Redesdale* (London: Athlone, 1985).
47 TNA FO372/20 21316/198/323 'Reports on the Mission of His Royal Highness Prince Arthur of Connaught, K.G. to Invest His Imperial Majesty the Emperor of Japan with the Most Noble Order of the Garter', Lampson (FO) memorandum 7 June 1906.
48 Redesdale, op. cit., pp.15–22.
49 Keene, op. cit., pp.634. This mishap is airbrushed from the accounts written by Yoshimura and Kimizuka. Prince Arthur referred to this mishap in a letter to his mother, see RA VIC/ADDA15/8090 Arthur to 'Darling Mama' 5 March 1906.
50 TNA FO345/60 Lampson to Lloyd Thomas 16 February 1929.
51 See for example, Phillimore papers, National Maritime Museum, Greenwich, PHIL/2/106, Willes (C-in-C China) to Phillimore 26 August 1881, Haldane papers, National Library of Scotland, Mss.20247, Haldane diary 6 April 1904, and Rumbold papers, Bodleian Library, Oxford, Rumbold dep.14, Rumbold to Rumbold 23 May 1909.
52 Donald Keene, *Emperor of Japan: Meiji and his World, 1852–1912* (New York: Columbia University Press, 2001) p.633.
53 TNA FO372/20 7064/198/323 Grey to MacDonald 27 February 1906 tel.10.
54 TNA FO372/21 17224/17224/323 Davidson (BP) to Grey 18 May 1906.
55 Redesdale, op. cit., pp.41–51. The following paragraph on the itinerary of the prince's visit is largely drawn from Redesdale's account
56 RA VIC/ADDA15/8090 Arthur to 'Darling Mama' 5 March 1906 and VIC/ADDA15/6463 Arthur to 'Darling Mama' Antipodes Day [18 March] 1906.
57 TNA FO372/20 21316/198/323 'Reports on the Mission of His Royal Highness Prince Arthur of Connaught, K.G. to Invest His Imperial Majesty the Emperor

of Japan with the Most Noble Order of the Garter', Lampson memorandum 7 June 1906.
58 See, for example, TNA FO372/20 12677/198/323 Lampson to Maycock 22 March 1906.
59 RA VIC/ADDA15/6492 Wyndham to 'Madame' 28 February 1906.
60 TNA FO372/20 13154/198/323 MacDonald to Grey 1 March 1906 no.43, and 13389/198/323 MacDonald to Grey 17 March 1906 no.55.
61 TNA FO372/20 9378/198/323 MacDonald to Grey 17 March 1906 tel.28.
62 Redesdale papers, Gloucestershire County Record Office, Gloucester, D2002/7/1/6 Grey to Redesdale 7 June 1906.
63 For Redesdale's writings, see Robert Morton, *A.B. Mitford and the Birth of Japan as a Modern State: Letters Home* (Folkestone: Renaissance Books, 2017).
64 P.F. Kornicki, 'General Sir Ian Hamilton (1853–1947) and the Russo-Japanese War', in Hugh Cortazzi (ed.), *Britain and Japan: Biographical Portraits* vol.VII (Folkestone: Global Oriental, 2010) pp.168–73.
65 TNA FO372/21 22977/22977/323 Grey minute n.d. [July 1906].
66 TNA FO372/61 9015/962/323 Lampson note 18 March 1907.
67 RA VIC/MAIN/X/24/53 Lampson to Davidson 2 April 1907.
68 RA VIC/MAIN/W/51/73 Hardinge (PUS FO) to Edward VII 24 April 1907.
69 RA VIC/MAIN/X/25/49 Davidson to Ponsonby 19 April 1907.
70 RA VIC/MAIN/X/25/59 Ponsonby to Davidson 21 April 1907.
71 RA VIC/MAIN/X/24/34 Lord Chamberlain's Office (LCO) memorandum 26 March 1907.
72 For the controversy, see the file TNA HO45/10533/150939.
73 RA VIC/MAIN/X/24/38 Ellis (LCO) to Davidson 26 March 1907, and TNA HO45/10533 150939/1 Lampson to Boyd (HO) 4 April 1907.
74 RA VIC/MAIN/X/25/51 Lampson to Davidson n.d. [April 1907].
75 TNA HO45/10533 150939/23 Duncan to Gladstone 11 June 1907.
76 *The Times*, 7 May 1907, p.9.
77 *The Times*, 10 May 1907, p.8.
78 *The Times*, 17 May 1907, p.10.
79 *The Times*, 22 May 1907, p.6.
80 *The Times*, 29 May 1907, p.8.
81 RA VIC/MAIN/X/26/37 Walsh (MC) to Davidson 11 May 1907 and VIC/MAIN/X/26/44 Walsh to Davidson 19 May 1907.
82 TNA FO372/61 18732/962/323 Lowther (Tokyo) to Grey 13 May 1907 no.108.
83 Morrison papers, Mitchell Library, Sydney, MSS.312, vol.51, Collins to Morrison 22 July 1907.

84 Ian Nish, *Alliance in Decline: A Study in Anglo-Japanese Relations 1908–1923* (London: Athlone, 1972) pp.28–36, and Yoshimura Michio, 'Jyōji go-sei taikanshiki zengo no kokusai jōsei to Nihon no taiō' [Japan's response to the international situation at the time of George V's coronation], *Seiji Keizai Shigaku*, 370 (1997) 61–78.
85 Nish, *Alliance in Decline*, p.84, and Yoshimura, 'Nichi-Ei kyūtei kōryu shi no ichimen', pp.318–19.
86 For Prince Fushimi Hiroyasu's arrival in Britain, see *The Times*, 10 March 1908, p.10. It is sometimes claimed that he was present continuously in Britain between 1907 and 1910, but, in fact, he had only come to Britain temporarily in 1907 as part of his father's suite.
87 *The Times*, 9 June 1909 p.12, and TNA FO372/168 23898/23898/323 Knollys to Tyrrell (FO) 24 June 1909.
88 TNA FO371/923 8274/8274/23 Grey note 3 March 1910.
89 *The Times*, 26 May 1910, p.8.
90 TNA FO372/250 17903/15261/350 Kato to Grey 19 May 1910, and FO372/255 20695/15261/350 MacDonald to Grey 23 May 1910 no.14 (Treaty).
91 TNA FO372/321 1966/43/350 MacDonald to Grey 14 January 1911 tel.-.
92 Yoshimura, 'Jyōji go-sei taikanshiki zengo no kokusai jōsei to Nihon no taiō', p.64.
93 *The Times*, 21 June 1911, p.13.
94 Yoshimura, 'Jyōji go-sei taikanshiki zengo no kokusai jōsei to Nihon no taiō', p.73.
95 TNA ADM116/1146 Brownrigg (NA Tokyo) to DNI 17 February 1911.
96 TNA FO372/378 26853/43/350 Rumbold (Tokyo) to Grey 23 June 1911 no.84.
97 TNA FO372/378 26853/43/350 Campbell (FO) minute 10 [July] 1911.
98 TNA FO372/370 33163/32166/323 Grey to MacDonald 7 August 1912 tel.-.
99 TNA FO372/370 33685/32166/323 MacDonald to Grey 9 August 1912 tel.-.
100 TNA FO372/370 33944/32166/323 Grey to MacDonald 12 August 1912 tel.6 (Treaty).
101 TNA FO372/370 34811/32166/323 Maycock minute 12 August 1912 and Grey to MacDonald 17 August 1912 tel.127.
102 TNA FO372/370 37400/32166/323 MacDonald to Grey 5 September 1912 tel.67.
103 TNA FO372/370 42249/32166/323 MacDonald to Grey 16 September 1912 no.224.
104 Arnold-Forster papers, Royal Navy Museum, Portsmouth, 2006.69 Arnold-Forster to 'Mother' 19 September 1912.
105 Methuen papers, Wiltshire and Swindon Record Office (WSRO), Chippenham, collection 1742, box 6348, Methuen to Aston 24 September 1912.
106 TNA FO371/1391 42250/38735/23 MacDonald to Grey 18 September 1912 no.225.

107 See Methuen papers, WSRO, collection 1742, box 6348, Methuen to Aston 24 September 1912.
108 TNA HO45/10533/150939 HO memorandum 24 September 1912.
109 TNA FO372/446 28063/1105/323 Maycock minute 11 June 1913.
110 TNA FO372/447 58115/58115/323 Greene (Tokyo) to Grey 8 December 1913 no.19 (Treaty).
111 TNA FO372/447 58115/58115/323 Grey to Greene 15 January 1914 no.1 (Treaty).
112 Nish, *Alliance in Decline*, pp.167–8.
113 Balfour papers, TNA, FO800/210 Piggott memorandum 11 November 1917. The only recipients of field marshal's batons prior to this were Wilhelm II (1901), Franz Josef (1903) and Nicholas II (1916), see Balfour papers, TNA, FO800/203 'Missions to Confer Military Decorations, etc., on Foreign Sovereigns' Field (FO) memorandum 4 April 1918.
114 Balfour papers, TNA, FO800/210 Malcolm (WO) to Malcolm (FO) 17 November 1917.
115 TNA FO371/3234 6083/6083/23 Greene to Balfour 10 January 1918 tel.20.
116 Nish, *Alliance in Decline*, pp.241–4.
117 RA PS/PSO/GV/PS/MAIN/24190/8 Stamfordham (KPS) note 1 April 1918.
118 RA PS/PSO/GV/PS/MAIN/24190/11 Derby to Stamfordham 4 April 1918.
119 *The Times*, 25 June 1918, p.5.
120 TNA FO371/3234 162924/6083/23 Greene to Balfour 16 July 1918 no.257.
121 TNA FO371/3234 140780/6083/23 Greene to Balfour 3 July 1918 no.239.
122 Balfour papers, TNA, FO800/203 Greene to Balfour 3 July 1918. See also Yoshimura, 'Nichi-Ei kyūtei kōryu shi no ichimen', pp.321–3 and Nish, *Alliance in Decline*, pp.246–7.
123 Chomondeley papers, Bodleian Library, University of Oxford, Ms. Eng lett c.583 Chomondeley to Christian 24 June 1918 f.88.
124 TNA FO371/3234 110161/6083/23 Greene to Balfour 19 June 1918 tel.658. For Terauchi's indiscretion, see Nish, *Alliance in Decline*, pp.245–6.
125 RA PS/PSO/GV/PS/MAIN/23106/1 Hardinge (PUS FO) to Stamfordham 31 May 1918. See also Nish, *Alliance in Decline*, p.247.
126 TNA FO371/3237 102925/96419/23 FO to Admiralty 12 June 1918, and 141300/96419/23 Admiralty to Foreign Office 14 August 1918.
127 RA MRH/MRH/MISC/114/5 Ponsonby to Douglas 9 October 1918.
128 RA PS/PSO/GV/C/O/2548 Queen Mary to Queen Alexandra 31 October 1918.
129 *The Times*, 2 November 1918, p.3.
130 *The Times*, 5 November, p.3, and *The Times*, 6 November p.4.

131 The standard account is Naoko Shimazu, *Japan, Race and Equality: The Racial Equality Proposal of 1919* (London: Routledge, 1998).
132 Hatano Masuru, 'Taishō junen kōtaishi hoō – sono kettei e no porosesu to saika [The Crown Prince's visit to Europe in Taishō 10 – the process and result of the decision], *Hogaku Kenkyū*, 66 (1993), 30–58. See also Ian Nish, 'Crown Prince Hirohito in Britain, May 1921', in Nish (ed.), *Britain and Japan*, pp.206–207.
133 RA PS/PSO/GV/C/P/510/12 Eliot (Tokyo) to Stamfordham 4 March 1921.
134 RA PS/PSO/GV/C/P/510/11 Eliot to King George V 2 February 1921.
135 PRO FO371/6687 F301/301/23 Wellesley (FO) minute 26 January 1921. The domestic debate in Japan is described in RA PS/PSO/GV/C/P/510/8 Eliot to King George V 2 February 1921.
136 TNA FO371/6687 F301/301/23 Lampson minute 26 January 1921.
137 RA PS/PSO/GV/C/P/510/8 Eliot to King George V 30 June 1920, and RA PS/GV/C/P/510/11 Eliot to King George V 2 February 1921.
138 PRO FO371/6687 F773/301/23 Curzon minute 25 February 1922.
139 PRO FO371/6690 F1441/301/23 Ponsonby to Crowe (FO PUS) 14 April 1921.
140 PRO FO371/6691 F1773/301/23 Curzon minute 9 May 1921. The Crown Prince also avoided any mention of the future of the alliance in his speech at the state banquet on 9 May, see *The Times*, 10 May 1921.
141 PRO FO371/6689 F1258/301/23 Lampson (FE Dept) minute 9 April 1921.
142 PRO FO371/6691 F1857/301/23 Newton (FE Dept) to Lampson 19 May 1921.
143 A diary account of the Crown Prince's visit was published as Yoshinori Futada and Setzsuzo Sawada, *The Crown Prince's European Tour* (Osaka: Osaka Mainichi, 1925). This is an English translation of the Japanese original. A number of accounts state that *Katori* and *Kashima* were cruisers, but this is to confuse them with later vessels of the same name.
144 Ibid., pp.59–62.
145 Curzon papers, India Office Library and Records (IOLR), BL, Eur.Mss F112/221b Stamfordham to Curzon 2 May 1921, and RA PS/PSO/GV/C/P/510/15 Stamfordham to Eliot 9 May 1921.
146 Futada and Sawada, op. cit., pp.67–9.
147 Large, op. cit., p.21.
148 Katherine, Duchess of Atholl, *Working Partnership: Being the Lives of John George, 8th Duke of Atholl, and of his Wife, Katharine Marjory Ramsay* (London: Arthur Baker Ltd, 1958) p.128.
149 Futada and Sawada, op. cit., pp.78–89.
150 RA GV/PRIV/GVD/1921: 9 May 1921, and Lord Riddell, *Intimate Diary of the Peace Conference and After 1918–1923* (London: Gollancz, 1933) pp.298–9.

151 Atholl papers, Blair Castle Archives (BC), Blair Castle, bundle 884, Murray to Murray 5 June 1921.

152 Large, op. cit., p.24.

153 Futada and Sawada, op. cit., p.70, and Large, op. cit., p.21.

154 Hatano, op. cit., pp.31–2. The emperor mentioned the visit to Blair Castle to Miles Lampson (who was later ennobled as Lord Killearn) in an audience during one of the latter's postwar visits to Japan, see TNA FO371/170758 FJ1051/53 Killearn to Home 5 September 1963.

155 The most critical and well-known revisionist biography of the Showa emperor in English is Herbert Bix, *Hirohito and the Making of Modern Japan* (New York: Harper Collins, 2000), but see also David Bergamini, *Japan's Imperial Conspiracy* (New York: William Morrow, 1971) and Edward Behr, *Hirohito: Behind the Myth* (London: Hamish Hamilton, 1989). For more sympathetic portraits, see Large, op.cit., passim and, more recently, Noriko Kawamura, *Emperor Hirohito and the Pacific War* (Seattle: University of Washington Press, 2015).

156 Hatano, op.cit., pp.54–5. See also the comments of the Imperial Household Minister, Makino Nobuaki, reported in Curzon papers, IOLR, BL, Eur.Mss F112/219b Eliot to Curzon 1 July 1921.

157 RA PS/PSO/GV/C/P510/17 Eliot to George V 23 September 1921.

158 TNA FO371/6709 F4294/4294/23 Eliot to Curzon 17 October 1921 no.538.

159 Stephen Large, *Emperor Hirohito and Showa Japan: A Political Biography* (London: Routledge, 1992) p.24.

160 Nish, *Alliance in Decline*, p.381.

161 TNA FO371/4470 A364/364/51 Tilley (FO) minute 29 January 1920.

162 Curzon papers, TNA, FO800/155 Campbell (FO) to Stamfordham 6 February 1920, and TNA FO371/5361 F1824/223/23 Cromer to Campbell 12 August 1920.

163 TNA FO371/6702 F2570/2518/23 Curzon minute 14 July 1921, and F2851/2518/23 Lampson 3 August 1921.

164 TNA FO371/6702 F3579/2518/23 Lampson to Thomas 5 October 1921, and RA EVIIIPWH/PS/VISOV/1921–2/INDJAP Thomas to Eliot 1 January 1922.

165 RA EVIIIPWH/PS/VISOV/1921–2/INDJAP Halsey to King George 14 April 1922 tel.-., and RA PS/PSO/GV/C/P/510/22 Eliot to Stamfordham 22 April 1922.

166 Mountbatten diary 12 April 1922, in Philip Ziegler (ed.), *The Diaries of Lord Louis Mountbatten 1920–22: Tours with the Prince of Wales* (London: Collins, 1987) p.277–8.

167 Sir Herbert Russell, *With the Prince in the East: A Record of the Royal Visit to India and Japan*, (London: Methuen, 1922) p.167. See also 8th Duchess of Atholl papers, BC, bundle 132, Thomas to Atholl 20 April 1922.

168 Mountbatten diary 15 April 1922, in Ziegler (ed.), op. cit., p.282.

169 Sir Percival Phillips, *The Prince of Wales' Eastern Book: A Pictorial Record of the Voyages of 'HMS Renown'* (London: Hodder & Stoughton, 1922) not paginated.
170 Russell, op. cit., p.171.
171 The Duke of Windsor, *A King's Story* (London: Cassell, 1951) p.179–80.
172 Ibid., p.177.
173 Ibid, p.179.
174 For the British suspicions of Ōtani, see TNA FO228/3211 'Secret Abstracts of Intelligence', General Staff Singapore report November 1917.
175 Phillips, op. cit., unpaginated.
176 Ibid.
177 RA PS/PSO/GV/C/P/510/25 Eliot to King George V 11 May 1922
178 Philip Ziegler, *King Edward VIII: The Official Biography* (London: Collins, 1990) p.146.
179 RA EVIIIPWH/PS/VISOV/1921–2/INDJAP Parlett to Thomas 10 June 1922, and Ziegler, op. cit., p.146.
180 Yoshimura, 'Nichi-Ei kyūtei kōryu shi no ichimen', pp.324–9.
181 Russell, op. cit., p.168.
182 Ibid, p.187.
183 Phillips, op. cit., unpaginated.
184 RA PS/PSO/GV/C/P/510/23 Eliot to King George V 27 April 1922.
185 Yoshimura, 'Nichi-Ei kyūtei kōryu shi no ichimen', p.327.
186 *Daily Chronicle*, 18 April 1922.
187 RA EVIIIPWH/PS/VISOV/1921–2/INDJAP Prince of Wales' speech at Tokyo Imperial University 13 April 1922.
188 RA EVIIIPWH/PS/VISOV/1921–2/INDJAP Prince of Wales' speech to the Japanese Parliament 13 April 1922.
189 Curzon papers, IOLR, BL, Eur. Mss F112/224a Eliot to Curzon 1 May 1922 and RA EVIIIPWH/PS/VISOV/1921–2/INDJAP Parlett to Thomas 10 June 1922.
190 Halsey papers, Hertfordshire Record Office, DE/HI/F67/14 Halsey to 'mother' 26 April 1922.
191 Curzon papers, IOLR, BL, Eur. Mss F112/224a Eliot to Curzon 1 May 1922 and Eliot to Curzon 23 May 1922. See also Ziegler, op. cit., pp.144–5.
192 Ragnar Colvin, *The Memoirs of Sir Ragnar Colvin KBE CB 1882–1954* (Durley: Wintershill Publications, 1992) p.86, and Curzon papers, IOLR, BL, Mss.Eur. F112/224a Eliot to Curzon 23 May 1922. See also Ziegler, op. cit., pp.144–5.
193 Mountbatten diary 9 May 1922, in Ziegler (ed.), op. cit., p.299, and Colvin, op. cit. p.86.
194 Large, op. cit. p.183.

195 TNA FO371/9230 F953/426/23 Eliot to Tyrrell (FO) 28 February 1923, and F1127/426/23 Stamfordham to Vansittart (FO) 16 April 1923, and Curzon papers, TNA FO800/155 Stamfordham to Vansittart 27 June 1923.
196 RA PS/PSO/GV/C/P/510/22 Eliot to King George V 8 December 1922.
197 RA PS/PSO/GV/C/P/510/33 Eliot to Curzon 10 February 1924.
198 RA PS/PSO/GV/C/P/510/34 Stamfordham to Eliot 12 April 1924.
199 Large, op. cit., pp.
200 PRO FO371/9234 F2280/2280/23 Wellesley minute 31 July 1923.
201 PRO FO371/10319 F4429/2384/23 Eliot to Chamberlain 27 November 1924 no.466, and Ashton- Gwatkin (FE Dept) minute 31 December 1924.
202 TNA FO371/10319 F2384/2384/23 King George V note n.d. [January 1925].
203 Ian Hamill, *The Strategic Illusion: the Singapore Base and the Defence of Australia and New Zealand* (Singapore: Singapore University Press, 1981) pp.99–107.
204 TNA FO371/10958 F129/9/61 Hardinge to Selby (FO) 7 January 1925, and *Hansard*, Fifth Series, HC, vol.180, c.1590 (23 February 1925).
205 RA/GV/PRIV/GVD/1925: 10 July 1925.
206 For the prince's Anglophilia, see Dorothy Britton, 'Prince and Princess Chichibu', in Hugh Cortazzi (ed.), *Britain and Japan: Biographical Portraits* vol.V, (Folkestone: Global Oriental, 2005) pp.23–5.
207 For the tensions in China in the 1920s, see Edmund S. K. Fung, *The Diplomacy of Imperial Retreat: Britain's South China Policy, 1924–1931* (Hong Kong: Oxford University Press, 1991) and Phoebe Chow, *Britain's Imperial Retreat from China, 1900–1931* (London: Routledge, 2017).
208 TNA ADM1/8692/257 Admiralty to C-in-China 22 August 1925 tel.606.
209 Chamberlain papers, Cadbury Research Room, Birmingham University Library (BUL), AC52/436 Grantham to Chamberlain 20 September 1925, and RA PS/PSO/GV/C/P/510/38 Eliot to King George V 25 September 1925
210 Eliot papers, TNA, FO800/255 Stamfordham to Eliot 28 October 1925.
211 Warren papers, Magdalen College, Oxford, MC: P414/C91/11 Tyrrell to Warren 25 January 1926. With kind permission from the President and Fellows of Magdalen College, Oxford.
212 Magdalen College papers, Magdalen College, Oxford, MC:PR/2/21 Warren to Tyrrell (draft) 29 December 1926.
213 TNA ADM1/8706/209 Fisher (DNI) minute 27 August 1926.
214 TNA FO262/1657 Tilley (Tokyo) to Chamberlain 25 February 1926 no.91 and Tilley to Clementi (GOV HK) 7 April 1926.
215 RA GV/PRIV/GVD/1925: 31 May 1926.
216 TNA FO372/2283 T16215/13338/379 Tilley to Chamberlain 25 December 1926 tel.173, and FO372/2404 F1268/2/379 Tilley to Chamberlain 29 January 1927 tel.54.

217 TNA FO372/2404 T1349/2/379 Chamberlain to Tilley 31 January 1927 tel.28, and *Hansard*, Fifth Series, HC, vol.202, cc.307–9 (10 February 1927).
218 See, for example, TNA FO372/1305 148618/148618/350D Curzon memorandum 2 November 1919, RA PS/PSO/GV/C/P/510/14 Stamfordham to Eliot 14 March 1921, and TNA FO372/1947 T3773/3773/350D Curzon minute n.d. [March 1922].
219 TNA FO372/2305 T1893/366/372 Mounsey (FO) minute 2 February 1927.
220 PRO FO372/2305 T1893/366/372 Chamberlain to Tilley 17 February tel.-.
221 PRO FO372/2305 T2226/366/372 Tilley to Chamberlain 19 February 1927 tel.-.
222 RA PS/PSO/GV/PS/MAIN/45786/B Chamberlain to Tilley 14 April 1927.
223 For Anglo-Japanese relations in this period, see Harumi Goto-Shibata, *Japan and Britain in Shanghai, 1925–31* (Basingstoke: St. Antony's/Macmillan, 1995) pp.137–8, and Ian Nish, 'Echoes of Alliance, 1920–30' in Ian Nish & Yoichi Kibata (eds.), *History of Anglo-Japanese Relations: The Political and Diplomatic Dimension, Vol.1, 1600–1930* (Basingstoke: Macmillan, 2000), pp.255–78.
224 RA PS/PSO/GV/C/M/2239/7 Chamberlain to Stamfordham 16 January 1927.
225 For the Nanjing 'outrages' see Chow, op. cit., pp.217–20.
226 RA PS/PSO/GV/PS/MAIN/45786/B Chamberlain to Tilley 14 April 1927.
227 Chamberlain papers, BUL, AC54/461 Tilley to Chamberlain 3 March 1927.
228 For the king's lobbying, see TNA FO371/12522 F1615/1615/23 King George V to Emperor Hirohito 25 December 1926 tel.-.
229 Chamberlain papers, BUL, AC54/449 King George V minute n.d. [March 1927?].
230 TNA ADM1/8706/209 NA (Tokyo) to Admiralty 4 March 1927 tel.45, and FO262/1682 Tilley to Wellesley 10 December 1927.
231 Chamberlain papers, TNA, FO800/261 Tilley to Chamberlain 9 June 1927.
232 Chamberlain papers, TNA, FO800/261 Stamfordham to Chamberlain 8 July 1927.
233 TNA FO372/2309 T11554/11319/372 Stamfordham to Tyrrell (FO PUS) 20 September 1927.
234 TNA FO372/2426 T3349/3349/372 Dormer (Tokyo) to Chamberlain 19 March 1928 tel.-.
235 TNA FO372/2426 T3349/3349/372 Chamberlain minute 22 March 1928, and Chamberlain papers, TNA, FO800/262 Tilley to Chamberlain 27 March 1928.
236 TNA FO262/1202 Tanaka memorandum 14 August 1928, and Tilley to Chamberlain 29 November 1928 no.490.
237 TNA FO345/60 Lampson (Peking) to Lloyd Thomas 16 February 1929.
238 TNA FO345/60 Lloyd Thomas to Kerr 19 February 1929.

239 TNA FO372/2526 T7948/452/372 Tilley to Chamberlain 3 June 1929 no.244.
240 *The Times*, 6 May 1929, p.15.
241 Sir John Tilley, *From London to Tokyo* (London: Hutchinson, 1942) pp.193–4.
242 TNA HW12/123 BJ.036512 London to Tokyo 18 October circulated 30 October 1929, and FO372/2526 T12903/452/372 Warner (Treaty Dept) 7 November 1929.
243 Warner papers, Hampshire Record Office, Winchester, 5M79/C9 Warner minute 15 May 1930.
244 TNA FO372/2685 T5475/972/379 Warner to Treasury 30 May 1930.
245 TNA FO372/2613 T7479/1305/372 Vansittart (FO PUS) minute 8 July 1930.
246 TNA WO32/3758 Stamfordham to Creedy (WO) 3 June 1930.
247 *The Times*, 27 June 1930, p.16, and *The Times*, 28 June 1930, p.9.
248 *The Times*, 28 June 1930, p.9.
249 *The Times*, 18 September 1930, p.15, and *The Times*, 26 March 1931, p.17.
250 MacDonald papers, TNA, PRO30/69/1753/1 diary entries 30 and 31 January 1932.
251 RA PS/PSO/GV/C/M/233/6 Wigram note 15 February 1932. See also C. Thorne, *The Limits of Foreign Policy: The West, the League and the Far Eastern Crisis of 1931–1933* (London: Hamish Hamilton, 1972) p.242 and p.257.
252 For Anglo-Japanese relations in the wake of the Manchurian crisis, see Ann Trotter, *Britain and East Asia, 1933–1937* (Cambridge: Cambridge University Press, 1975) pp.3–22, and Gill Bennett, 'British Policy in the Far East 1933–1936: Treasury and Foreign Office', *Modern Asian Studies*, 26 (1992) 545–68.
253 *The Times*, 3 May 1934, p.16.
254 TNA FO372/3065 Randall (FE Dept) minute 23 April 1934.
255 Cadogan papers, Churchill Archive Centre, Churchill College, Cambridge, ACAD1/2 diary entry 20 January 1934.
256 For Lindley's letters to Wigram (KPS), see RA PS/PSO/GV/PS/510 42–57; delete'?'
257 RA PS/PSO/GV/PS/MAIN/55310 Montagu-Douglas-Scott (FBI) to Wigram 8 August 1934, and Hardinge to Montagu-Douglas-Scott 9 August 1934.
258 RA GEO.V. M2433/4 Wigram to Vansittart 28 September 1934.
259 TNA FO371/19243 F4922/6/10 Leith-Ross (Treasury) to Vansittart 29 July 1935.
260 Hosoya Chihiro, '1934-nen no nichi-ei fukashin kyōtei mondai, *Kokusai Seiji* (1977) 77–8.
261 TNA FO372/3149 T6783/54/379 Clive (Tokyo) to Simon 7 May 1935 no.253, and RA PS/PSO/GV/C/P/510/62 Clive to Wigram 10 May 1935.
262 TNA FO262/1938 vol.1, Clive to Eden 22 January 1936 tel.30.

PART ONE

Pl. 1 Prince Alfred, Duke of Edinburgh photographed in Hong Kong in 1869, a few weeks after he had left Japan.

Pl. 2 Front entrance and side wings of the Enryōkan guest-house completed in 1869 for the Duke of Edinburgh's visit to Tokyo.

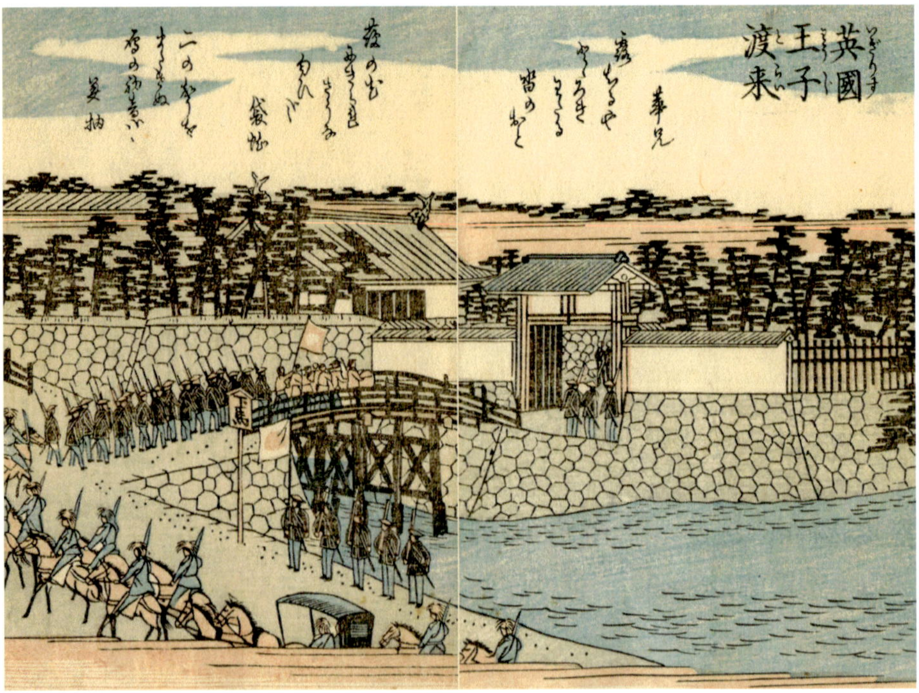

Pl. 3 Woodblock print by Ichiryūsai (Hiroshige III) showing the Duke of Edinburgh with escort entering the palace precincts.

Pl. 4 Watercolour painting by Nicholas Chevalier of the Duke's audience with the Emperor in the Waterfall-viewing pavilion in the Fukiage Garden of the Imperial Palace, dated 4 September 1869.

Pl. 5 Photograph of Prince Higashi-Fushimi taken some time between 1868 and 1876.

Pl. 6 Photograph of H.M.S. *Bacchante* on its voyage around the world.

Pl. 7 Prince George (on the right) with fellow midshipmen on H.M.S. *Bacchante* in 1879.

Pl. 8 Photograph of Emperor Meiji presented to Captain Lord Scott, captain of the *Bacchante*.

Pl. 9 The two princes photographed with their party at the back of the Enryōkan in Tokyo, 1881.

Pl. 10 The two princes and their party at the Nishi-Honganji temple in Kyoto.

Pl. 11 From *The Graphic*: 'In Japan, 1881: Prince George and the tattooing artist.'

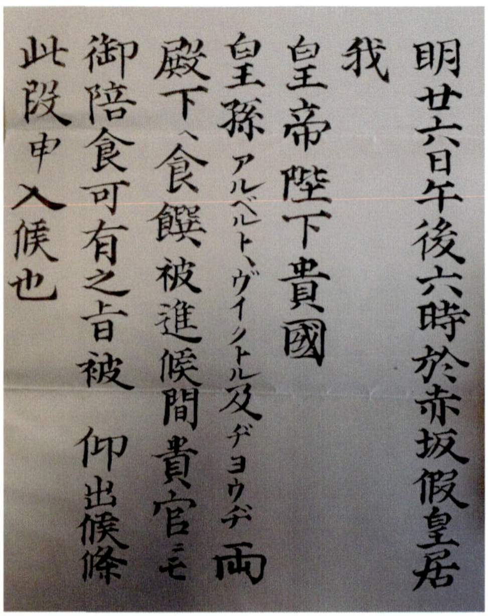

明廿六日午後六時於赤坂假皇居
我
皇帝陛下貴國
皇孫アルベルト、ヴイクトル及ジヨウヂ両
殿下ヘ食饌被進候間貴官ニモ
御陪食可有之旨被　仰出候條
此段申入候也

Pl. 12 Letter from the imperial palace inviting the two princes to dinner on 26 October 1881

Pl. 13 From *The Graphic*, 14 June 1890: 'The Duke and Duchess of Connaught buying furs at Nikko.'

Pl. 14 Prince Arisugawa Takehito and his suite attending the Diamond Jubilee of Queen Victoria in 1897.

PART TWO

Pl. 15 The conferring of the Order of the Garter by Prince Connaught on Emperor Meiji, 20 February 1906.

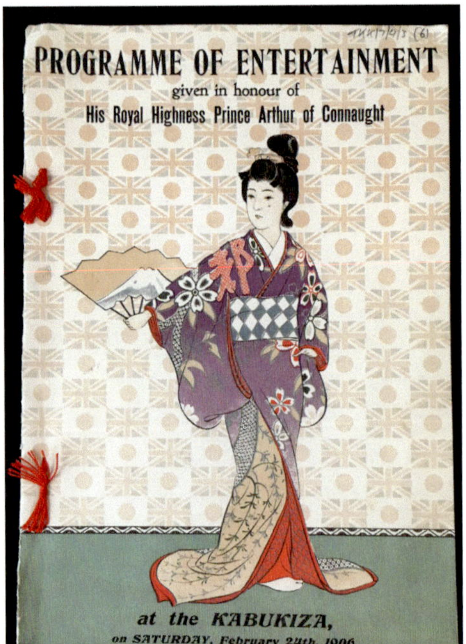

Pl. 16 Cover of the *Programme of Entertainment* given in honour of Prince Arthur of Connaught at the Kabukiza.

Pl. 17 The Imperial Japanese Navy battleship *Katori* arriving at Portsmouth on 9 May 1921 carrying Crown Prince Hirohito for a tour of Europe.

Pl. 18 Crown Prince Hirohito photographed on board the *Katori*, May 1921.

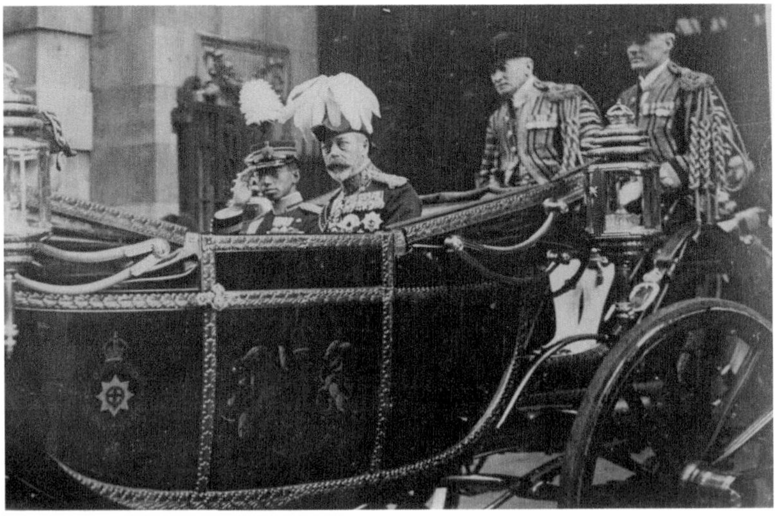

Pl. 19 King George V and Crown Prince Hirohito in the state carriage at Grosvenor Place, London, May 1921.

Pl. 20 Crown Prince Hirohito at the National Gallery, London, May 1921.

Pl. 21 Crown Prince Hirohito responds to an address of welcome by Sir John Baddeley, the Lord Mayor, on behalf of the City of London at the Guildhall, 11 May 1921.

Pl. 22 Japanese commemorative postcard. Crown Prince Hirohito is greeted by King George V at Victoria Station, 9 May 1921.

Pl. 23 Japanese postcard commemorating Crown Prince Hirohito's visit to Europe, 1921. From left to right: Crown Prince Hirohito, Edward, Prince of Wales, Prince Kotohito Kan-in, the Duke of Connaught.

Pl. 24 Japanese commemorative postcard. Edward, Prince of Wales, accompanied by Prince Higashi-Fushimi, on their way in the imperial limousine to visit the Imperial University, Tokyo, 13 April 1922.

Pl.25 Japanese commemorative postcard. Wearing the uniform of a Japanese General, Edward, Prince of Wales, at the Imperial Japanese Army parade ground at Yoyogi.

Pl. 26 Japanese commemorative postcard. Wearing the dress uniform of the Welsh Guards, Edward, Prince of Wales, attending the Imperial cherry garden party, April 1922. On the left is Crown Prince Hirohito, centre is Empress Teimei.

Pl. 27 Japanese commemorative postcard. Prince George, Duke of Gloucester, rides with Prince Chichibu to the Imperial villa at Kasumigaseki to present the Order of the Garter to Emperor Hirohito, 2 May 1929.

Pl. 28 Japanese commemorative postcard. Prince George, Duke of Gloucester, with Prince Chichibu leaving Yokohama on board SS *Empress of Asia,* 23 May 1929.

Pl. 29 Prince and Princess (pictured) Chichibu attend a garden party at the Hurlingham Club, London, on 23 May 1937.

Pl. 30 Prince and Princess Chichibu photographed on the seafront at Hove, East Sussex, April 1937.

PART THREE

Pl. 31 Crown Prince Akihito attends the coronation of Queen Elizabeth II at Westminster Abbey, 2 June 1953.

Pl. 32 Princess Alexandra during an official visit to Japan in October 1961 photographed on a duck-netting expedition with Prince Hitachi at one of the imperial preserves near Tokyo.

Pl. 33 Ambassador John Pilcher at Haneda airport welcomes Prince Charles on an official visit to Japan, April 1970 in connection with Expo '70 in Osaka. Elizabeth Cortazzi is introduced to Prince Charles (pictured) with Hugh Cortazzi to her right.

Pl. 34 Ambassador John Pilcher introduces Prince Charles to a leading Kabuki actor (*onnagata*) at the British Embassy, Tokyo, during the Prince's official visit to Japan, April 1970.

Pl. 35 Queen Elizabeth II rides with Emperor Hirohito in the state carriage during the state visit of the Emperor and Empress, October 1971.

Pl. 36 Formal portrait taken during the imperial state visit to Britain, October 1971.
From left to right: Prince Philip, Duke of Edinburgh, Queen Elizabeth, the Queen Mother, Empress Nagako, Emperor Hirohito, Queen Elizabeth II.

Pl. 37 The Emperor and Empress visiting Kew Gardens.

Pl. 38 The Emperor lays a wreath at the Tomb of the Unknown Warrior, Westminster Abbey, October 1971.

Pl. 39 Emperor Hirohito and Empress Nagako with Queen Elizabeth II and the Duke of Edinburgh before the banquet given by the Queen at the British Embassy, Tokyo, marking the state visit in May 1975.

Pl. 40 The Queen making her address at the banquet she hosted at the British Embassy, Tokyo, during the state visit in May 1975.

Pl. 41 Queen Elizabeth II plants a commemorative oak tree at the Akasaka Detached Palace, Tokyo, during her state visit to Japan in May 1975. The Akasaka Detached Palace is an Imperial Palace in Tokyo, originally built as an official residence for the Crown Prince at the beginning of the twentieth century.

Pl. 42 The Queen and Duke of Edinburgh watch women divers collecting pearl oysters at the Toba pearl farm, near Ise, Mie Prefecture, during the state visit, May 1975.

Pl. 43 Crown Prince Akihito and Crown Princess Michiko visit Stoke Poges church, scene of Gray's *Elegy Written in a Country Churchyard*, during a visit to Windsor in June 1976.

Pl. 44 Dressed in miner's overalls and helmet, Crown Prince Akihito visits the Deep Navigation Coal Mine in South Wales, June 1976.

Pl. 45 The Crown Prince and Princess arriving at Ascot, accompanied by members of the royal family, June 1976.

Pl.46 The Crown Prince and Princess attend a dinner at Trinity House, London, given by the Secretary of State for Foreign Affairs and his wife, 19 June 1976. Also featured are Sir Hugh and Lady Elizabeth Cortazzi.

Pl. 47 Photograph of Prince Hiro (Naruhito) with Dr Highfield at a lock on the River Thames, 1984, during the time he was studying at Oxford. Inset: Prince Hiro attends an event at the University of Essex.

Pl. 48 Prince Philip, the Duke of Edinburgh, welcomes the Crown Prince and Princess to a reception hosted by Ambassador Sir Hugh Cortazzi at the British Embassy, during a visit on behalf of the World Wildlife Fund, November 1982.

Pl. 49 Crown Prince Naruhito speaking at a reception at London's Guildhall marking the centenary of the Japan Society, September 1991.

Pl. 50 Emperor Akihito and the Empress riding in the state carriages along The Mall during their State Visit to the United Kingdom, May 1998.

Pl.51 Emperor Akihito inspects the guard of honour at Horse Guards, May 1998.

Pl.52 The Emperor and Empress are welcomed at the state banquet at Buckingham Palace, May 1998.

Pl.53 The Imperial Party visit the newly renovated Chokushi-Mon and Japanese gardens at the Royal Botanic Gardens, Kew, May 1998.

Pl.54 At Kew, the Emperor and Empress (pictured) talk to participants of the JET (Japan Exchange and Training programme, May 1998.)

Pl.55 The Prince of Wales with the Emperor (pictured) and Empress at Cardiff Castle where they met British managers of Japanese companies and members of the Japanese community in Wales, May 1998.

Pl. 56 Emperor Akihito speaks at a reception at the Grosvenor House Hotel, given by the Japan Society, the Japan Association, the Nippon Club and the Japanese Chamber of Commerce and Industry, May 1998.

Pl. 57 The Empress adds her signature to the Japan Society Visitors' Book, May 1998.

Pl. 58 Prince William, the Duke of Cambridge, is welcomed to the Imperial Palace by the Emperor and Empress on his arrival in Japan at the end of February 2015.

Pl. 59 Crown Prince Naruhito welcomes Prince William, February 2015.

Pl. 60 Prince William visits Smile Kids Park in Sendai with Prime Minister Abe Shinzo, February 2015.

263 TNA FO372/3187 T5207/751/379 Clive to Mounsey (FO) 31 January 1936.
264 TNA FO262/1938 vol.1, Clive to Eden 31 January 1936 no.45.
265 RA PS/PSO/GVI/PS/COR/01000/015/051 Clive to Vansittart 22 February 1936
266 RA PS/PSO/GVI/PS/COR/01000/015/051 Clive to Vansittart 22 February 1936 and RA PS/PSO/GVI/PS/COR/01000/015/064 Clive to Vansittart 21 May 1936.
267 *The Times*, 20 October 1936, p.15.
268 TNA CAB23/87 5(37) Cabinet meeting 3 February 1937. For this incident, see Greg Kennedy, 'The Keelung Incident and Britain's Far Eastern Strategic Foreign Policy, 1936–37' , in Greg Kennedy and Keith Neilson (eds*) Incidents and International Relations: People, Power, and Personalities* (Westport: Praeger, 2002) pp.146–50 .
269 Sainoji/Harada diary (US State Department translation), SOAS Library, microfilm 4611/2, diary entry 12 March 1937.
270 PS/PSO/GVI/PS/COR/01000/103/01 Mounsey (FO) to Lascelles (BP) 12 January 1937.
271 TNA FO371/21029 F324/28/23 Clive to Eden 16 January 1937 tel.17.
272 TNA FO371/21029 F1106/28/23 Clive to Eden 23 February 1937 tel.81.
273 RA PS/GVI/C/053/JAP/6 Clive to Wigram 1 March 1937.
274 TNA FO371/21029 F1745/28/23 Clive to Cadogan (FO) 18 February 1937.
275 TNA FO371/21029 F1366/28/23 Clive to Eden 6 March 1937 and Cadogan minute 8 March 1937.
276 TNA FO372/3233 T3833/1/379 Bland (Treaty Dept) to Gabriel (LCO) 17 March 1937.
277 TNA FO372/3234 T6849/1/379 Bland minute 30 April 1937.
278 *The Times*, 14 April 1937, p.11.
279 *The Times*, 20 May 1937, p.18.
280 TNA FO372/3239 T9419/1650/379 Clive to Eden 20 May 1937 no.278.
281 RA PS/PSO/GVI/PS/COR/01000/015/068 Hirohito to George VI 30 June 1937.
282 For Anglo-Japanese relations and the opening of the Sino-Japanese War, see Bradford A. Lee, *Britain and the Sino-Japanese War, 1937–1939,* (Stanford: Stanford University Press, 1973), Peter Lowe, *Great Britain and the Origins of the Pacific War: A Study of British Policy in East Asia, 1937–1941* (Oxford: Clarendon, 1977), and Antony Best, *Britain, Japan and Pearl Harbor: Avoiding War in East Asia, 1936–41* (London: Routledge, 1995).
283 RA PS/PSO/GVI/C/040/20 Chichibu to George VI 16 September 1937.
284 RA PS/PSO/GVI/C/040/25-6 Harvey (FO) to Hardinge (KPS) 29 September 1937. Both Eden and the Prime Minister, Neville Chamberlain, approved the Foreign Office draft before it was forwarded to the king.

285 Sainoji/Harada diary (US State Department translation), SOAS Library, microfilm 4611/2, diary entry 3 November 1937.
286 RA PS/PSO/GVI/C/040/42 Hoyer-Millar (FO) to Hardinge 3 January 1938.
287 RA PS/PSO/GVI/C/120/01 Hardinge to Cadogan (FO) 26 August 1939, and RA PS/PSO/GVI/C/120/02 Hardinge note 28 August 1939.
288 Diary entry 25 August 1939, in *Kido Kōichi Diary* (Washington DC: State Department, 1977) p.234.
289 TNA FO371/29713 F12796/86/23 Craigie (Tokyo) to Eden 27 November 1941 tel.2415.
290 TNA FO371/29713 F12796/86/23 Cadogan (FO PUS) minute 2 December 1941.
291 See Waldo Heinrichs, *American Ambassador: Joseph C. Grew and the Development of the United States Diplomatic Tradition* (New York: Oxford University Press) pp.357–8.
292 RA PS/PSO/GVI/C/130/35 Hardinge to Sargent (FO) 10 December 1941 and PS/PSO/GVI/C/130/40 Hardinge memorandum 23 December 1941.

PART THREE

Renewing and Developing Royal Relations in a Changed World: 1945–2018

HUGH CORTAZZI

FOLLOWING THE OUTBREAK of hostilities in December 1941, the Japanese invasion of Malaya was followed by the sinking of the two British capital ships, HMS *Prince of Wales* and HMS *Repulse*, and then by the surrender of Hong Kong on Christmas Day. As the war in the Far East unfolded, British resentment against Japan intensified. The humiliation of the British surrender of Singapore in February 1942 could not easily be forgotten, but as confirmation was received of Japanese maltreatment of prisoners of war and civilian internees, feelings against the Japanese emperor in whose name Japanese soldiers were fighting became angry and there were calls for him to be tried and punished once victory had been attained. No one in Britain gave any real thought in 1945 to reviving the relationship between the British royal and the Japanese imperial families and courts. The priority was survival and recovery. There could be no going back to the pre-war world. The balance of power had radically changed as a result of the war. Monarchical systems were being superseded, and if monarchies were to survive in the post-war world they would have to change and adapt.

THE BRITISH MONARCHY

The British monarchy had come out of the war with its popularity and prestige enhanced by the identification of King George VI and his queen with the war effort and the sufferings of British people in the blitz and in battles which had only been won through suffering and sacrifice. But the old hierarchies and stuffy court system of the past could not be revived in their old form in an age of austerity and under the Labour government that came to power in August 1945. The British loved pageantry, but there was no money left for ostentatious show. Changes were inevitable, but they took time to work their way through the system. Many changes did not come about until the accession of Queen Elizabeth II in 1952 on the death of King George VI. Prince Philip, the Duke of Edinburgh, in particular recognized that if the monarchy did not adapt to the post-war world its existence would be questioned. Royalty could not continue a gilded life cocooned from the realities facing working people. It had to show a human face.

This could not be achieved quickly. The presentation of debutantes to the sovereign, for instance, was only ended in 1958 when the queen abolished the practice, which had become an anachronism. The Society 'season' during which balls and dances were organized for young ladies of aristocratic or wealthy lineage that had followed the ceremony gradually faded, although some sporting events such as Royal Ascot, Henley Royal Regatta and the tennis championships at Wimbledon are still popular features of the English summer. While King Edward VII and King George V were strict about formal dress and protocol, as the present reign has progressed greater informality has become not only acceptable (except in the royal enclosure at Ascot) but the norm for the younger members of the royal family.

The British nobility have kept their titles and many still retain their country mansions. Some, such as the Duke of Westminster, are among the wealthiest people in Britain because of their property holdings, but the old nobility has ceased to exercise any significant political role. Those with hereditary titles who used automatically to sit in the House of Lords lost this right by an Act of Parliament in 1999 and now only ninety-two hereditary peers, elected by other hereditary peers under the terms of the act, can sit in the Lords. Hereditary aristocrats are far outnumbered by successful businessmen, bankers and representatives of non-governmental organizations who have been given life peerages. The House of Lords thus consists largely of life peers created either for distinguished service in various fields or more often for their political affiliation and loss of ministerial office or seat in the House of Commons.

The powers of the British sovereign are not set out in any constitutional document but have evolved over time. Queen Victoria frequently interfered in matters of state and allowed her personal and conservative preferences to influence her attitude towards her ministers. Her son, King Edward VII, tried to play an active role in foreign affairs not least through his family connections with European royalty. King George V thought that he retained the right to veto legislation and was reluctant to accept in 1911 that the powers of the Lords should be curtailed. In practice, he never tried to go against the advice of his ministers. He was embarrassed during the First World War by his German ancestry and name (Saxe-Coburg-Gotha) and in 1917 adopted the family name of Windsor, thus identifying the royal family with Britain.

King George VI's and Queen Elizabeth's morale-boosting activities in the Second World War and the decision not to evacuate the two princesses to Canada helped to secure a sense of the royal family as symbols of the nation rather than political actors (although inviting the then prime minister, Neville Chamberlain, onto the balcony of Buckingham Palace after the signature of the Munich Agreement in 1938 had for a time identified the monarchy with the subsequently discredited policy of appeasement).

The royal prerogative, a body of customary authority, privilege, and immunity, and the source of many of the executive powers of the British government, theoretically still gives extensive powers to the sovereign, but in exercising the royal prerogative the sovereign now only acts on the advice of ministers and there remain very few matters on which the sovereign retains total discretion. These include appointments to the Orders of the Garter, the Order of Merit, the Order of the Thistle and the Royal Victorian Order. Other honours including life peerages, knighthoods and other orders conferred by the sovereign are only granted on the recommendation of the government.

The British sovereign's powers are thus by tradition and usage limited and controlled through the government which is responsible to parliament and by the courts. The sovereign, however, has the right to be consulted and to advise. This right is exercised through her weekly private meetings with the prime minister of the day. As the twentieth century developed, it became increasingly difficult to imagine any occasion on which the sovereign would wish or feel able to exercise the royal prerogative and insist on any course of action against the wishes and advice of ministers. Such action would provoke a constitutional crisis and jeopardize the future of the monarchy.

The sovereign retains the power to call on an individual politician to form the government. By tradition the sovereign calls on the individual who commands a majority in the House of Commons and who is accordingly the leader of the party with the largest number of seats in the House. Until 1965, the sovereign could theoretically face a dilemma if the Conservatives were the majority party as its leader had until then had been chosen through intra-party consultations and the final decision might have fallen to the sovereign. Now, all party leaders are elected and this problem does not arise. If there were no party capable of commanding a majority the sovereign would by tradition ask the incumbent prime minister to continue in office. The sovereign retains the power to call a general election but only does so if this is requested by the prime minister of the day.

The British sovereign's status and nominal powers today are little different from what they were in 1945. Britain as well as the composition of its peoples has, however, changed enormously. Some institutions such as the royal court have altered almost beyond recognition. The hereditary peerage no longer counts politically and the monarchy remains the only hereditary institution in Britain, but its powers are limited by tradition and the practical and political imperatives of British parliamentary democracy as it developed over the twentieth century.

THE JAPANESE MONARCHY

While the British monarchy has evolved gradually, the Japanese monarchy in the immediate post-war years faced possible extinction and Japan had to find a way to survive and prosper. The imperial institution came through the trauma of the war diminished but alive, and post-war Japan went from ruin and destruction to prosperity and world influence.

By the beginning of 1945 it was apparent to all but the most blinkered and brainwashed among Japan's military leaders that Japan could not win the war and faced total destruction. The almost complete devastation of Tokyo and other Japanese cities in the air raids of the spring of 1945 and the threat of starvation of the Japanese people simply entrenched in the military suicidal attitudes and expressions of loyalty to the emperor. Even after the dropping of atomic bombs on Hiroshima and Nagasaki the diehards sought to continue the war.

Why did the emperor not intervene to stop the war until 15 August 1945? Under the Japanese constitution granted by the Meiji Emperor in 1889, the emperor of Japan 'in a line of Emperors unbroken for ages eternal' was 'sacred and inviolable'. Only the emperor could initiate amendments to the constitution. He had the power to issue ordinances both regular and emergency, and the power unconditionally to declare war, make peace and conclude a treaty. But the Meiji Emperor, his son the Taisho Emperor and his grandson the Showa Emperor, whose given name was Hirohito, had delegated the business of government to others. The Taisho Emperor was a sick man and incapable of exercising power, so Crown Prince Hirohito was named prince regent (*sesshō*) on 25 November 1921.

Hirohito was brought up in the stifling atmosphere of court life. Sir John Pilcher, British ambassador in Tokyo at the time of the Japanese state visit to

Britain in 1971, declared that the Emperor Hirohito was 'by temperament and inclination essentially the mild, but dedicated professor', whose specialized subject was marine biology.[1] He was 'the least endowed by nature and upbringing to stand up to the pretensions of his turbulent military subjects and both physically and morally unequipped to cut them down…The shameful rape of Nanking, the disgraceful treatment of prisoners of war and fellow Asians may have moved him, but not to the point of horror they should have evoked.'[2]

Emperor Hirohito thought of himself as a constitutional monarch who 'cannot of his own volition interfere or intervene in the jurisdiction for which ministers of state are responsible'. After the government decides on a given course of action, 'I have no choice but to approve it or not. To do otherwise would clearly be destroying the constitution.' In August 1945, he intervened for peace, but only because the government had asked him to intervene.[3]

In August 1945, the Imperial War Council was evenly split on whether to accept or reject the terms of the Potsdam Declaration calling for Japan's unconditional surrender and asked the emperor to decide. The emperor decided for acceptance. This meant surrender. The emperor's broadcast on 15 August was unprecedented and was only made after attempts had been made by diehards to stop the broadcast and destroy the recording. The broadcast was in archaic language and euphemistically stated that 'the war situation has developed not necessarily to Japan's advantage', so many on the allied side feared that Japanese forces, might not understand and might not obey their emperor, but loyalty was too ingrained for disobedience and resistance ended.

The emperor's future seemed uncertain. Some on the allied side argued that he should be tried and executed as a war criminal, but Japan specialists advised that the imperial institution should be preserved. Without it, Japan would become politically unstable, they argued. General MacArthur, the Supreme Commander of the Allied Powers responsible for the post-war occupation of Japan, accepted this advice and saw the emperor as a symbol of the continuity and cohesion of the Japanese people. Accordingly, when the emperor made a formal call on MacArthur in Tokyo on 27 September 1945, it was clear that he would not be prosecuted as a war criminal, but he was obliged to disassociate himself from state Shinto, which was proscribed by an Occupation directive of December 1945. This was followed by an Imperial rescript of 1 January 1946 which rejected the concept that the emperor was divine and that 'the Japanese people are superior to other races and fated to rule the world'.

In the new constitution of May 1946, which is considered by some Japanese to have been based on an American draft and then imposed on the Japanese people, the emperor was to be 'the symbol of the state and of the unity of the people'. He was to derive his position from the will of the people with whom sovereign power remains. The Cabinet was to be responsible for all acts of the emperor in matters of state, and the emperor might only act in matters of state at all within clearly defined limits. The emperor might only appoint the prime minister as designated by the Diet and the chief judge of the supreme court as designated by the Cabinet. He might neither receive property nor make gifts therefrom without the authorization of the Diet. The preamble to the Constitution set the tone of all that followed but did not even mention the emperor. It reads in part: 'we the Japanese people . . . do proclaim that sovereign power resides with the people and do firmly establish this Constitution'. This omission was, in Sir John Pilcher's view, a deliberate attempt by the drafters to demote the emperor from his pre-war status.[4]

The Imperial Household law enacted in 1947 drastically reduced the size of the imperial family, which was limited to the emperor's immediate family, his widowed mother, and the families of his three brothers. It abolished the collateral lines of the imperial family that had traditionally provided a pool of potential successors to the throne if the main imperial family failed to produce an heir. The fifty-one members of the eleven cadet branches renounced their imperial status, and they were formally removed from the Imperial Household register and became ordinary citizens on 14 October 1947. All princesses ceased to be imperial on marriage and became ordinary citizens. The ban on a princess acceding to the throne was retained.

The abolition of State Shinto did not preclude the emperor from performing his priestly Shinto duties such as the spring rice planting (*otaue*) ceremony and the rice harvest festival (*niinamesai*). Whatever the emperor's legal status, Japanese, especially the older generation, continued to see him as more than just the symbol of Japan. He remained for many Japanese, according to Sir John Pilcher, as 'the living link with the past, the unbroken thread in Japanese history'.

After the war, the Japanese Imperial Household Ministry was downgraded to the status of an agency and the imperial court became a shadow of what it had been before the war. Imperial garden parties and New Year ceremonies were resumed, however. The *Kunaichō* (Imperial Household Agency) continued to deal with the ceremonies and events involving the emperor and members of the imperial family. These included such traditional events as the annual court poetry competitions and duck-netting at imperial preserves organized as entertainment for visiting VIPs and ambassadors, but the resources available to the Agency in the austerity which Japan faced in the years after the end of the war were strictly limited.

The most important task facing the Imperial Household Agency was how to adapt the imperial institution to the post-war world and to bring the emperor into greater contact with the Japanese people. To this end the emperor attended sporting festivals and undertook tours to various Japanese prefectures, but he found it difficult to make personal contacts and Japanese whom he met were generally inhibited in their contacts with a sovereign who had hitherto been a figure of awe and reverence.

Although the Japanese emperor is no longer the titular head of state, he is generally so regarded outside Japan and by many Japanese who still see him as more than just a symbol. He cannot take any action which could be regarded as having any political implications, but his continued existence may be seen as a restraining influence against extreme change. The decision by Emperor Hirohito not to visit the Yasukuni shrine after convicted Japanese war criminals were enshrined with the Japanese war dead can be seen as a silent rebuke to Japanese government ministers who visited the shrine in their official capacity. Emperor Akihito's visits to countries and places that had suffered greatly as a result of Japanese actions in the Second World War have also been seen by some as a silent rebuke to Japan's historical revisionists.

A FRESH START

So long as Japan remained under allied (in practical terms mostly American) occupation, the resumption of contacts between British royalty and the Japanese imperial house was not feasible. The British public continued to feel resentment towards Japan, primarily because of Japanese ill-treatment of British prisoners of war. The latter had lobbied hard for compensation and the British government had pressed their case in the negotiations for the peace treaty signed in San Francisco in 1951, which came into force in April 1952 following ratification. But the compensation provisions of Article 16 of the treaty yielded a meager pittance. The Japanese government failed to recognize at the time and in subsequent years that a generous gesture towards former prisoners of war would have won significant goodwill towards Japan. Instead they stuck obstinately to the legal position that the terms of the peace treaty fulfilled their legal obligations. Sadly, this issue continued to cast a shadow on relations between the two monarchies until the end of the twentieth century.

The British royal family could not ignore the prisoner-of-war issue or that of the Japanese treatment of the civilian populations of Hong Kong, Singapore and Malaya. Prince Philip, Duke of Edinburgh, had served in the Royal Navy during the war and had been serving on HMS *Whelp* in the British Pacific Fleet when Japan surrendered (he had thus visited Japan for the first time in September 1945). His uncle, Lord Louis Mountbatten, had headed the South

East Asia Command in the battles against Japanese forces in South-East Asia. Other members of the royal family had close connections with other branches of the services and army regiments. However, once diplomatic relations were reestablished after the peace treaty came into force, the question of royal/imperial relations could not be ignored.

The Foreign Office maintained during the Occupation that the emperor was 'the greatest asset we hold in the control of Japan' and was firmly opposed to indicting the emperor for war crimes.[5] The United Kingdom Liaison Mission in Tokyo during the Occupation argued in 1948 that Britain 'should act to enhance the role of the court and improve British influence by taking advantage of the royal connection'.[6] When the question of a tutor for Crown Prince Akihito came up, the initial suggestion was for a British tutor, but the Americans preempted this through the appointment of Elizabeth Vining, an American Quaker, as his tutor.

In January 1952, the grand master of ceremonies to the imperial court, Matsudaira Yasumasa, was sent to Britain and other European monarchies to inspect how they managed their constitutional duties. The Foreign Office saw this as a good opportunity to reopen contacts and arranged meetings for him with Foreign Office and Buckingham Palace officials responsible for protocol issues. Sir Esler Dening, who was head of the British Liaison Mission in Japan and about to take up his appointment as the first British ambassador to Japan after the war, recommended to the foreign secretary in March 1952 that Britain should take advantage of Japan's long-standing admiration of British institutions, including the monarchy, to improve its standing in Tokyo.[7]

The death of King George VI and the accession of his daughter Elizabeth as queen in February 1952 provided the catalyst for a new relationship. The Foreign Office started to prepare for the coronation in early 1952. Monarchs do not attend the coronations of fellow monarchs and John Pilcher in the Foreign Office, in a minute dated 24 July 1952, suggested that it would be good if the crown prince were to represent the emperor. In Tokyo the then Japanese prime minister, Yoshida Shigeru, strongly recommended this and, according to a letter from Dening, 'the Imperial Household were not opposed to it'. Dening was officially informed of the selection of the crown prince to represent the emperor on 9 September 1952. British and Japanese alike saw the visit as a prime opportunity for restoring relations between the British royal and Japanese imperial families and helping the normalization of relations between Britain and Japan. It was not, however, an easy decision in view of the hostility towards Japan in Britain at that time not only because of the Japanese maltreatment of prisoners of war but also because of British fears of unfair competition from Japan in textiles and other products. The Japanese decided that the crown prince should also visit the USA and that, in addition to touring important countries such as France and Germany, he should also visit European countries with constitutional monarchies and restore relations with European royalty.

One problem had to be set aside for the moment. Emperor Hirohito had been made a Knight of the Garter in 1929, but this honour had been withdrawn during the war and his banner had been removed from St George's chapel in Windsor. Anthony Eden, the foreign secretary, considered that British public opinion precluded a restoration of the honour at this time and the Japanese wisely did not press the issue on this occasion.[8]

CROWN PRINCE AKIHITO ATTENDS THE CORONATION IN 1953[9]

Careful and detailed plans for the tour were drawn up and a budget allocated despite Japan's then exiguous foreign exchange reserves. Experienced diplomats and palace officials were nominated to accompany the crown prince. The head of the suite was the Grand Chamberlain Mitani Takanobu, assisted by Matsui Akira from the Foreign Ministry and by the Vice-Grand Master of Ceremonies, Kikkawa Shigekuni. Dening suggested that while in Britain the crown prince should be accompanied by David Symon, a young second secretary in the embassy who had been a language student. David, who was an able athlete, visited the crown prince a number of times before his departure in order to give the prince an opportunity to practise his English and learn more about Britain. They also spoke about sport in view of the prince's interest in tennis and other sports.

The British were particularly concerned to ensure that suitable preparations were made to deal with the press, both Japanese and British. The Foreign Office thought that the Japanese embassy in London had not done enough to cultivate the British press and were relieved when Henry Shimanouchi was appointed to deal with the media. He spoke fluent English even though he had never been to Britain and his main experience had been in the United States.

The Japanese were naturally much concerned about the security arrangements, but were told firmly by Scotland Yard that it would take good care of these and that it did not want or need hordes of Japanese security personnel to accompany the prince. The Japanese did not press the point.

Dening, in his despatch to the foreign secretary reporting the crown prince's departure from Japan, strongly urged that Britain should welcome him:

> Since the Crown Prince is still young and impressionable, since he can by no stretch of the imagination bear any responsibility for what Japan did in the war, and since the Japanese people set much store by him, I venture to hope that his reception in the United Kingdom will be kindly and that everything possible will be done to enable him to carry away, when he leaves the United Kingdom, the best possible memories of our country and people.

The crown prince arrived at Southampton from the United States on 27 April 1953 on board the *Queen Elizabeth*. Asakai Kōichirō, the Japanese minister in London, who had met the party in New York, warned them that there was still strong anti-Japanese sentiment in Britain and British newspapers had published articles suggesting that the prince would not be welcome. He also reported that the invitation to visit Newcastle would not take place because of opposition in the City Assembly. However, when the Japanese ambassador in London, Matsumoto Shun'ichi, came on board to greet the prince he looked cheerful. Overnight, the attitude of the press had completely changed and the newspapers that morning carried articles welcoming the prince; there had not been one critical article. Members of the Japanese embassy in London and members of the Japanese community also came to greet the prince. Major-General Francis Piggott, who had spent several years in Japan before the war, represented the Japan Society. There were many press representatives and photographers there too. The prince read a brief message in English in which he expressed his pleasure in visiting Britain and noted: 'My father has told me of the happy days he spent here when he visited your country 32 years ago.' At Waterloo Station he was greeted by Lord Selkirk in his capacity as Lord-in-Waiting, as well as by Sir Robert Craigie, chairman of the Japan Society and the last pre-war ambassador to Japan, and Sir Edward Crowe, chairman of the Japan Association.

On 29 April the Japanese ambassador gave a reception at his residence at 23 Kensington Palace Gardens, 'in the presence of the Crown Prince', to celebrate the emperor's birthday. On the following day the prince visited the British Museum and *The Times* building, but his most important engagement was lunch at No. 10 Downing Street as guest of the prime minister, Sir Winston Churchill. Clement Attlee, the former prime minister and leader of the opposition, and other politicians were among the guests who included the press barons, Lords Beaverbrook, Kemsley and Rothermere. The Japan specialists invited were Arthur Waley and Sir George Sansom.

The Prime Minister proposed the toast to the emperor and spoke briefly without notes. Sir George Sansom, after obtaining clearance from the prime minister's private secretary, sent an account of Churchill's speech to the Japanese prime ninister, Yoshida Shigeru:

> I think you may be interested in a summary of the Prime Minister's speech, though no paraphrase ever does justice to his spoken words. It was a short, unprepared speech, which we English guests at the luncheon found very moving and which I am sure gave pleasure to H.I.H. and the Japanese guests. We heard the voice of a wise statesman speaking out of his many years of experience to a young man who one day must undertake great responsibilities in his own country. Sir Winston Churchill pointed out the diversity of political opinions represented by those present – government, parliament, trade unions, the press – and said that this was characteristic of English life. The English, he said, are a people who, while they may disagree vigorously among themselves, are united in cherishing and upholding the English way of life, 'which we will defend with all the breath in our bodies and all the blood in our veins'. We owe much of the continuity and stability of English life to our institutions, particularly to our constitutional monarchy. The Sovereign 'reigns but does not govern'. The Sovereign can do no wrong and if statesmen make blunders they are replaced by the people and the parliament, which the people elect. Having spoken of the affection and the trust inspired in the English people by our young Queen the Prime Minister addressed the Crown Prince directly, hoping that H.I.H. would enjoy his visit to this country and would profit by the view of English life which it would afford. He said that the Crown Prince was fortunate in that he was a young man. Those who had to look back on the past must inevitably have a memory not only of successes, but also of the errors and misfortunes which attend human affairs. Young men like H.I.H. could look forward to a life of achievement.
>
> I think that these were the main points of the Prime Minister's speech, though he did give some entertaining reminiscences, including some memories of what his mother had seen and heard in Japan in 1894. He recalled that at that time Japan was more esteemed for her recent naval and military progress than for her age-long achievement in the arts. He wished that the nations of the world could devote more of their resources to works of art than to the construction of aircraft and battleships.

Altogether the party was most successful, the atmosphere most genial. Montague Brown, the prime minister's private secretary, noted Churchill's advice to the prince on leaving, 'to ignore any local discordant notes in his welcome to this country'.

The fact that this lunch was held so soon after the crown prince had reached Britain at a very busy time in the run-up to the Coronation underlines the determination of the British government to do all they could to ensure that the prince was given a warm welcome in Britain and was shown due honour. The government were conscious of the continuing resentment against Japan and a great deal of effort was put by the government into organizing the very full and comprehensive programme arranged for the crown prince, whose stay lasted an unprecedented five weeks.

After the crown prince had left Britain on his European tour, Churchill wrote on 25 June in reply to a message from the prince sent on 10 June 1953:

> I trust he found his stay amongst us both agreeable and profitable. Her Majesty's Government and the British people were glad and honoured to be afforded this opportunity of meeting His Imperial Highness during a visit which I feel sure will have greatly contributed to Anglo-Japanese understanding.

The queen received the crown prince on 5 May and he attended a royal garden party on 28 May. The prince also met the queen during his visit to Epsom on 6 June to see the Derby. Matsui Akira recorded that the attitude of British royalty had been extremely friendly and he noted that at Epsom the queen had invited the crown prince to sit with her to watch the race. At his audience to say farewell, Matsui noted that the queen had said:

> I do hope that your Highness has enjoyed your visit. I do not know His Majesty the Emperor but please tell him on your return to Japan that I am most grateful that your Highness was able to attend my coronation.

The crown prince's attendance at the coronation ceremony on 2 June, which lasted over three hours, was, of course, the main purpose of his visit. The Foreign Office despatch of 18 June 1953 about the visit recorded that the crown prince:

> . . . was particularly thrilled to sit among members of other royal houses and representatives of other heads of state at one of the two state banquets given at Buckingham Palace for official guests at the Coronation. The pomp and splendour of this occasion undoubtedly impressed him, perhaps more so than the Coronation service itself where, although he had an excellent seat, his view was obscured by his neighbours in the choir stalls.[10]

The service certainly greatly impressed members of his suite. Matsui noted that although there were said to have been some changes in the ceremonial it reflected many centuries of tradition and was an impressive ritual accompanied by solemn music and magnificent costumes. It made him think that he was looking at a medieval picture scroll (*emakimono*). The coronation throne, the crown, the sceptre and the jewels forming the regalia all seemed to have a traditional significance and he felt the power of tradition in Britain. They had learnt in their travels in European countries that the system of holding a coronation had not been preserved in other European monarchies. He felt that rather than suggesting the divine right of kings, the coronation service emphasized that the British monarchy reflected the will of God and the consent of the people and that the royal prerogative derived from on high and not from the sovereign herself. Mitani Takanobu, the head of the suite, in his memoirs stated that the words of the service did not simply stress that this was an occasion for celebration and joy, but rather emphasized the weight of responsibility falling on her. Matsui noted that the visits, which she made to every part of Britain during coronation week, underlined the recognition by the people of the queen as the sovereign. Matsui was impressed by the intimate and friendly way in which the queen had behaved. In common parlance it was very democratic. He had heard so often people commenting of the queen 'So simple and nice.' In Britain, it seemed to him that, while an ancient system of important and dignified ceremonial was maintained, daily life at court went on in a natural and ordinary way. This seemed also to be the case in other European monarchies.

The Foreign Office despatch recorded that the suite had declared that the crown prince was greatly moved by the dignity, informality and charm of the royal family: 'There is no doubt that he will perpetuate that admiration for the British Royal Family, which has become traditional in the Japanese Imperial Household.'[11]

The Japan Society gave a dinner in honour of the crown prince on 4 May 1953 at the Hyde Park Hotel attended by over 200 members and guests. Before the loyal toasts, the poet Edmund Blunden was asked to recite the poem he had written to mark the visit. Like so many poems written to order, it sounds banal to modern readers and its rhymes forced. The chairman of the Japan Society, Sir Robert Craigie, gave the main speech to which the crown prince replied briefly stressing how honoured he felt to be attending the coronation as proxy for his father and proposed a toast to the Society.

After his audience with the Queen, the Crown Prince began his tour of Britain going first to Edinburgh. He went on to visit the Duke of Buccleuch at Bowhill, Selkirk, where he was shown the duke's hounds. He went next to Blair Atholl to be greeted by the Duke of Atholl and was shown the room in the castle where his father had stayed in 1921. On 9 May, the prince returned to England to stay at Cragside, the home of Lord and Lady Armstrong, where his father had stayed in 1921.

A visit to Newcastle and the Vickers-Armstrong works there (Vickers Maxim and Sons of Barrow-in-Furness had built Admiral Togo's battleship *Mikasa* in 1896) had been planned, but this was cancelled when a proposed civic reception was strongly opposed by the city's Labour Party, the Newcastle and District branch of the Far East Prisoner-of-War (POW) Association and local trade union branches. The lord mayor of Newcastle, Mrs Grant, who felt that Newcastle had been discourteous to the Prince, attended a dinner at Cragside in his honour. Wearing her full regalia and expressing her regret she declared: 'This gold chain round my neck is the symbol of Newcastle. When your Highness sees this it means that you have been welcomed in Newcastle.'

The prince apparently enjoyed his stay at Cragside. He played tennis and billiards. He saw the lighthouse and the bird sanctuary and was present at a garden party. On his way back to London he visited Durham and was guided round the cathedral and castle by Louis Allen who had studied Japanese during the war and served in the Burma campaign, about which he later wrote an account in his book *Burma: The Longest War* (1984).

One of his first visits after his return was to Windsor Castle and Eton College. Four days had then been set aside for a visit to Oxford. This had to be cut down as the Prince developed a feverish cold. As a result, he missed a visit to Stratford-on-Avon and some other events including one strongly advocated by General Piggott, a visit to Lords to watch cricket. The prince was sufficiently recovered to visit the general's home at Cranleigh. Two days were then spent in a visit to Cambridge where he stayed at Trinity with the Master (later Lord) and Lady Adrian. On his return to London, the queen and crown prince among other events attended a dinner given by the prime minister at Lancaster House and an evening reception at Buckingham Palace. He also visited various London sights including the Houses of Parliament.

The Japanese press assiduously followed the prince's schedule. Twenty-four reporters and cameramen from thirteen news organizations accompanied him. They carefully investigated local reactions to his visit. In Japan there was much interest in how he was received in Britain and in the role of the monarchy in Britain, which might have pointers for Japan. The Japanese press representatives, according to Henry Shimanouchi, had 'a tendency to look for grievances where few or none existed: their own lack of English prevented them from sharing in the full sense of the Coronation story and in consequence they were inclined to fall back on the occasional press manifestations of hostility, the difficulties in Newcastle, and the like'.

The Times reported frequently and factually on the crown prince's tour of Britain. But for the British media the prince was just one of many VIPs invited to the coronation. The prince faced a battery of cameras on his arrival and photographers followed him around (for instance, they photographed him buying a hat at Locke's in St James's) but they eventually got bored and only photographed the more important items in his programme, such as his visit to the Derby at Epsom when many photographs were taken of the two royal personages sitting together. Inevitably the prisoner-of-war issue cast a shadow over the crown prince's tour but apart from the cancellation of the visit to Newcastle this issue did not lead to any other unfortunate incidents.

Dening reported on 21 October 1953 that the emperor, at a luncheon party for heads of mission in Tokyo from countries which the prince had visited, had 'referred in the warmest terms to the reception which the Crown Prince had received, in particular from the Royal Family, during his visit to England'. Dening added that afterwards he had talked with the crown prince himself:

> I was at once struck, not only with the marked improvement in his English, but with his ease of manner and the greater confidence which he had acquired in the course of his tour. . . he now both smiles and laughs more readily and seems to take greater pleasure in conversation.

According to Matsui, the suite also believed that the visit had been both generally enjoyable and a success. Relations with the British royal family had been re-established. The queen had been gracious and friendly. The British government had worked hard to provide a varied and interesting programme.

The prince, still a young man of only nineteen, behaved with decorum. He displayed the warmth of his personality and charmed his hosts by his natural friendliness. This visit was a symbol of the reacceptance of Japan in the post-war world and was as significant as a state visit.

FOLLOWING UP: PRINCESS ALEXANDRA'S VISIT TO JAPAN IN 1961

The ice had been broken, but the thaw took time. Wartime resentment against Japan continued to fester. Japanese competition in textiles and sundry goods intensified and British manufacturers in industries affected condemned what they called Japanese 'sweated labour'. Britain faced an uncertain economic future. The empire was being dismantled and there were manifold uncertainties about Britain's future role in the word. As a result, royal relations with Japan did not receive the priority that the embassy in Tokyo and the political department in the Foreign Office would have liked them to be given.

An opportunity was, however, presented in 1961, when the University of Hong Kong was due to celebrate its fiftieth anniversary and a royal visit to the colony to attend the celebration was proposed. At a meeting of the Royal Visits Committee in the Cabinet Office, the queen's young cousin Princess Alexandra of Kent was selected as the queen's representative on this occasion. The Foreign Office representative on the committee suggested that the princess might go on to Japan and make an official visit.[12] This suggestion was put to the Japanese who gave it a warm welcome.

In 1961 I had returned to Tokyo as a first secretary in the chancery and the ambassador, Sir Oscar Morland, asked me to deal with the arrangements which needed to be agreed in detail with the Imperial Household Agency. The Agency saw this visit as an important step forward in relations between the two monarchies and went to a great deal of trouble to ensure that the visit was a success in both personal and public relations terms. When a preliminary plan for the visit had been drawn up and sent to London, Sir Philip Hay, the Princess's comptroller, and Group Captain Stack of the Queen's Flight made a reconnaissance visit to go over the ground. (Inevitably, this was called the haystack visit.)

The princess, who was born on Christmas Day 1936, was twenty-four when she made her official visit to Japan in October 1961. She was young, pretty and elegant. She had an infectious smile and charmed all who met her. On arrival at Haneda airport on a Britannia aircraft of the Queen's flight, she was met by Princess Chichibu on behalf of the emperor and by members of the Japanese suite who were to accompany her on her tour in Japan. Sir Oscar and Lady Morland greeted her and accompanied her to the embassy where she stayed while in Tokyo.

The emperor and empress hosted a lunch for her, and it was indicated to His Majesty beforehand that Britain would not object if he wore his Order of the Garter on this occasion.[13] The Crown Prince, his brother Prince Hitachi and Princess Chichibu accompanied the princess on a duck-netting expedition at one of the imperial preserves near Tokyo where a lunch of wild duck and saké was served (Pl. 32). As Princess Chichibu was patron of the Japan Red Cross, the two princesses visited the Red Cross Hospital together. Princess Chichibu was also patron of the Japan British Society in Tokyo, which gave a reception for the princess.

The royal train was provided to take her to Kyoto where she was put up in the Sento palace, which was used for state guests. The palace has a fine Japanese garden with a lake, which looked ethereal in the mist and rains that fell one day. In Kyoto she was entertained by geisha dances, *kemari* (imperial court football in traditional costumes) and a Japanese tea ceremony. A visit to Nara included a visit to the Hōryūji to see some of the oldest wooden buildings in the world. She also visited Mikimoto Pearl Island at Toba where she viewed Japanese women divers collecting oysters in which seeds had been implanted so that pearls would grow naturally in the shells. The Japanese press pursued her everywhere, much to the irritation of Sir Philip Hay, and I had difficulty in preventing photographers from ruining the visit. The Japanese journalists were fascinated by her youth, charm and informality, which were different from the formal and staid protocol of the imperial court. Those involved with the visit in both Japan and Britain agreed that the visit had been a great success and the way was now open for further visits both ways.

In the 1960s, Britain began to put an increased effort into penetrating the Japanese market for British products. Japanese curiosity in British royalty seemed insatiable and the Board of Trade and the embassy in Tokyo decided to capitalize on this. For this reason, and because of her popularity in Japan, Princess Alexandra was subsequently asked to open a British trade fair in Tokyo in 1965. She made a third visit to Japan in 1997 as part of the final tour to Asia of the Royal Yacht *Britannia* which went to Hong Kong on the occasion of the hand-over of the colony to China at the end of June 1997. A reception was given on the yacht which was about to be decommissioned. Eminent Japanese were invited on board and Sir David Wright, then British ambassador to Japan, gave a dinner in Princess Alexandra's honour attended by three imperial princesses, Princess Nobuko of Mikasa, Princess Takamado and Princess Nori.

PRINCESS CHICHIBU: BRITAIN'S FAVOURITE JAPANESE PRINCESS

Princess Chichibu reciprocated Princess Alexandra's 1961 visit to Japan by making an official visit to Britain in July 1962 as a guest of the government. Princess Chichibu (1909–1995), whose given name was Setsuko, was a staunch friend of Britain. She was born in Walton-on-Thames when her father, Matsudaira Tsuneo, was first secretary at the Japanese embassy in London. Her family soon moved to Washington. After graduating from High School in Washington DC, 'with enormous reluctance' she agreed to marry into the imperial family, but she and Prince Chichibu turned out 'to have much in common – not least their shared nostalgia for the Western part of their education'.[14] As already mentioned above, Prince Chichibu

(Yasuhito, 1902–1953) had studied briefly at Magdalen College, Oxford in 1926. He went up to Magdalen in the Michaelmas Term of 1926, but had to return to Japan on the death of his father, the Taisho Emperor, to participate in the formal mourning ceremonies. He never returned to Oxford although he retained fond memories of his time at Oxford and after his death Princess Chichibu kept in regular contact with the college. He was also a mountaineer and climbed various mountains in Europe.

Prince and Princess Chichibu had represented Emperor Hirohito at the coronation of King George VI in 1937 and had been entertained by the Japan Society. Prince Chichibu developed tuberculosis during the war and despite spending much time at their country house at Gotemba in the Hakone mountains he died in 1953. On his death, his widow took over the role of imperial patron of the Japan British Society in Tokyo and in this capacity did all she could to further Anglo-Japanese understanding. She attended all the main functions of the Society and, as recounted above, often represented the emperor in greeting British royal visitors, who in turn were happy to call and take tea with the princess in her small house in the imperial compound at Akasaka. She also did much to promote the Japan Red Cross, of which she was patron, and the Japanese Anti-Tuberculosis Association.

In July 1962, as Princess Alexandra was recovering from an operation, Princess Chichibu was met on arrival by the Duke of Kent. The Queen and Prince Philip gave a dinner for her. After dinner the queen herself showed Princess Chichibu the new gallery of royal treasures and the princess was made a Dame Grand Cross of the Royal Victorian Order (she was also given a GCMG by Princess Margaret on the latter's visit to Japan in 1978 – see below.) The queen asked her to join the royal party at the garden party held on the following day. In her capacity as Commander-in-Chief of the Red Cross, Princess Anne, the Princess Royal, also entertained her to tea. Princess Marina, the mother of the Duke of Kent, gave a theatre party for her and the prime minister gave a lunch in her honour.

In London, Princess Chichibu visited the British Red Cross and attended a garden party given by the Japan Society and other Japan-related organizations. She also made visits to Kew, the Tate Gallery and the Design Centre. From London she went to the King Edward VII Sanatorium at Midhurst and had lunch at Petworth House. On the following day, she visited Magdalen College at Oxford where her late husband had studied briefly before the war. She then travelled to Scotland by night train in the royal coach specially made available for her use, and there she visited Edinburgh and the Highlands.

The Foreign Office official report on the visit noted the 'high degree of royal participation in the visit'. On her return to Tokyo, Princess Chichibu said that she had been 'impressed by the warm welcome extended her by the Royal Family, the Government and people of Great Britain'.[15] Princess Chichibu was invited to revisit London in early 1967 for the seventy-fifth anniversary of the Japan Society. She was the guest of honour at the anniversary banquet at the Savoy Hotel on 30 January 1967. The princess presented the Society with a silver vase duly inscribed.

On another visit to Britain, a reception in her honour was given by the Japan Society at the Banqueting Hall in Whitehall on 14 June 1974. The Prince of Wales was the guest of honour on this occasion: a photograph of Prince Charles shaking hands with the princess formed the frontispiece to the *Japan Society Bulletin* in October 1974,

When the Great Japan Exhibition was held at the Royal Academy in Piccadilly from 24 October 1981 to 21 February 1982, Princess Alexandra and Princess Chichibu jointly opened what was indeed 'a significant and unprecedented event in UK-Japanese cultural relations'. [16] It contributed to the improvement in the climate of opinion towards Japan in Britain and 'opened many eyes to some of the great achievements of Japanese art and culture'.

Dorothy Britton declared in her obituary of the Princess:

> Princess Chichibu charmed everyone she met. 'She is so considerate', people would say time and time again. Her gentleness and consideration for others, so typical of the aristocracy of old Japan, was combined with a lively enthusiasm and easy familiarity with Western ways. She excelled in the delicate balance between dignity and spontaneity, and between the traditional and the modern in Japanese culture.

PRINCE AND PRINCESS HITACHI'S OFFICIAL VISIT TO BRITAIN IN 1965

When it was intimated to the Foreign Office in 1965 that Prince Hitachi (Masahito, born 1935), the younger brother of Crown Prince Akihito, and his wife Princess Hanako wished to visit Britain that year following their marriage in 1964, it was decided that, in view of the splendid welcome given to Princess Alexandra, this visit should also be treated as an official one made at the invitation of the British government.[17] The prince and princess having stated that 'they wished to visit the United Kingdom and to see as many places of interest as was possible in the time available', a 'heavy programme' was prepared at the request of the Japanese ambassador. Diana Makgill of the Protocol Department tried to lighten the programme, but the Japanese were insistent.[18] She found some members of the prince and princess's suite tiresome and 'inclined to dictate what their Imperial Highnesses could and could not do'. In spite of this, she thought, 'the Prince and Princess really enjoyed themselves on the whole although the Princess naturally got very bored going round ceaseless biochemical laboratories'. The official despatch declared: 'It was fairly obvious throughout that the Japanese authorities held different views from Their Imperial Highnesses, who would have enjoyed less formal arrangements and more free time for shopping and seeing things of personal interest to themselves.'[19]

The programme included a visit to Scotland. This went well, although a one-day strike at Edinburgh airport necessitated a tiring two-hour drive to Prestwick after a long day of official visits. The highlight of the visit was undoubtedly the lunch given by the queen on 3 November.[20] This was attended by Princess Alexandra and her husband, the Hon. Angus Oglivy, who then hosted a luncheon for their highnesses the following day in his capacity as president of the Cancer Research Fund, for cancer research was a particular interest of the prince. Press coverage was 'very slight but sympathetic. The princess attracted the attention of the Society columnists rather than that of the serious commentators.' The Foreign Office concluded that:

> Although the visit did not break new ground as did Princess Chichibu's in 1962, it once more confirmed that Anglo-Japanese relations had moved away from the post-war period when bitter memories prevented all but the most formal contacts. That this visit by members of the imperial family could take place as a matter of normal course is a noteworthy illustration of the further deepening of the friendly relations between the two countries which has marked the development of Anglo-Japanese relations over the past few years.[21]

Prince Hitachi, in his capacity as honorary patron of the Japan Art Association, visited Britain again in 2011 with Princess Hitachi to mark the announcement of the 2011 laureates for the *Praemium Imperiale* awards given by the Japan Art Association for distinguished contributions to the Arts (Theatre/Film, Architecture, Sculpture, Painting and Music). They arrived on 6 July and left on 13 July. Their programme included a visit to Oxford where the prince was able to examine the collections of the Oxford University Museum of Natural History, followed by lunch and a tour of Magdalen College. The prince also took the opportunity to make visits to the London School of Hygiene and Tropical Medicine and the Natural History Museum. In the context of the *Praemium Imperiale* awards they attended a reception at Buckingham Palace and had an audience with the queen on 11 July and were the guests of honour at the awards dinner at the British Museum on 12 July.

PRINCESS MARGARET VISITS TOKYO IN 1969 FOR BRITISH WEEK

Japanese department stores tended in the 1960s to sell limited quantities of British consumer goods at relatively high prices. The British embassy, wanting to expand exports and noting the way in which the department stores promoted sales by organizing special events, proposed to department store managers that they hold British exhibitions to increase interest in British goods. The Board of Trade, having run a successful British Week in stores in Hong Kong, set their sights on Tokyo and a large-scale British Week was organized in Tokyo in 1969.[22] All the main department stores in Tokyo made the unprecedented decision to hold simultaneous British exhibitions and sales in the week beginning 26 September 1969. As an incentive, a promise was made that all the exhibitions would be visited during British Week by Princess Margaret, the queen's younger sister.

At the same time, an exhibition of British scientific and medical instruments was arranged at the Tokyo Science Museum and a special 'Britain in Tokyo' exhibition, organized by the Central Office of Information, was opened in the Budōkan, the headquarters and spiritual home of Japanese martial arts, especially judo, close to the Science Museum and the Imperial Palace. The opening ceremony was held at the National Theatre on the morning of Friday 26 September 1969 in the presence of Princess Margaret and her husband, the Earl of Snowdon, and Princess Chichibu and various Japanese and British VIPs. After a few brief speeches, Princess Margaret declared British Week open. The band of the Royal Marines played appropriate music and the trumpeters blew a special fanfare. The guests then boarded London double-decker buses parked in the theatre forecourt and were driven to the Budōkan for the opening of the 'Britain in Tokyo Exhibition', which included a pub serving British beer.

Princess Margaret and Lord Snowdon kept up a hectic pace over nine days. As promised, Princess Margaret visited every department store that had pledged its support by offering British goods for sale during the week. Apart from their visits in direct support of British Week, the princess and her husband attended various functions including a Japan-British Society lunch as well as a white-tie dinner at the embassy hosted by the ambassador, Sir John Pilcher, and Lady Pilcher, a gala fashion show, a ball arranged by the Loyal Societies (St George, St Andrew and St David) and the Japanese premiere of the *Battle of Britain* film.

Princess Margaret and Lord Snowdon had arrived in Japan on Saturday 20 September. This enabled them to pay a formal call on the emperor and empress, who entertained them to lunch, and to have tea with Princess Chichibu. They were also invited to dinner by the Japanese prime minister, Satō Eisaku .

Prince William of Gloucester had joined the staff of the embassy towards the end of 1968. Sir John Pilcher decided that he should work in the commercial department, which was particularly busy with preparations for British Week. As head of the department, I asked Prince William to organize his cousin's programme. Princess Margaret and Lord Snowdon naturally took the opportunity to call on their cousin and inspect the small house which had been rented for him. Prince William, who was keen on flying his own aircraft, returned to Britain shortly after British Week was over. He died in 1972 in an aircraft accident.

Princess Margaret paid a brief visit to Japan in October 1978, after a visit to Australia and Tuvalu, where she had planned to attend the independence celebrations, but had fallen ill. This was mainly ceremonial, and included the presentation of the GCMG to Princess Chichibu, as reported elsewhere.

PRINCE CHARLES, THE PRINCE OF WALES, AT EXPO '70 IN OSAKA

Sir John Pilcher, the British ambassador, in his report on Expo '70, noted that the emperor had been 'precluded by the constitution from opening the exhibition, since the experts decreed that to do so would have been a political act'.[23] It was accordingly the crown prince 'who pressed the button that set the lunacy in motion'.

Sir John observed ironically of the British pavilion:

> Even the Central Office of Information, from which no insanity could possibly – it goes without saying – emanate have produced a sober contribution...Not a bandbox certainly but a tailor's flat cardboard box of considerable dimensions, suspended from four vermilion gantries. The squashed superstructure of some giant ship with cranes at rest?
>
> No moving staircase rushes viewers up; they proceed appropriately by staid gangway into the belly of some stranded dirigible. But here too the viewer is treated for good measure to a vast Union Jack atop the box. The terrestrial being, however, is at least led on by the splendid calligraphy from the hand of the erudite Governor of Osaka, proclaiming unmistakably in huge vermilion characters 'Britain'.

Sir John did not record Prince Charles's reaction to the British Pavilion when he was taken on a visit to Expo '70 during his first official visit to Japan in April 1970. The visit lasted five days during which the prince had dinner with the emperor and empress and visited Crown Prince Akihito and Princess Michiko, who had their young son Prince Hiro (later Prince Naruhito) with them. Sir John Pilcher, who was fascinated by aspects of Japanese culture and had studied Japanese as a young language student in the consular service in Kyoto, which he knew well and loved, guided the prince round some of his favourite temples and gardens and introduced him to the Kabuki theatre and a famous *onnagata* (Pl. 33). Sir John asked the Rolls Royce representative to lend a Rolls Royce car for this stage of the trip. Duncan Fraser, the head of Rolls Royce in Japan and then chairman of the British Chamber of Commerce, recalled that when the prince thanked him for the loan, he asked with a twinkle in his eye 'why his mother's car was so much bigger than mine'.[24]

SHOWA EMPEROR'S STATE VISIT TO BRITAIN[25]

The Shōwa emperor (Hirohito) and the empress made a state visit to Britain on 5–8 October 1971. The visit was not only the first Japanese state visit to Britain, but it was also the first time that a reigning emperor had ever travelled abroad. It helped to reaffirm relations between the British royal and the Japanese imperial families and underlined the British government's wish to end the hostility towards Japan which had continued in some parts of the media and among former prisoners of war since the end of the Second World War.

In April 1966, Sir Francis Rundall, the British ambassador in Tokyo, who was on home leave at the time, asked about the possibility of the queen making a state visit to Japan.[26] This immediately led to the question of whether the emperor could respond by visiting Britain. Although it seemed to officials in London most unlikely that the emperor would be allowed to leave the country, it was decided to make it clear to the Japanese authorities that a visit by the emperor as part of an exchange of state visits would be welcomed. This message was passed by Sir Francis to Harada, the then grand master of ceremonies in the Imperial Household Agency, on 18 August 1966. Rundall reported that this news was received with 'considerable gratification but it did not appear that the Imperial Household ... had begun to contemplate the Emperor making a trip abroad'. The ambassador was told 'a great deal about the age old tradition' that the emperor did not travel outside Japan.[27] However, it was reported in the English-language papers in Japan that on 31 August 1970 the emperor had said that he would like to visit Europe, and the household began to think about the possibility. In October 1970, despite some doubts in Britain about the wisdom of issuing an invitation in the light of continuing anti-Japanese sentiments, the two governments agreed that the state visit would be part of an exchange of state visits.

Sir John Pilcher handed the formal invitation from the queen, dated 8 February 1971, to the Japanese foreign minister. It was recognized in London that the visit would be soured if the emperor were not formally restored to the list of members of the Order of the Garter and the queen so instructed in May of that year. No action was taken to restore the emperor's former rank of field marshal in the British army as this would have been inappropriate, not least because of Article 9 of the Japanese constitution of 1947.[28]

The invitation from Britain was an important factor for the Japanese government in deciding to allow the emperor to travel abroad. But Sir John Pilcher thought that the visit to Europe 'was basically inspired by the desire of the Emperor to relive happy moments he recalled from his only other journey abroad as Crown Prince in 1921'. That he had particularly warm memories of King George V and of Prince Edward, then Prince of Wales and briefly King Edward VIII, was shown by his request for a meeting in Paris with the Duke and Duchess of Windsor, on whom he made an unprecedented call at their mansion in the Bois de Boulogne the day before he flew to London.

The Imperial Household Agency wished their Majesties to see 'how other royal families tackled the problems of the contemporary age'. Pilcher also thought that forward-thinking Japanese who wanted Japanese leaders to become more international in outlook had encouraged the trip. He noted that the right-wing disliked 'the idea of this manifest divinity and repository of all the Japanese virtues and traditions leaving the Empire of the Gods'. Conversely, the left-wing 'saw in the trip a nefarious plot on the part of the Imperial Household Agency, in league with reactionaries and militarists, to enhance the position of the Emperor in the eyes of his subjects and pave the way for a recrudescence of the manic nationalism of the past'.

The Japanese government when planning the tour saw it as an opportunity to return state visits from Belgium and West Germany and royal visits from the Netherlands. So, within the short space of seventeen days, the imperial party met US President Nixon at Anchorage, paid state visits to Brussels, London and Bonn, made unofficial visits to Copenhagen and Amsterdam and private visits to Paris and Geneva.

Sir John Pilcher noted that the development of personality had never been an aim of Japanese education and that Emperor Hirohito, having been moulded by men like General Nogi and Admiral Tōgo, 'was never allowed to develop as an individual as a result of the policy of the military to emphasize the mystique and seclusion of the living divinity'. Pilcher rejected the view that 'the stuffier courtiers of the Imperial Household Agency prevent members of the Imperial Family from making due impact upon the people, because they remain petrified in the tradition of the divinity hedging them around, which they wish to preserve'. He believed that the Household were 'longing to discover how best to organize an Imperial life in tune with the times'.[29]

The emperor, he recorded, was not a 'leader on a white horse'. Instead, perhaps partly as a result of his myopia, he had developed an enthusiasm for science, and in his preferred subject of marine biology and to a lesser extent botany he had built a reputation as a scholar. 'Much mystification surrounded his publications on these subjects until recently, but now they are published openly.' Sir John described the emperor as:

> ... by temperament and inclination essentially the mild, but dedicated professor. No extrovert he: knowledge must be prised out of him. Words come hardly to him, though his delivery is emphatic.[30] Timid reserve characterizes him; the ambiguity of silence would be more his forte than the withering rebuke. He is essentially a man of peace, diffident and almost humble about his own role, sceptical probably about its holy attributes. He was thus the least endowed by nature and upbringing to stand up to the pretensions of his turbulent military subjects and both physically and morally unequipped to cut them down.

Pilcher thought that the emperor's finest hour came in August 1945 when 'he brought himself to the point of commanding the unthinkable: surrender. This required a toughness of fibre which events had hitherto not revealed in him.'

The empress, Sir John wrote, 'smiling and good humoured, accommodates herself to the Emperor's scientific pursuits, while attending to her own love of painting and music', mainly Beethoven and Chopin.

The Emperor's constitutional duties had become essentially ceremonial. During Expo '70 in Osaka, he had given twenty-one formal banquets for important foreign visitors, including the Prince of Wales. Their majesties in practice lived a very homely life in their private residence where the Emperor 'who neither smokes nor drinks' spent the evenings watching television, enjoying serials and sumo. His existence is dominated by duty and he led 'a life of bourgeois respectability and tranquility'.

The official programme included all the usual ceremonial occasions of other State visits, but there were some special features designed to cater to the emperor's particular interests. The Japanese were pleased by the fact that their majesties were invited to spend three nights at Buckingham Palace instead of the usual two. Princess Margaret met them on their arrival on the morning of Tuesday 5 October at Gatwick Airport. They then travelled by special train to Victoria station where they were greeted by the queen, the Duke of Edinburgh and other VIPs. From Victoria, the queen and the emperor, the Duke of Edinburgh and the empress proceeded by horse-drawn carriages up Victoria Street, Whitehall and the Mall to Buckingham Palace (Pl. 35). 'The Flags flew, the bands played; and the crowds remained silent.' The only overt protest came when a man with a personal grievance that had nothing to do with Japan, threw his coat towards the carriage in which the emperor was travelling.

After the customary private luncheon at Buckingham Palace, the emperor laid a wreath on the tomb of the unknown warrior in Westminster Abbey (Pl. 38). (The decision to include this in the programme aroused some controversy.) The emperor and the empress called on Queen Elizabeth, the Queen Mother, at Clarence House. On their way by carriage to Clarence House, a single demonstrator used abusive language. Later the emperor received addresses from the chairman and members of the Greater London Council and from the lord mayor, aldermen and councillors of the City of London. That evening their majesties attended a state banquet given in their honour at the palace. The queen in her speech referred briefly to the bad relations of the past.[31] The emperor in his speech did not respond to this point. There was some criticism in both Japan and Britain that the issues had not been faced, but 'the Imperial Household Agency declared that His Majesty could not have done so because that would have been a political act, from which he is precluded by the Constitution'.

The second day of the visit began by the emperor receiving heads of diplomatic missions in London. The emperor then visited the Royal Society, where he was formally admitted as a Fellow, having been elected on 13 May 1971, by the President, Professor A.L. Hodgkin, and signed the Charter book. A special exhibit was arranged for this occasion. The emperor was clearly delighted by this recognition of his scholarly achievements. The emperor and empress were then entertained to luncheon by Sir Alec Douglas-Home, the foreign secretary, in the Great Hall at Hampton Court Palace. They went on to Kew Gardens (Pl. 37), where the Emperor planted a cryptomeria tree which was sadly destroyed soon afterwards by a protester, much to the chagrin of the Japanese. That evening, their majesties attended the lord mayor of London's banquet at the Guildhall where the queen was represented by the Duke and Duchess of Kent. Edward Heath, the Prime Minister, was able to have a lengthy conversation at the dinner with Mr Fukuda Takeo, the Japanese foreign minister, who accompanied their majesties on their tour.

The morning of the third day (Thursday 7 October) of the visit began with a visit to the Linnaean Society where the emperor was received by the President, Professor A.J.E. Cave, and autographed the page in the Roll and Charter Book where he had signed during his visit as crown prince in 1921. They then visited the London Zoo, 'where the antics of Chi-Chi, the giant panda, appeared to divert the emperor more than other events of the visit'. In the afternoon, the emperor visited the Natural History Museum while the empress went to the British Museum to view a collection of calligraphy and prints. They went on to attend a reception at Claridge's hosted by Japan-related organizations in London, where Sir Norman Brain, then chairman of the Japan Society, gave a speech of welcome. The day ended with a return banquet at the Japanese embassy hosted by their majesties. On Friday, 8 October, the emperor and the empress left for Amsterdam for an unofficial visit to the Netherlands, where there were more signs of anti-Japanese feelings than there had been in London.

The Japanese media reported in detail on the tour. The large number of Japanese press representatives, around 150, caused difficulties, not least because facilities for press coverage were restricted at many of the places visited by the emperor and empress, but also because of 'the excessive, often frantic involvement of the Japanese embassy in the shape of a team of eight to ten officers'. Sir John Pilcher reported that:

> ... the Imperial progress was followed ardently on television and was seen as a splendid series of theatrical occurrences, among which the events in Britain, because of the pomp and circumstance and the brilliance of the weather, very markedly stole the show. Only the Japanese flag floating above the Lorelei during the Imperial progress on the Rhine came near to evoking the enthusiasm which the carriage procession immediately called forth ... what most touched Japanese viewers on television and readers of the copious accounts in the Press was the enormous trouble taken by Her Majesty The Queen, His Royal Highness the Duke of Edinburgh and the Royal Household in making flawless preparations. This more than outweighed any shock of realization that the misdeeds of the past still remain a1live.[32]

The British media, which had experienced many state visits, inevitably did not pay as much attention as the Japanese to the details of the visit. *The Times*, in a measured leader on 5 October 1971, headed 'A Very Special Visit', said: 'The Emperor's present visit to western Europe is a voyage of exploration to see where Japan might find firm ground elsewhere outside her own unsettled region.' After discussing the Anglo-Japanese alliance, the writer referred to the atomic bombs dropped on Hiroshima and Nagasaki which 'had left a residue of pacifism which is still strong'. *The Economist*, in a leader in its issue dated 2 October 1971, concluded that: 'If the emperor's trip abroad is an attempt to pull down some of the psychological barriers it must be welcomed. The Emperor Hirohito in his own person is a symbol of the fact that the past need not be irrevocable.' *The Guardian*, in a leader on 8 October marking the end of the visit, concluded that, 'By his visit the Emperor has tried to secure a better working relationship between Japan and the countries on his itinerary. It is understanding that is still lacking.' *The Daily Telegraph* on the same day sounded a sourer note: 'Silent streets and noisy arguments, curiosity and angry controversy – such has been the reception of the Emperor of Japan here ... His utterances have been platitudinously bland, as though our two countries had enjoyed unbrokenly good relations during his long reign ... the controversy really centres round the personality of the Emperor himself.'[33] This last comment was probably inspired by the publication that year of David Bergamini's book, *Japan's Imperial Conspiracy*. By and large, the British media and public were not hostile.

The Foreign Office noted that:

> Much credit is due to the responsible attitude taken by the Executive Council of the Federation of Far Eastern Prisoners of War, who made it known publicly once the State Visit was announced that, as an expression of respect to the Queen, the Council did not wish to be associated with any demonstrations which might take place during the Emperor's visit and that the Federation's name was not to be used in any sensational press features. The extent of the Executive Council's control over the activities of its members can be gauged from the fact that the Federation's annual reunion was held at the Festival Hall only three days before the Emperor's arrival. There were no formal demonstrations.[34]

The Foreign Office described the public attitude towards the visit as marked by coolness. 'The routes were only fairly well lined with onlookers but there was no applause.' The conclusion as set out in the official report on the visit sent to Tokyo on 9 November 1971 was:

> The relative coolness of public reaction to the visit did not prevent it from being a success. In fact there were only three individual public demonstrations throughout the stay. When we recall the number of placards outside Claridge's Hotel for virtually any distinguished foreign visitor I think we have done very well. It was perhaps a good thing that the Japanese should realize that it will take some time yet to work themselves back into favour.

> In retrospect perhaps the best thing about the visit was that it took place at all. A precedent has been created: never again will it be the first time the Emperor has travelled abroad.[35]

Sir John Pilcher, the British ambassador in Tokyo, who had accompanied their majesties to London, largely shared this view. In his despatch of 5 November 1971, which crossed with that from the Foreign Office, he concluded as follows:

> The visit gave immense pleasure but it has administered a jolt to the memory. It was a certain shock to the Japanese to find that Europeans had not quite forgiven them for the humiliations to which they were exposed. The Japanese are used to resentment for a variety of political reasons, but the American example had led them to suppose that the last war had been forgiven and largely forgotten... In these circumstances it strikes *me* as commendable that the Japanese Press and people took as calmly as they did the incidents which occurred.[36]

Sir John thought that the Japanese people were relieved to find that their majesties had returned from their strenuous journey in more relaxed form than before their departure:

> They were delighted to learn that the beaming face of the Empress had broken through to some extent the barriers of race, culture and education. The impassive myopia of His Majesty, which may have been the real cause of the lack of enthusiasm of the crowds, was not commented upon.[37]

Pilcher noted that the visit had taken place when Japan was reeling from what were called the Nixon shocks:

> The American ascendancy has lost its magic...China and South East Asia have long memories and have not forgiven past Japanese misdeeds. Now Europe reveals itself to be equally resentful. If this realization leads to redoubled efforts to gain the fair opinion of the world, no harm will have been done. It should not, however, be allowed to make the Japanese turn in on themselves...It would not be wise to cold shoulder the world's third economic power...If the visit encourages the healthy outward-looking tendency of young Japanese, it will have made a real contribution. It may help to diminish Japanese insularity and egocentricity.[38]

State visits in the modern world are largely symbolic. This is especially so in the case of Japan where, under Article 1 of the Constitution, the emperor is defined as 'the symbol of the State and of the unity of the people'. The state visit in 1971 could not by itself heal the wounds in the relationship between Britain and Japan, but it marked a significant step towards reconciliation and renewal of old friendships. The next step was for the queen to return the compliment by making a state visit to Japan

THE QUEEN'S STATE VISIT TO JAPAN IN 1975

The queen and Prince Philip made a state visit to Japan from 7 to 12 May 1975. This was the first state visit to Japan by a British monarch and the Japanese authorities made unprecedented efforts to make the queen and Prince Philip welcome. The schedule agreed for the visit was a hard and tight one. The queen clearly took a personal interest in the details of the programme.[39] It must have been exhausting for the royal couple who made every effort to make it the success it undoubtedly was. Huge crowds of Japanese wanted to see the queen and to ensure the security of the visitors the Japanese authorities brought in large numbers of extra police to control the crowds.

On arrival at Haneda airport, Princess Chichibu and the Japanese foreign Minister, Miyazawa Kiichi, greeted the queen and Prince Philip and a twenty-one-gun salute was fired.[40] The main arrival ceremony was held at the government guest house in Akasaka, where Emperor Hirohito and Empress Nagako warmly welcomed the visitors (Pl. 39) and a Self-Defence Forces band played the British and Japanese national anthems. The emperor then introduced the queen and Prince Philip to other members of the imperial family, prime minister Miki Takeo and other dignitaries and the queen reviewed the honour guard.

Following this twenty-minute ceremony, the queen and the emperor in a black Rolls Royce, followed by Prince Philip with the empress in a similar car, proceeded to the imperial palace where gifts were exchanged. The queen gave the emperor a decorative porcelain plate by Bernard Leach, the British potter who had worked and studied in Japan, and a microscope in recognition of the emperor's scientific interests. The emperor gave the queen a painting by Higashiyama Kaii. They then strolled briefly in the palace garden where azaleas were in bloom.

A state banquet was held that evening at the imperial palace. In his speech the emperor expressed the hope that the two 'lands of history and tradition' would 'proceed in closer cooperation' towards peace, and progress in culture and welfare. The queen in reply declared that she 'looked forward immensely to learning, not only about Japan's rich cultural heritage, but also her modern technology, and how you succeed in keeping both old and new in reasonable harmony. She stressed that 'we must all continue to develop our bilateral trade. This has been and will be the bedrock of our relations.' Both nations had 'everything to gain from closer commercial and financial links'.

The visit coincided with a transport slowdown and strikes. This was rather ironic as many Japanese businessmen had got into the habit of criticizing Britain for its strike record and what they termed the *eikokubyō* or 'English disease' of poor labour relations. Despite the congestion, crowds lined the streets from the guest house to the palace.

The second day of the visit began with a display in an annex to the guest house of examples of various schools of *ikebana* (flower arrangement).[41] The rest of the day was devoted to various official functions and engagements in Tokyo, including a meeting with the heads of diplomatic missions in Tokyo and a visit to the Japanese Diet, a lunch given by Japanese economic organizations (Keidanren) and a dinner given by the Japanese prime minister. The guest list at the lunch at Tokyo Kaikan 'was unbelievable. Every person present was the head of his own business organization. Every famous Japanese manufacturer you have ever heard of…was there.'[42] Dokō Toshio, the venerable president of the Keidanren, gave 'a 'charming and helpful speech' in English. The queen in her reply was forthright about the importance of the trading relationship.

In the afternoon there was a garden party in Shinjuku Gyoen (park) for members of the British Commonwealth who were entertained while they waited for the queen by the band of the Gordon Highlanders which had been flown up from Singapore. The queen had gone from the lunch to NHK television studios where she had watched the screening of a samurai play involving sword fighting and tense drama. Following this the queen watched a sports exhibition at the Yoyogi gymnasium including a judo bout. Perhaps because the performance had been so exciting the queen was running late.[43] When the queen's motorcade of some twenty cars with outriders appeared in the park there was great excitement. 'Both The Queen and Prince Philip were absolutely marvellous about talking to people and went round for at least an hour though still running quite late'. When the royal couple left to get ready for dinner with the Prime Minister there were loud cheers.

On the third day, there was a wreath-laying visit to the British Commonwealth war graves cemetery at Hodogaya outside Yokohama.[44] The queen and Prince Philip then made separate industrial visits, the queen to a Canon factory and the duke by helicopter to a shipyard in Yokosuka. Both companies were deeply gratified, not least for the publicity that they received from the visits. While Prince Philip lunched with the Japan Academy, the queen attended a lunch given by the Japan British Society. There were only places for 650, but there had been over 800 applications and a ballot had had to be run, which led to the disappointment of the unlucky ones. Princess Chichibu, imperial patron of the Society, greeted the queen on behalf of the Society.

The queen and Prince Philip, who joined her, then made a fifteen minute slow drive to the National Theatre in an open convertible Cadillac (specially purchased for the occasion) along a carefully planned route to enable the crowds of well-wishers to see her. At the National Theatre they were joined in an unprecedented gesture by the emperor and empress as well as by the crown prince and princess for a performance of Japanese classical *bugaku* and a kabuki dance by Nakamura Utaemon and other kabuki actors.[45]

After the performance the queen and Prince Philip drove to the British Embassy nearby to meet the staff and their spouses. Prince Philip then managed to fit in a visit to the British Export Marketing Centre, which had been opened by the Duke of Kent. The prince, according to Ben Thorne, the director of the Centre, 'was thoroughly at home in the Exhibition and enjoyed his trip round immensely. Although he had no more than twenty to twenty-five minutes in the Centre he talked to everybody in the Exhibition without exception. People to whom he talked for maybe twenty or thirty seconds were quite convinced that they had five minutes with him. It is a splendid technique.' The prince also met the council of the British Chamber of Commerce in Japan.

That evening the queen's return dinner for the emperor and empress was held at the British ambassador's residence (Pl. 40). Following the dinner attended by some sixty VIPs there was a white tie and decorations reception and ball to which 400 guests had been invited.[46] The reception began with a trumpet fanfare announcing the arrival of the queen and Prince Philip who were joined by the Crown Prince and Princess. The queen and the crown prince went round one way, Prince Philip and the crown princess went round the other way. After about fifteen minutes the dancing began in the ballroom. The queen was led onto the floor by the crown prince while Prince Philip led the crown princess to music played by the band of the Gordon Highlanders. Ben Thorne and his wife were much impressed by the style of the Crown Prince and Princess when dancing together. 'In white tie and tails they looked like a "Come Dancing" team on television.'

The reception guests, who included the then reigning sumo champion Wajima, Kabuki actors and leaders of Japanese fashion as well as industrialists, were regaled in the marquee erected in the garden with what was described as 'breakfast' which consisted of all the traditional elements of an English breakfast except porridge. Around midnight the crown prince and princess departed followed shortly after by the queen and Prince Philip.

On the fourth day, the royal visitors were due to travel to Kyoto by super-express train, but because of the strike the Japanese government decided that they should fly to Osaka in their chartered Boeing 707. In fact, the strike was called off and members of the suite and luggage went to Kyoto as planned by train.[47] At Osaka airport the queen and Prince Philip were met by the governor of Osaka and other local VIPs. They then drove to Kyoto where they partook of an informal lunch at the Sento Gosho (palace with a fine Japanese garden). In Kyoto they visited the Ryōanji and the Katsura detached palace.[48] They attended a tea ceremony and a reception given by the Japan British Society of the Kansai. They ended the day with a traditional Kyoto-style dinner at the famous Tsuruya restaurant, given by Ambassador Nakamura, who headed the Japanese suite of honour. They stayed that night at the Omiya Palace.

On their fifth day they first visited the Kyoto Imperial Palace, where they watched a performance of *kemari* (Japanese court football) with players in traditional costumes.[49] Before taking a train from Kyoto to Tsu, a brief call was made at the Nishi-Honganji temple, where King George V had stayed when a teenager in 1881. From Tsu the royal couple were escorted to the Ise Grand Shrines. Normally only the emperor and empress are admitted to the inner sanctum, but a special exception was made for the British monarch and her consort. At a stable attached to the shrine, the queen saw a thirteen-year-old stallion called Yamaisamaru who, she was told, was 69.73 per cent British and to whom she fed a carrot. The decision to include a visit to Ise in the programme was not welcomed by all Japanese.[50] A small Japanese group protested to the Japanese government and the British embassy at the inclusion of this visit in the programme. They alleged that the visit would encourage 'reactionary forces such as militarists, the Liberal-Democratic Party and those who advocate revival of the autocratic Emperor system and state Shintoism'. A group of Japanese Protestants also protested to British ministers and to the Archbishop of Canterbury.[51] The official British response was to point out that the Queen's visit to Ise was no different from her visits to temples and palaces in Kyoto and had no religious significance.[52]

After visiting the Ise shrines, the royal couple visited Toba pearl farm, a popular tourist attraction, and watched the women divers collecting pearl oysters (Pl. 42). In the evening at the Toba International Hotel there was an informal supper for the team accompanying the royal party.[53]

On the sixth and final day of their visit they travelled by train to Tokyo, changing at Nagoya from the branch line from Tsu on to the *Shinkansen* ('bullet train') to Tokyo. They were driven to the guest house at Akasaka where they took leave of their hosts and thanked all concerned with the organization of their programme. Princess Chichibu was at the airport to see them off. Their aircraft departed at 4.15 p.m.

The visit had marked a significant step in Anglo-Japanese relations and had cemented relations between the British royal and Japanese imperial families. The relationship inevitably was different from that with European royalty with whom there were long-standing family ties. Sir Fred Warner, the British ambassador, considered that 'all members of the Imperial Family greatly enjoyed the visit and helped ensure its success'.[54] 'The programme', Sir Fred noted, 'had provided a wide range of opportunities for The Queen to have contacts in the political, economic and cultural fields.' To the surprise of the Japanese authorities, 'The most overwhelming reaction was … the enthusiasm of the Japanese people who watched the visit, live and on television, in unprecedented numbers.' Over a million people gathered to see them go by. The television scored more viewers than at any time in its history. People searched the channels for continuous reports of the visit and the ratings show that about 75 million people watched the television broadcast of the Queen's speech at the Palace. Queen-viewing became a national pastime.'

The visit greatly increased Japanese interest in Britain. It created, Sir Fred said, 'an enormous fund of goodwill and interest which can be tapped in many fields, not least that of trade.' He went on as follows:

> There is the emotional response of the ordinary consumer, who is more likely to be interested in buying British if the goods are there and the price is right. There is also renewed interest among decision-makers in the business community, but this can obviously only be turned to advantage by proper effort – by offering goods at attractive prices and restoring our tarnished reputation for reliability. There is interest in our institutions, which can grow with offers of scholarships and academic exchanges, and a revived interest in English as the Japanese have heard it spoken by The Queen. The unspoken fear amongst our friends is that Britain will not be able to follow up the opportunities that have been created – that we have done what we do best and that what follows may be an anti-climax.

The visit also stimulated British interest in Japan. British media, which had not yet got over all their prejudices and looked for signs of exotica in Japan, sent a large contingent of reporters to follow the visit.[55] The BBC also saw the visit as an occasion for producing documentaries about Japan.

Among the reasons for the queen's popularity with the Japanese was that she was accessible while the Japanese emperor, although he had tried hard through his travels in Japan to make contact with his people, was remote and hedged around by protocol.

The arrangements for the visit had involved many man-hours and had not been made without some problems. These arose mainly from the bureaucratic and unimaginative rigidities of officials of the imperial household.[56] The Imperial Household Agency sought to ensure that the programme for the queen's visit did not invite 'critical comparison with the Emperor's own cloistered life and that of other members of the Imperial Family'. In particular they objected to the proposal for an open car drive through the streets of Tokyo. The queen had, however, told her ambassador that 'she would like to do an open-car drive through the centre of Tokyo – something she always tried to do on state visits as it gave a great number of people an opportunity to see her.'[57] The Japanese demurred: this was unprecedented. The emperor never did such a thing and the British were told that the emperor would prefer that this plan was not insisted on. 'The Queen did insist. It was what she definitely wished to do.' The Japanese after lots of argument said she could do the drive but only if she went in a bullet-proof car at 40 mph. The ambassador had to tell the Japanese that this was not acceptable to the queen. Finally, after weeks of toing and froing and moments when it almost seemed that the visit would have to be aborted, the Japanese side agreed to the drive. It became in fact one of the highlights of the visit.

CROWN PRINCE AKIHITO'S OFFICIAL TOUR OF BRITAIN, 1976

In his despatch on the state visit of the queen, Sir Fred Warner had noted that the Crown Prince remained 'in the shadows…The Kunaichō [Imperial Household Agency] have always feared that any active life by the crown prince would build up his popularity at the expense of that of his father.'[58] During her state visit to Japan in 1975, the queen invited the crown prince and princess to stay with her at Windsor in 1976 and attend the races at Ascot. The British government decided (I was then deputy under-secretary in the Foreign and Commonwealth Office [FCO]) to invite their imperial highnesses to stay a few days in Britain as government guests. The invitation was accepted and plans were drawn up in discussions between the FCO and the Japanese embassy in London for a programme of visits in England, Scotland and Wales

The crown prince and princess visited Britain between 15 and 24 June 1976. They spent the nights of 16 and 17 June as guests of the queen at Windsor Castle where the queen hosted dinners in their honour. She also took them to Ascot as her guests at the Royal Ascot race meetings (Pl. 45). After leaving Windsor, the crown prince and princess stayed at Claridge's while they were in London. Unfortunately, it was an exceptionally hot June and Claridge's in those days did not have air-conditioning. The imperial couple bore the heat with fortitude and appeared to enjoy their visit. I accompanied the couple on most of their visits and do not recall any unfortunate incidents or signs of resentment and hostility such as left an unfortunate impression during their state visit as emperor and empress in 1998.

Both the prince and princess made visits in England to Stoke Poges church which the crown princess wanted to see as a result of her study of English literature and Grey's famous elegy (Pl. 43). The crown prince visited the Thames water treatment plant at Beckton while the crown princess went to the British Red Cross. Both visited Stoke Mandeville Sports Stadium for the disabled. The crown prince attached particular importance to this visit as sporting activities for the disabled has been one of his life-long interests. He had been honorary president of the Paralympics which had been held in Tokyo in 1964 immediately following the Tokyo Olympics that year.

On 18 June, after a short trip on the Thames, the couple attended a dinner given by the Secretary of State for Foreign Affairs and Mrs Crosland at Trinity House (Pl. 46). On 19 June, they flew to Edinburgh where the crown prince visited the Royal Scottish Museum and the crown princess Edinburgh University's School of Scottish Studies. They both visited Edinburgh Castle and then went on to St Andrews to visit the marine laboratory of the University. They stayed two nights at Scone Palace, the home of the Earl and Countess of Mansfield. In addition to a visit to Blair Castle for lunch with the Duke of Atholl, the couple made a tour by car through the Highlands. On 21 June they lunched with the Earl and Countess of Moray at Doune Park and then flew from Glasgow to Cardiff, where they stayed with the Lord Lieutenant and Lady Traherne at Coedarhydglyn. In South Wales the crown prince visited the Deep Navigation Coal Mine where he was dressed in miner's overalls and helmet and went down to the depths of the mine; he coped well with the heat (Pl. 44). The crown princess meanwhile visited Tintern Abbey and Chepstow Castle. After lunch with the lord mayor and lady mayoress of Cardiff, the imperial couple viewed the Welsh Folk Museum at St Fagan's Castle and went on to the United World College of the Atlantic at St Donat's Castle where they met some Japanese students. That evening they attended a 'medieval banquet' in Cardiff Castle, where their host was Lord Goronwy-Roberts, minister of state in the Foreign Office. As this involved eating off gravy-covered bread plates the crown princess must have had some difficulty in avoiding soiling the fine kimono she was wearing.

After returning by train to London they visited the Natural History Museum and called on the Duke and Duchess of Gloucester at Kensington Palace.

Finally, before leaving on Thursday, 24 June 1976, they visited Kew Gardens.[59] The visit helped to cement relations with the royal family and underlined the growing improvement in Anglo-Japanese relations.

JAPANESE IMPERIAL PRINCES AND PRINCESSES AT UNIVERSITIES IN BRITAIN

A significant number of members of the Japanese imperial family have studied at British universities, especially at Oxford. The most important of those who studied at Oxford is the present Crown Prince Naruhito (Crown Prince Naruhito is due to replace his father Akihito as emperor on 1 May 2019) and his wife Princess Masako, who before her marriage and while in the Japanese diplomatic service had studied at Balliol College in Oxford from 1988 to 1990. They were preceded at Oxford by Prince Chichibu (Yasuhito, 1902–1953), who had studied briefly at Magdalen College in 1925, and by Prince Tomohito of Mikasa (1946–2012) who was at Magdalen College, Oxford from 1968 to 1970, where he studied East Asian international relations and rowed for the first eight. He thoroughly enjoyed his time at Oxford having a lively social life and making friends with his fellow students.

Prince Mikasa Takahito (1915–2016), father of Tomohito and youngest brother of Emperor Hirohito, had pursued advanced studies in archaeology, Middle Eastern studies, and Semitic languages at the University of Tokyo. Prince Mikasa was fluent in Hebrew and was much interested in Judaism. From 1954 until his death in 2016, he directed the Japanese Society for Middle East Studies. He was honorary president of the Japan Society of Orientology. The prince held visiting and guest faculty appointments in Middle Eastern studies and archaeology at various universities in Japan and abroad. From 18 April 1975 to 29 August 1975 he was a visiting professor at the School of Oriental and African Languages (SOAS) in London.

Princess Akiko of Mikasa, elder daughter of the late Prince Tomohito of Mikasa and Princess Nobuko (who studied at Rosslyn House College in 1973) came first to Oxford in 2001 for a year abroad during her undergraduate degree at Gakushuin University. She studied Japanese art history at Merton College and later, on graduation, in 2004 returned to Merton to study, under Dame Jessica Rawson, for her D. Phil. at the Faculty of Oriental Studies until 2010. She was co-supervised for her doctorate by Tim Clark at the British Museum, and became very familiar with the Japanese collection there, since her research topic was 'The William Anderson Collection at the British Museum - Western Interest in Japanese Art in the Nineteenth Century. William Anderson (1842–1900).'[60] Princess Akiko became the second member of the imperial family to be awarded a doctorate (2011). Princess Tsuguko of Takamado, the eldest daughter of the late Prince Takamado and Princess Hisako (née Tottori, who herself was a graduate of, and studied for her MA at, Cambridge University) studied at the University of Edinburgh from 2004 to 2008.

Prince Fumihito (Akishino), known at that time as Prince Aya (born 1965), who had studied law and biology at Gakushuin University, studied at St John's College, Oxford, from October 1988 to June 1990, when he returned to Japan to marry Kiko Kawashima.[61] At St John's he concentrated on research into the taxonomy of fish, and later, in 1996, he received a PhD degree in ornithology from the Graduate University for Advanced Studies.[62] While he was at Oxford the Prime Minister, Margaret Thatcher, and her husband gave a lunch in his honour on 22 April 1989; Prince Edward, Earl of Wessex, was among the guests. The queen invited him to tea at Buckingham Palace on 12 July 1989.

Princess Mako (born 1991), the elder daughter of Prince Akishino, studied English at University College Dublin for one month in 2010. She graduated from the International Christian University in Tokyo in 2014 with a Bachelor's degree in Art and Cultural Heritage. On 17 September 2014, she left for the United Kingdom where she studied museology at the University of Leicester for a year, receiving a Master's degree in Museum Studies in January 2016. She also studied art history at the University of Edinburgh for nine months, from September 2012 to May 2013.

Princess Kako (born 1994), the younger daughter of Prince Akishino, decided to follow in the footsteps of her elder sister. She went to the United Kingdom in autumn 2017 to begin studying for a degree at the University of Leeds where she is doing a combination of Performing Arts and Psychology. Princess Aiko, the only daughter of Crown Prince Naruhito and Crown Princess Masako, attended a three-week summer school at Eton College in 2018.

The most important of all the imperial princes who studied in Britain was Prince Naruhito (Hiro) who became crown prince in 1989 on the death of his grandfather, the Shōwa Emperor. He did post-graduate studies at Merton College, Oxford from 1983 to 1985. The prince wrote a memoir about his time at Oxford for his friends at Gakushuin (the post-war university which developed from the pre-war Peers College). This was published in 1993 under the title *Thames to tomo ni*, which I translated as *The Thames and I*.[63] The English translation was published by Global Oriental in 2006 with a foreword by the Prince of Wales.

When I was British ambassador in Tokyo, I had become friendly with Abe Isao, Grand Master of the Ceremonies in the Imperial Household Agency, who had been Japanese ambassador to Belgium. One day he mentioned to me that thought was being given to the future education of Prince Hiro (Naruhito), the elder son of Crown Prince Akihito and second-in-line to the throne. He needed some exposure to the world outside Japan. I immediately wondered whether the answer might be for the prince to follow in the footsteps of his great uncle Prince Chichibu, who had remembered fondly his days at Magdalen College, Oxford. But perhaps another college might suit the Prince better as his security and privacy had to be guaranteed. I promised to consult in strict confidence Sir Rex Richards, the vice-chancellor of Oxford University, who was visiting Japan. When I put this idea to him he immediately suggested that the college of which he was the warden could be the appropriate place for the prince. It was Merton, one of the smallest colleges. Merton would introduce the prince to Oxford's history and traditions and provide him not only with an opportunity to study his chosen subject but also to mix with a selection of scholars and undergraduates from various backgrounds and nationality in the intimacy of a small community. Security, which would be provided by VIP protection officers, should not be a problem. As the prince's memoir *The Thames and I* shows, the arrangements worked well and his stay was both successful and enjoyable.

Prince Hiro, as he was called at the time, arrived in London on 21 June 1983. He spent his first ten days staying with the then Japanese ambassador and Mrs Hirahara at their residence in Kensington Palace Gardens. This gave him an opportunity to recover from jet lag and see some of the sights of London, including the House of Parliament.

One of his first calls was on Princess Alexandra, who recalled with pleasure her first visit to Japan in 1961. On the following day, he called at Buckingham Palace where the queen, who had Princes Andrew and Edward with her, had invited him to tea. He enjoyed 'a pleasant time in a relaxed atmosphere'. He 'felt rather nervous but the conversation was very informal'. He 'wondered how "Tea" was served in England but the Queen kindly poured the tea herself'. On 24 June Princess Anne at her house in Gloucestershire invited him to lunch. He made a courtesy call on Princess Margaret and signed the book at the queen mother's residence. He attended a garden party at Buckingham Palace and in the royal tea tent was able to talk informally with the queen and the Duke of Edinburgh. The queen told him of how, when she attended the opening of the NEC factory near Edinburgh, she had had to 'wear an overall which looked like a space suit.' The duke, who was Chancellor of Cambridge University, asked him humorously why he had chosen Oxford.

Prince Hiro was introduced by Sir Rex Richards to Professor Peter Mathias from All Souls, who would be his academic supervisor, and Dr Roger Highfield, a fellow of Merton, who would be his tutor. Both, through their hard work and commitment to the prince's welfare and studies, played important roles in ensuring that his stay at Oxford was successful.

He needed first to improve his knowledge of the English language and thus his ability to converse freely with his fellow students. For this purpose, he went to stay with Colonel Tom Hall and Mrs Hall at their house in Chiselhampton near Oxford. Colonel Hall, who had been a Gentleman at Arms in the queen's bodyguard, ran a language school that had a branch school in Japan. The prince had one-to-one tuition each morning and afternoon with Mr and Mrs Corcos over three months. He was able to play tennis and swim in the Halls' pool and generally live a normal life 'below the clouds'. While at first no doubt he found English family life and cuisine strange, he soon adapted. He had to learn such ordinary things as filling up a car with petrol, buying stamps and going to a bank, which he had never done before and probably never would do again after he returned to Japan. Guessing that the prince while at Oxford would have occasion to visit a pub, Colonel Hall took him to three pubs in succession so that he knew how to order beer and understood the meaning of the phrase 'a pub crawl'.

The prince's identity was not generally known in the village and he was simply called Hiro when they were out and about. At the local village fete he joined in 'a game involving throwing Wellington boots'. Prince Hiro threw his boot with much vigour but it flew sideways across a wall and grazed a farmer working in a field. This caused much laughter. The prince commented in his memoir how 'important and precious' it was 'to have the opportunity to be able to go privately at one's own pace where one wants'. He enjoyed English country life although he suffered from hay fever and never got use to what one of his teachers called a 'good country smell'.

During his stay with Colonel Hall he made various expeditions including visits to Stonehenge and Stratford-on-Avon. On one trip from Abingdon to Clifton Hampden he became fascinated by the operation of the canal lock at Culham. Perhaps this sowed the seed for the thesis that he eventually wrote about the history of water transport in eighteenth-century England centring on the River Thames.

When the university term was about to begin, he moved to Merton College where, after he had signed the register, the Warden showed him to his rooms. Carrying his suitcase, he found these on the second floor where he had a study looking south over Christ Church Meadow, while from his bedroom he could look down on the peaceful college garden. He was fortunate in having a bathroom to himself across the corridor. But there was no central heating and never enough hot water for a good hot bath. To cope with the cold, he had to buy an electric heater and use an electric blanket Colonel Hall had given him.

The prince's first day in college must have been an ordeal, meeting and getting to know his fellow students and learning how they lived. He soon got used to meals in the college dining hall with its English institutional food, but living in college involved various chores. He recalled that 'One of my biggest tasks at weekends was doing my washing.' There were three washing machines and a drier in the basement:

> All I had to do was to put my washing in the machine, pouring the appropriate quantity of detergent and insert the money, but as I was not used to the procedure it was a bit of a puzzle for me. The first time I used the machines I made a major mistake. As instructed I put in my washing, the detergent and the money. I gathered that the washing would be ready in forty minutes, so I went back to the basement forty minutes later, only to find that there were soap suds all around. When I looked carefully I discovered that soap suds had clearly come from the machine I had been using. There was another student near the machine who asked: 'Is this yours? The soapsuds have overflown.' I had overloaded the machine with washing. I apologized to him and did my best to get over the difficulties I had caused. I still have a good laugh at my mishap.

He also learnt to iron his own shirts. 'Immediately after I began at Oxford I went into the city and bought an iron and an iron-stand. I learnt how to use the iron from one of my police escorts. I did not find it too difficult to learn and while I was studying at Oxford I did all my own ironing.'

The prince, who was unassuming and happy to mix informally with his fellows, made various friends among the other students:

> Shortly after I went up to Merton I got to know a very pleasant couple. The man had come up to Oxford at the same time as I had and was reading English Literature at Merton. The girl was doing research at a different university, but they were always together and no one doubted that she was also at Merton. P and his fiancée were very kind to me while I was at Oxford and they greatly helped to make my stay at Oxford so enjoyable. I got to know P at the first MCR [middle common room, for graduate students such as the prince, who had graduated from Gakushuin] dinner after term began. Thereafter they often came to my room for a chat. P was learning to play the *shakuhachi* (a Japanese five-holed bamboo wind instrument) and his fiancée was interested in Japanese design. They both showed great interest in Japan. One day they asked what was the word for 'lazy' in Japanese. I told them that the appropriate word was *namakemono*, P. immediately memorized the word and pointing at his fiancée called her *namakemono*. They still use some Japanese words when they write to me these days. They also asked me what was the Japanese for 'Your Royal Highness'. I explained that the word was *denka* and said that this should not be confused with the electric light in the ceiling to which I pointed and which was called *denki* in Japanese. Afterwards I

> regretted saying this but it was too late and thereafter the two of them teased me by referring to me as *denki* and pointing at the light said it was *denka*. One day P came round with his *shakuhachi* and persuaded me to blow into it, but I could not get a peep out of it. He then produced some good sounds from the instrument and declared in his typical way, as he blew into the instrument, 'I am Samurai'.

P and his friend introduced the prince to various Oxford pubs including the *Perch*, the *Trout* and the *White Heart*. He was also invited by members of the MCR to go to wine bars.

> We did not know one cocktail from another; so we each ordered a different one and, though this was rather bad behaviour, sampled by drinking through straws those ordered by others. I also went to a disco in the city to see what it was like, here I made a real blunder. I remember that it occurred on a Saturday evening. I was with another man who was a member of the MCR and who apparently liked discos. We were stopped at the door and when I asked why I was told that on that evening people in T-shirts and jeans were not admitted. As usual I was in jeans and my companion was wearing a T-shirt. The door-keeper pointed to my police escort who was behind us and said 'You will do!' He was not wearing a tie, but he was wearing a blazer and thus apparently qualified. While I was at Oxford I tried as far as possible to be like other students and certainly did not explain who I was. So I gave up and went weakly away.

But while socializing was an important part of life at Oxford, the prince was there to study and learn about the world outside Japan. During his two years at Oxford, the prince, who was a serious and conscientious student, attended university lectures, read books recommended to him, did research and wrote essays. At Gakushuin he had studied history and had become interested in the transportation system in medieval Japan. When he arrived in Oxford he had not yet decided on a particular theme for research, but from the beginning of his stay in Britain he was fascinated by British canals, their locks and their connection with British rivers. During his stay in Britain he visited many canals in the southern counties. The Thames flowed through Oxford and near Chiselhampton and transport on it attracted his interest (Pl. 47). These were among the factors which led to the decision taken at the beginning of his second term at Oxford that he should do research on transport on the Thames during the eighteenth century. The first step was to discover what records were available. So he explored Oxfordshire County Record Office and the Bodleian Library. Later he visited other record offices including those at Reading, in Gloucestershire and Buckinghamshire as well as the Public Record Office at Kew (now the National Archives). Prince

Hiro was greatly helped in his research by Professor Mathias and Dr Highfield, but he clearly worked hard and delved deeply into his chosen theme:

> Based on the historical materials which I had collected during my two years at Oxford, I analysed the state of water transport on the Thames, concentrating on the people who had been involved in improvements to the river and navigation on it, and on the transport of agricultural commodities including coal and malt.

He gives a rough sketch of his thesis and his conclusions in his memoir, *The Thames and I* (pp. 123–126). His thesis was published by Oxford University Press in 1989 under the title *The Thames as Highway: a study of navigation and traffic on the upper Thames in the eighteenth century*.

Dr Highfield taught him about Oxford and Western culture. He took the prince on long walks around Oxford explaining the places they visited and their history and culture. With Dr Highfield he saw a number of operas including *Fidelio*, where he was struck by the scene in which the heroine sings while ironing. He was invited by Prince Charles and Princess Diana to Covent Garden to see *Boris Godunov* and much enjoyed his two visits to Glyndebourne. He also saw lots of films and plays. The prince greatly enjoyed classical music and had learnt to play the viola:

> I had wanted to find opportunities to play from the time I entered the college, but my hopes were fulfilled much earlier than I expected. I cannot remember exactly when one morning at breakfast a student sitting next to me chanced to remark that he was studying music. I told him a little nervously that I played the viola and said that I was hoping to be able to play in a chamber-music group. He was a post-graduate student named W; he undertook to find others to join the two of us. On 26 November 1983 we had our first meeting as a quartet in Merton's summer house.

They began mainly with Haydn quartets but went on to play works by Mozart and Beethoven. One day he was asked to play the viola in a Mozart trio for clarinet, viola and piano, the delightful *Kegelstatt* trio. They practised hard and performed it at a concert at Merton in March 1984. 'In the second movement the viola has a prominent role but there are some difficult passages. I managed these alright and the third movement went without any problems.'

Prince Hiro was young and keen to take part in sports. He tried rowing:

> I enjoyed going on the Thames in the boat, but I think that the other members of the crew supported me as a beginner and I realized that it would be difficult for me to become a team member and practise regularly.

He particularly enjoyed tennis. 'I was chosen to play for Merton and thus had the opportunity to take part in competitive matches with other colleges.' He became 'number three seed in Merton's team of six'. He was nowhere near as big and brawny as some of his opponents, but he had stamina. 'I have fond memories of the matches against other colleges in which I played for Merton and I shall never forget the many friends I made as a result of playing tennis on grass courts. I recall the captain of tennis who, irrespective of the results, would always say to me after the game: "Well done Hiro".'

Prince Hiro enjoyed jogging, cycling and mountain climbing. In the summer of 1984 he climbed Ben Nevis during a leisurely holiday in Scotland and in 1985 he tackled Snowdon and Scafell Pike in the Lake District. He commented: 'British mountains are not particularly high but you get the feeling that you are among high mountains perhaps because Britain lies in such a northerly latitude.'

He also tried golf but 'found more attraction in sports where I have to move around more'. He was invited by the queen to Royal Ascot in both 1984 and 1985 and watched the races from the royal box. 'Although I did not understand much about racing I saw the races from start to finish and was overwhelmed by the atmosphere.' He was much impressed 'by how relaxed the Queen seemed. For the first time in my life I had a bet on a horse race, but it was a spectacular failure. As it was only a one pound bet it did not have any serious effect on my purse.' He was also invited by the queen to stay at Balmoral.

The prince wanted to see as much as he could of Britain during his stay. He was entertained by a number of aristocratic friends of his father, including the Earl and Countess of Mansfield, who owned Scone Palace in Scotland, and Lord and Lady Saye and Sele, who owned Broughton Castle which was not far from Oxford. On one occasion he stayed incognito in a B&B.

He was well served by his two Metropolitan Police escorts, Roger Bacon and Bruce Ayer:

> They took it in weekly turns to occupy the room next to mine and to provide round the clock protection. As far as I was concerned they did more than provide protection. They were excellent guides to English life. They made all sorts of arrangements for me and helped me with my understanding of documents which were difficult to read...During the two years they were with me I never had any unpleasant moments. They provided me with every possible help during this time and I shall never forget all they did for me.

Prince Hiro's parents, Crown Prince Akihito and Crown Princess Michiko, were understandably interested in seeing how he was getting on. He met them first in Belgium in February 1984 when they stopped off there before a tour of

Africa. They fitted in a visit to London on their way home and Prince Hiro was able to give them a short tour of Oxford. He was able to meet them again in Bergen when they were visiting Norway. He 'was impressed by the strength of the friendly ties between the Japanese Imperial and Norwegian Royal families'. During his stay in Britain he visited thirteen European countries and managed to meet most of the European royalty. When he visited the King of Spain in Majorca, at his request the king arranged for him to see the house where Chopin had lived with Georges Sand. He 'recognized that the warm welcome he received from European royalty was due to the friendly relations, which my parents had built up with them over the years'.

Among his impressions of Britain were the following: 'in Britain the old and the new exist harmoniously side by side ... I felt that, while the British attach importance to old traditions they also have the ability to innovate.' He 'could not avoid feeling the weight of tradition at Oxford', but 'while at first sight there was something incompatible between the old and the new in Britain, British society had been sufficiently flexible and discerning to ensure that there was no confrontation between the two'.

He believed that 'the British usually take a long-term view of things. I felt that the character of the British people lies in generally not forcing the pace when dealing with immediate problems and in thinking about the future implications of what they do.' He also noted:

> The British attach a great deal of importance to their private life and to their own space and time...The British like to enjoy their holidays to the full, It seemed to me that they look on their vacations as an important opportunity to store up energy for their future work, In brief, on the basis of their traditional individualist beliefs, they defend firmly what they regard as strictly personal. There is a tacit understanding that certain areas are mutually inviolable. Is not this the difference of identity between people who live in spaces which are separated from the outside by stone and those who live in spaces separated by very thin partitions made of substances like paper and wood, which can easily be penetrated by anyone?

He also observed 'how adept the British are at social relationships, and the way they show consideration for others by, for instance, holding doors open for people behind them. I was also often aware of their inconspicuous acts of warmth and sympathy for the disabled.' Moreover, he was struck by the attitude of the British and continental people towards 'light':

> In England the winters are cold and the skies cloudy...When I was in my rooms in college I felt the cold and the draughts coming through the cracks and often

> longed for the warmth of life in Japan with its well-heated rooms.[64] One consolation in winter was the fact that the grass remained green throughout the year. If winter seemed long the spring was lovely.

He thought that 'the clothes generally worn by British people were sober and lacking in colour. The fact that this did not seem out of harmony was, I thought, because it was appropriate to the British climate.' 'When back in Tokyo I began to feel my thankfulness for sunshine gradually ebbing away.'

At the conclusion of his memoir Prince Hiro wrote:

> Looking back it seemed to me that the two years had passed in a flash but I had learnt a great deal. I had had many interesting experiences not least at Oxford. Among my experiences were, of course doing my own laundry and ironing! I had been able to see Britain from the inside and meet many people. Through these meetings I had learnt much about British society. I had also, seeing it from the outside, reappraised my own country. All these were irreplaceable experiences for me.

Prince Hiro, or to give him his proper name Prince Naruhito, succeeded his father as crown prince in 1989 when Emperor Hirohito died. As crown prince he returned to Britain on visits in 1991 and 2001 (see below).

THE PRINCE AND PRINCESS OF WALES OFFICIAL VISIT TO JAPAN IN MAY 1986

Prince Charles, the Prince of Wales, had made his first visit to Japan in 1970. In 1986 he and Diana made a six-day visit to Japan as official guests of the Japanese government. This was the most important British royal visit after the queen's state visit in 1975. The royal couple began their tour with an unofficial visit to the Kansai. They arrived at Osaka on the afternoon of Thursday 8 May and went on to Kyoto where they stayed at the Omiya Palace. The following day was spent in Kyoto where they first visited the Shūgakuin detached palace with its fine garden on the slopes of Mt Hiei. Prince Hiro (Naruhito) acted as their guide explaining that the garden had been created before Bach and Handel were born. They went on to visit the Shisendō, a small and secluded temple and garden, to which Sir John Pilcher, the then British ambassador who had studied Japanese in Kyoto before the war, had introduced the prince on his 1970 visit. After a brief rest they went to the Nijō Castle where they attended a garden party jointly hosted by the governor and the mayor of Kyoto and the Kyoto Chamber of Commerce and Industry. They also took part in a tea ceremony performed at Nijō by the tea master Sen Soshitsu and sampled *matcha* (Japanese green powdered tea). Princess Diana was presented with a long-sleeved kimono (*furisode*) with patterns of pine trees, bamboo, plum trees, cranes, waterfalls and pomegranates on a coral-pink background which was said to have taken 100 days to make. Large crowds, estimated at over 100,000, thronged the streets of Kyoto to catch a glimpse of the royal couple.

Their next engagement was a visit to an exhibition of Kyoto products and crafts where they viewed demonstrations of ceramics, dyeing and weaving performed by three outstanding Kyoto artists. In the early evening they were present at a reception hosted by the Kansai Japan-British Society before a Japanese style dinner given in their honour by the then Japanese foreign minister, Abe Shintarō (father of current Prime Minister Abe Shinzō).

On Saturday 10 May, they visited a colour TV plant of Matsushita Electrical Industries (Panasonic) at Ibaraki in Osaka Prefecture. They went on to the Kobe plant of Kawasaki Heavy Industries which had close connections with Rolls Royce. They then flew to Haneda (Tokyo airport) where they viewed a British-made flight simulator used by All Nippon Airways (ANA) in the training of flight crews. Thereafter they were escorted to the Akasaka official guest house where Prime Minister Nakasone Yasuhiro greeted them at an official fifteen-minute welcoming ceremony during which the British and Japanese national anthems were played. The Prime Minister accompanied by his wife introduced them to some of the 400 guests. Afterwards they went into the guest house where they shook hands and chatted informally with some hundred Japanese and foreign journalists. That evening, Crown Prince Akihito and Crown Princess Michiko, who had attended the wedding of the Prince and Princess of Wales in 1981, gave a dinner in their honour.

On Sunday 11 May, the royal couple, following the example set by the queen and Prince Philip, drove in an open-top car slowly along Aoyama enabling large crowds to see them. The glamour of Princess Diana attracted much attention and publicity. The royal couple also went to the Kokugikan to see parts of the spring sumo tournament where they met some of Japan's champion wrestlers.

On Monday 12 May, their first engagement was a visit to the Nissan car plant at Zama outside Tokyo, where the chairman, Ishihara Takashi, who had played an important role in Nissan's decision to invest in Sunderland, welcomed them and guided them around.[65] During the visit the royal couple painted the right eye of a Daruma image to signify their wishes for the success of the investment where production would shortly begin. Princess Diana, according to a report in the *Japan Times* of 13 May, appeared to have been particularly impressed by the fact that all the robots working in the body assembly shop were named after popular actresses and singers and by the fact that pin-ups on the robots were clothed. When they were given two dozen clockwork miniatures of four car models for their children, Princess Diana jokingly said that since they were given so many toys she must have more children.

On their return to Tokyo from Zama, Prime Minister Nakasone and his wife hosted a lunch for them in a Japanese pavilion within the guest house compound. There, according to the *Japan Times*, the princess enjoyed feeding the carp and the prince commended *umeshu* (plum wine) in which they drank toasts. The paper reported that 'a wide range of topics ranging from civilization and natural environment to sumo and Zen' had been discussed.

After lunch the royal couple went on to the Diet where the Prince of Wales gave a speech in the lower house chamber to members of both houses of the Diet. The prince began by quoting Fukuzawa Yukichi, the philosopher modernist who established Keio University and who was one of the first Japanese to visit Britain in the nineteenth century. He had found the British parliament a 'perplexing institution':

> He learned that there were bands of men called political parties who were always fighting one another. His perplexity was compounded when he found that the enemies were to be seen later at the same table eating and drinking with one another...Although he may not have appreciated it at the time, Fukuzawa had in fact identified an essential feature of parliamentary democracy: the mutual tolerance of conflicting points of view...The political institutions of Japan and Britain have evolved along different paths. But we can be justly proud that the present systems of government in our two countries rest on this common principle.

The prince praised Japan as 'a strong and stable bastion, which contributes to the defence of our most cherished ideals of freedom, democracy and all our Western values'. Referring to the roles Japanese and Europeans should play in international society, the prince said:

> At a time when there is division and conflict in the world, the accent needs to be placed on interdependence and solidarity. This is where Japanese and Europeans, with our democratic traditions, our skills and talents, can play a special role together.

The prince thought that Japan could have a unique role to play in terms of mediation in the religious, racial or ideological conflicts and wars which plague the world:

> We are in dire need of more tolerance and in this field the Japanese are particularly gifted because you can communicate easily. You have a sharp eye for observation and are wise enough to listen instead of scatter words in the winds.

While highly valuing the relationship between Japan and Britain, the prince said that there is a 'fundamental problem' that needs to be overcome between the Japanese and non-Japanese people:

> It lies deeper than the problem of balance of trade. It is first of all a problem of communication and cultural gap. We need to exchange more of our cultures and by doing so enrich our creativity.

The people of the two countries needed to have 'direct experience' by visiting the other country instead of just watching television and reading books about each other so that they can deepen mutual understanding. The prince concluded by saying of his visit:

> We will gather many fond memories and will, in turn, pass them on to our children, in the hope that our two countries will grow closer together in mutual understanding and partnership.

After talking with leaders of various parties in the Diet, the royal couple attended a reception hosted by the Japan-British Parliamentarians league. They then went on to the Kabukiza theatre where they saw Onoe Kikugorō's famous play *Kanjinchō* and talked with the actors Ichikawa Danjūrō, who played the part of Benkei, and Onoe Kikugorō, who played the part of Yoshitsune.

That evening they attended a dinner and reception at the British embassy. Some sixty people attended the dinner and some 400 celebrities were invited to the subsequent reception, much on the lines of the similar occasion during the queen's state visit. Crown Prince Akihito and his son, Prince Naruhito (Hiro), attended the dinner.

On Tuesday 13 May, the last day of their visit, the royal couple visited the British embassy to meet members of the staff and then went to NHK broadcasting studios. While Princess Diana, accompanied by Princess Chichibu and Princess Mikasa, visited the Japanese Red Cross Hospital and met some of the children there, the Prince of Wales officially opened the new British Council building in Iidabashi. The royal couple were then the guests of honour at a luncheon hosted by the *Keidanren* (Federation of Economic Organizations) at the New Otani Hotel. Later Prince Charles met Japanese members of the Anglo-Japanese 20th Century Group (now called 21st Century Group).

Their final engagement was an audience with the emperor to whom they presented two books on marine animals in Britain. The audience was followed by a banquet in the palace attended by a total of sixty guests. The emperor had on his right Princess Diana who had Prince Hiro on her other side. Prince

Charles sat between the Crown Prince and Princess Chichibu. While dinner was being served a *gagaku* orchestra played six pieces of classical Japanese music. When the dinner ended the royal couple left for Haneda airport to board their aircraft to return home. It had been a successful and significant visit that helped to maintain close relations between the two monarchies and to promote British interests especially in trade, inward investment and cultural relations.

END OF THE SHŌWA ERA AND THE INAUGURATION OF HIS SUCCESSOR

Emperor Hirohito's health had been declining for some time. In 1987 he had had abdominal surgery and duodenal cancer had been diagnosed. In September 1988, he collapsed and his health worsened. So his death on 7 January 1989 came as no surprise. The state funeral took place on 24 February 1989. The state ceremonies were held at Shinjuku Gyoen in a specially constructed funeral hall. The official guests, who included presidents and monarchs from around the world, were seated in two white tents in front of the funeral hall. Because it was cold and wet many guests used hand warmers and blankets to keep warm during the three-hour Shinto and state ceremonies.[66] At the state ceremony, after Prime Minister Takeshita had given a eulogy, the foreign dignitaries approached the altar and paid their respects by bowing. There were some protests against the inclusion of Shinto rites in the ceremonies on the grounds that their inclusion violated the constitutional separation of state and religion.

Prince Philip, who arrived flying his own plane from Kenya, represented the queen at the funeral. Geoffrey Howe, the British foreign secretary, represented the government. Both were accommodated at the British embassy. Before departing from Japan Prince Philip visited the Commonwealth War Graves Cemetery at Hodogaya.

The emperor's illness and death had unfortunately aroused a good deal of anti-Japanese sentiment in parts of the British media, particularly *The Sun,* which condemned the dying emperor as a war criminal declaring: 'Hell is waiting for this truly vile emperor.' This aroused right-wing fanatics in Tokyo, who plastered obscene anti-British slogans such as 'Queen Elizabeth you must go to hell' on a dustcart which was driven through the streets of Tokyo, stopping outside the British embassy where insults were broadcast over loudspeakers. Sir John Whitehead, the British ambassador lodged a strong protest.

At the enthronement of the Heisei Emperor on 12 November 1990, the Prince of Wales and Princess Diana represented the queen. The prince took with him Dr Carmen Blacker, a Japanese scholar at Cambridge University who specialized in Japanese religion. Her extensive knowledge of Japan and its ancient rituals spurred the prince's interest and helped him to understand what the rituals represented and how they had developed. Extracts from her diary, including an account of some of the rituals associated with the enthronement, have now been published.[67] On Armistice Day, Sunday 11 November 1990, the royal couple attended a remembrance service at the Commonwealth War Graves Cemetery at Hodogaya.

The prince and princess arrived in Japan on 9 November and left on 14 November 1990. Sir John Whitehead, the British ambassador, noted that while 158 countries were represented, 'attendance at the Enthronement while substantial was less high-powered than that at the funeral of the Showa Emperor in early 1989. The Japanese were in less self-congratulatory mood about their emergence on the international stage. A political role consistent with their economic strength still eludes them, as their activities over the Gulf crisis have shown.'

The ceremonies were in two parts. The *Sokui-no-Rei* or solemn proclamation of the emperor's new reign was:

> a brief, solemn, slow-moving occasion, conjuring up visions of ancient Japanese scroll-paintings of court life, but lacking the drama and pageantry of our own Royal occasions. It was nevertheless modern in spoken content, both Emperor and Prime Minister speaking strictly in accordance with the post-war constitution. The open Rolls-Royce parade on the same day was a festive and happy occasion, even though it generated modest rather than overwhelming enthusiasm by the people. The ceremony was an entirely Japanese and Shinto affair, although here too an effort was made to demythologize, but not to demystify the occasion. Security was very tight. There were a number of minor incidents, the responsibility of extreme left-wing groups, but only one serious bomb attack in which a policeman was killed. The whole occasion was greeted with only modest enthusiasm by the Japanese people.

Sir John concluded his telegram reporting the ceremonies and the royal visit in the following words:

> By contrast there was much affection for and fascination with the Prince and Princess of Wales, whose visits to the ceremony and related occasions and to other functions stole the media show. And UK interests – the UK 90 cultural festival, exports and industrial collaboration – were usefully promoted. The visit has helped to further our bilateral relationship with Japan.

CROWN PRINCE NARUHITO AND JAPANESE CULTURE IN BRITAIN

The Japan Society celebrated its centenary in 1991. A large-scale Japan Festival in the United Kingdom was held to mark the occasion. The Prince of Wales and the crown prince agreed to become royal patrons and graced various events during the Festival. The aim of the Festival, apart from promoting greater knowledge and understanding of Japanese culture, was to demystify Japan and clear away misconceptions.

David Barrie, who was executive director of the festival, gave his account in a lecture which he gave to the Society on 18 February 1992 under the title 'Behind the Scenes at the Japan Festival 1991'.[68] As Barrie explained, the festival included over sixty official events in some 200 venues across the country. As the chairman of the Japan Society from 1985 to 1995, I wanted the Society to celebrate its centenary in style. Martin Campbell White and Sir Ian Hunter of Harold Holt, a prominent concert agency, embraced the idea and an organizing committee was established. Sir Peter Parker, whom I had known from Japanese studies during the war and who had wide business contacts, agreed to chair the committee. He proved to be an enthusiastic and efficient leader and he gathered significant sponsorship. Saba Shōichi, a former chairman of Toshiba with many links to Britain, chaired a Japan committee for the festival. We were fortunate in securing at an early stage royal and imperial patronage. This and the presence of our patrons at festival events significantly helped to make the festival the success it undoubtedly was.

The festival was opened at a ceremony at the Victoria and Albert Museum on 16 September 1991.[69] After opening words from Sir Peter Parker, the Prince of Wales noted that 'never before in Britain had such a concentrated effort been made to explore and celebrate the many facets of a single foreign culture'. The festival offered 'the opportunity to discover, explore and enjoy an astonishingly wide cross-section of Japanese culture, popular and high-brow, ancient and modern – from Sumo wrestling to Noh theatre, from archery on horseback (*yabusame*) to avant-garde Art'. The prince gave a special welcome to the festival's education programme. He had visited Japan on a number of occasions and he vividly recalled the warmth of the hospitality extended to him and his wife on his visit.

Mr Saba Shōichi then spoke briefly on behalf of the Japan Committee and invited the crown prince to speak. The crown prince started by saying that he had 'always observed relations between the two countries closely and with great interest', especially since his days at Oxford. He recalled 'the great contributions the [Japan] Society has made by fostering for many years, the bond between our two countries. It is also a great occasion to strengthen our relations for the future.'

After the speeches the Prince of Wales presented the prime minister (John Major) and the foreign secretary (Douglas Hurd) and other cabinet ministers and VIPs to the crown prince. Later in the day the two princes returned to the Victoria and Albert Museum to open the festival's flagship exhibition and then went over to the Science Museum to open the robotics exhibition. That evening the crown prince attended a performance at the Royal Festival Hall by the Saito Kinen Orchestra conducted by Seiji Ozawa.

On the following morning both princes met again at Holland Park where they opened the Kyoto Garden, a beautiful and permanent reminder of the festival. The princes toured the garden before taking tea prepared by the Urasenke school of tea ceremony and viewing an ikebana exhibit in the Orangery. In the course of his week-long programme in the United Kingdom, the prince attended Japan Festival events in Scotland, Wales, Northern Ireland and Newcastle (during his visit to the North-East of England, he returned to Cragside, the Armstrong mansion that his father had visited in 1953).

On the evening of 17 September, the lord mayor of London, Sir Alexander Graham, gave a reception at the Guildhall to mark the Japan Society's centenary. In his speech of welcome the lord mayor stressed the British welcome to Japanese investment and paid a 'tribute to the contribution that Japanese companies and institutions have made to the smooth and efficient operation of our reconstructed [post 'big-bang'] financial markets in the City of London'.

As chairman of the Japan Society, I responded and expressed the Society's thanks to a number of lord mayors of London who had entertained members of the Society. The Japan Festival demonstrated Japan's cultural achievements. I hoped that it would help to further mutual understanding, 'But it must not be a one-off event. There needs to be a consistent follow-up.'

The crown prince in his concluding speech recalled 'with great pleasure' the evening in 1984 when he was a student at Merton College and the Society had invited him to the annual dinner. He also recalled the farewell reception that the Society had given for him shortly before his return to Japan 'on this date exactly six years ago'. He hoped that the Japan Society 'with its long traditions will continue to prosper over the coming years'.

The crown prince returned to Britain ten years later in support of 'Japan 2001'.[70] This lasted for eleven months beginning in May 2001 with a *Matsuri* in Hyde Park and opening concerts and exhibitions. As Christopher Purvis, its chief executive, explained, 'the emphasis shifted to outdoor events in the summer. There was a great autumn season of theatre and museums. And then we actually extended right through to March 2002 in order to allow school exchanges at the end of the Japanese academic year. At the final count there were 2,087 events attended by 3 million different people, many of whom attended more than one event.' Much emphasis was placed on 'grass roots' events. 'Events happened if people wanted them to happen and were willing to make them happen.'

It was agreed fairly early on in the preparation process that the joint patrons of Japan 2001 would be the Prince of Wales and the crown prince of Japan. It was considered to be important to have the support of the two royal families for the success of the whole year. It was also decided that the majority of events during the year would be self-defining. The organizers would give encouragement by the provision of grants but would not directly manage each event. The exception to this general rule was the '*Matsuri* – Japan in the Park'. It was important to put on a major event to launch the festival and this had to be directly managed. It was held over the weekend 19 and 20 May 2001. The presence on the Sunday of the Prince of Wales and the crown prince was an important ingredient in the success of the *Matsuri* – creating a dynamic start to the whole year. Approximately 215,000 people attended over the weekend. There was a happy, more or less spontaneous, participation by the two princes in the *odori* (dance).

On the evening of 20 May there was a concert of the Philharmonia Orchestra conducted by Vladimir Ashkenazy with Suwanai Akiko playing. The occasion was used to hold an opening reception for all the corporate sponsors of Japan 2001. The crown prince and the Duke of Gloucester, royal patron of the Japan Society, were the guests of honour.

HEISEI EMPEROR (AKIHITO) STATE VISIT TO BRITAIN 1998

The state visit of Emperor Akihito to Britain in 1998 was the most significant event of the Heisei era in terms of relations between the two monarchies. The 1971 Japanese state visit of Emperor Hirohito and Empress Nagako had created a precedent, and following the queen's state visit to Japan in 1975 it was the Japanese turn to repay the compliment. Britain responded by arranging a visit with all the pomp and ceremony for which the British Royal Household is famed.

As crown prince, Emperor Akihito had been in Britain in 1953 to attend the queen's coronation, and after his stay at Windsor in 1976, he had made an official visit to Britain in 1981 to attend the wedding of the Prince and Princess of Wales; on this occasion he had also made brief tours of Scotland and Wales (see above).

The programme of the state visit followed the trusted pattern of state visits with variations to take account of Japanese interests and the personal interests of the emperor and empress. During the visit, the emperor, as his father and grandfather before him, was made a Knight of the Garter.

The preparations for the state visit of the Heisei Emperor in 1998 were dominated by three considerations. First, by that time, the policy initiated by

Prime Minister Thatcher in seeking to encourage Japanese inward investment into the UK had achieved significant success. Although she had left power many years before, successor governments had espoused her policy and wished to signify this through the state visit. Secondly, the emperor's scientific and research credentials had been widely welcomed and were thought to be worthy of recognition by learned institutions in the UK. Thirdly, and most sensitively, any state visit from Japan was likely to provoke hostile attention from organizations representing Far Eastern Prisoners of War (FEPOWs), dissatisfied with the continuing failure of successive Japanese governments to offer either an apology or compensation for their treatment of the former prisoners of war.

The first two of the considerations mentioned above were easily and constructively accommodated. Much attention was paid to the representatives of Japanese companies that had invested in the UK in events involving the emperor and empress. The visit to Cardiff was presented as recognition both of the strength of devolution in the UK and the role played by Japanese companies in the Welsh economy. As for the emperor's scientific and research credentials, these were fully acknowledged by his interaction with learned societies during the visit. However, efforts which had been made in the years before the state visit to take the sting out of the justified resentment and anger on the part of the prisoners of war and their representatives had not been successful. Much work had been done in 1994–1995 to negotiate the text of an apology to be used by both governments on the 50th anniversary of the end of the Pacific War. The negotiations on the language of the apology were conducted by David Wright on the FCO side, as the then deputy under-secretary responsible for UK foreign policy outside Europe and the Middle East, and on the Japanese side, by Numata Sadaaki, minister in the Japanese embassy in London.

Ironically, that work, which had seen both governments working harmoniously to find language to satisfy both sides, proved nugatory when the then Japanese Prime Minister Murayama failed to use the joint statement at the time planned. All that notwithstanding, the terms of the apology were never likely to satisfy the UK FEPOWs' aspirations both in terms of language and also the possibility of financial compensation.

Nevertheless, the work was important in preparatory terms for the UK government in advance of the state visit. There was a general election in 1997 which brought the Labour Party to power led by Tony Blair. He visited Japan at the beginning of 1998 for the UK Festival in Japan and during his talks in Tokyo on that visit, the handling of the FEPOWs' aspirations played an important part. The visit concluded with the appearance of an article in *The Sun* about the issue, the text of which had been heavily influenced by contributions from the UK officials responsible for the visit.

Sadly, these efforts failed to draw the sting from the FEPOWs issue during planning for the state visit. The FEPOW organisation had enlisted the support of legal specialists familiar with cases involving claims deriving from conflict. This added to their platform and the attention paid to their claims by the UK media. It became clear before the state visit took place that the FEPOWs would not be persuaded from registering a public protest at the emperor's visit as it was taking place and particularly would not be dissuaded by the argument that they risked embarrassing the queen.

The protest took place on the first day of the state visit following the formal arrival ceremonies at Horse Guards Parade. As the carriage procession bearing the imperial and royal couples reached the Mall, a body of FEPOWs which had gathered ostensibly to view the procession turned their backs on the imperial and royal couples as they passed by. It was little more than a fleeting moment in the procession and indeed in the entire state visit. But it attracted and secured much media attention and was widely viewed in the UK.

That was, however, very much the end of the matter in terms of what passed off as a successful state visit with the aim of demonstrating the strength of the political, business, cultural and scientific relationship between the UK and Japan. The demonstration on the Mall did not detract from any of these objectives, nor did it seem to affect the sense of enjoyment which the emperor and empress showed about their reception in the UK.

Since that time and naturally given the passage of time since the Second World War, the FEPOWs issue has ceased to occupy the prominent position in bilateral relations which it held in the 1980s and 1990s. In part, this is because economic growth in China, Korea and South East Asia has resulted in their indigenous bitterness about the Japanese occupation in the Second World War becoming a less significant issue in those nations' relationships with Japan. As far as the UK is concerned, some benefit and alleviation in bitterness has been achieved through an imaginative scheme, supported by both the UK and Japanese governments, to arrange visits to Japan for the grandchildren of FEPOWs which gave them an opportunity to observe Japanese life and customs for themselves. This scheme has developed further by bringing high school students from both countries together to participate jointly in scientific research projects. This scheme has been promoted through Cambridge University and schools in East Anglia. It has not only brought teenagers together from both countries, it has also given them a chance to work together in academically productive work, as well as experiencing life in their respective countries.

Emperor Akihito and Empress Michiko, through their earlier visits and through their sons, Prince Naruhito and Fumihito, who had enjoyed their time at Oxford, had an understanding of and affection for Britain. Fortunately, the sour response of some of the tabloid press did not deter them from making later visits to Britain. In 2012, relatively soon after he had undergone heart surgery, the emperor and empress made a five-day visit to Britain, to attend a lunch at Windsor Castle to mark the queen's diamond jubilee: he was one of only two reigning monarchs to have attended the Coronation.[71]

The emperor and empress arrived at Heathrow from Portugal on Monday 25 May. The following morning, they received the traditional welcome by the queen and the Duke of Edinburgh on the Horse Guards Parade and then, after the emperor had reviewed the Guard of Honour, the queen with the emperor in one carriage and the empress with the Duke of Edinburgh in the second carriage were driven with the members of their suite in open carriages in a ceremonial procession to Buckingham Palace. (There had been rain and for this reason the coaches used for the royal and imperial couples were closed.) While they were welcomed by many groups of onlookers with Japanese flags, a group of former prisoners of war turned their backs in protest against their ill treatment during the war, but the protests, such as they were, were peaceful.[72]

After the customary lunch at Buckingham Palace, where the emperor and empress stayed, they went to Westminster Abbey to lay a wreath on the tomb of the unknown warrior before taking tea with the Queen Mother at Clarence House. In the evening they were the guests of honour at a state banquet. In his speech in reply to the queen, the emperor expressed his sorrow for the suffering inflicted during the war and his sadness that bilateral relations had been marred:

> The Empress and I can never forget the many kinds of suffering so many people have undergone because of the war… At the thought of the scars of war that they bear, our hearts are filled with deep sorrow and pain. All through our visit here this thought will never leave our minds…At the same time may we express our profound respect and gratitude to those people who, despite such past sufferings, looking towards the future, have dedicated immeasurable efforts to the cause of friendship between our two countries. I sincerely hope that our two peoples can continue to strive for true mutual understanding and can join hands in the cause of world peace and prosperity.

On Wednesday, the imperial couple flew in an RAF aircraft to Cardiff where on arrival Prince Charles greeted them. A welcoming ceremony was held at Cardiff Castle and the couple watched a performance of Welsh singing and dancing. The decision to include a visit to Wales in their itinerary underlined the importance Britain attached to Japanese investment and the role that the Prince of Wales had played in promoting Japanese interest in Wales.

That evening they attended a banquet at the Guildhall where they were received by an honour guard and the playing of the Japanese national anthem. Before dinner the couple were taken to the library where they were shown the Magna Carta, one of the City of London's treasures. Their first engagement on Thursday 28 May was a visit to the Royal Botanic Gardens at Kew where they viewed the recently restored copy of the Chokushimon and the Japanese gardens and chatted informally with British participants in the Japan Exchange and Teaching (JET) programme. From Kew they returned to central London for lunch at No. 10 Downing Street with the Prime Minister, Tony Blair and Mrs Blair. In the afternoon, they visited the Royal Society where the emperor was presented with the King Charles II Medal and Certificate in recognition of his scientific research. That evening they gave a return banquet and reception at the Victoria and Albert Museum.

They had a varied schedule on Friday 29 May, the last day of their official visit. The emperor went first to the Linnean Society of which he is an honorary member. He spoke there with fellow ichthyologists and viewed an exhibit on gobies. Meanwhile the empress visited the National Headquarters of the British Red Cross Society where she met volunteers and members of the staff. They then together attended a reception given by the Japan Society, the Nippon Club, the Japanese Chamber of Commerce and Industry and the Japan Association at Grosvenor House Hotel and talked with members of these organizations. In the afternoon the emperor, as an honorary member of Royal Zoological Society, as his father had done on his state visit in 1971, went to the zoo in Regent's Park.

They stayed on in Britain privately in Buckinghamshire for two further nights. The emperor, who is a keen naturalist, spent some time on Saturday 30 May visiting Wells Farm in Little Milton which maintains a conservationist farm policy. The empress, who was much interested in English literature, took advantage of their proximity to Oxford by visiting the Bodleian Library. On Sunday 31 they departed for Copenhagen to pay a state visit to Denmark.

THE PRINCE OF WALES AND THE DUCHESS OF CORNWALL'S OFFICIAL VISIT TO JAPAN IN OCTOBER 2008.

As described above the Prince of Wales had visited Japan in 1970 for Expo '70, had made an official visit with Princess Diana in 1986 and had attended Emperor Akihito's enthronement ceremonies together with Princess Diana in 1990. He was invited to pay a further official visit with his wife Camilla, Duchess of Cornwall, to mark the 150th anniversary of the signing of the Treaty of Amity and Commerce between Britain and Japan in 1858. Their visit, which lasted five days, began on 27 October 2008.

This royal trip had a strongly environmental theme. The financial crisis had burst on the world the previous month, and the centrepiece of the royal programme was a speech given by the Prince at the Miraikan (Science Museum) in Tokyo, in which he argued that the need to address the 'climate crunch' as well as the 'credit crunch' had to be a crucial element of the world's response to financial instability. His speech concluded with a thirty-second projection on a giant screen behind him of the Miraikan's 'geo-cosmos' simulation of the pace of global warming between 1900 and 2100.

The prince also attended a round-table meeting between senior business representatives from his Corporate Leaders' Group on Climate Change (including senior advisers from Shell, Johnson Matthey and Standard Chartered Bank) and Japanese industry. The session ended with a sense that Japanese companies – who had been hesitant about setting ambitious, holistic targets on emissions reductions – were attracted by working more closely with foreign firms in this area, and this helped the inevitably slow process of getting Japanese government and industry to think creatively about how to contribute to the United Nations process that culminated in the Paris agreement of 2015.

The prince focused in his speech on the link between deforestation and climate change – it was a theme also of his visit immediately afterwards to Indonesia – and he was able to travel out of Tokyo, together with Princess Takamado, to visit the Afan Woodland Conservation Project in Nagano, run by C. W. Nicol, a Welsh-born, Japanese-naturalised environmentalist, who had reforested farmland which had been left as derelict scrub after the Second World War, and reintroduced principles of sustainable management. The prince also met Japanese schoolchildren working as climate change champions on a visit to Sharp's energy-saving technology R&D centre.

The royal couple were also guests of honour at a special reception to mark 'U.K. Japan 2008' year during which a series of over 300 events, performances and exhibitions focused on the arts, science and creative industries were arranged by the British embassy and British Council. In addition, while in Tokyo the royal couple visited Keiō University which had been founded by Fukuzawa Yukichi, whose writings the prince had cited in a speech to members of the Diet during his 1986 visit. At the university they viewed displays of traditional arts.

Prior to their official visit to Tokyo, the Prince of Wales and the Duchess of Cornwall visited Nara, which the prince had not been able to do on his previous visits to Japan. In Nara they went to the Tōdaiji Temple and the Shōsōin (Imperial Treasure House), where they saw preservation work on artefacts preserved from the Heian period.

In Tokyo the royal couple had private dinners with the emperor and empress, and with the crown prince and crown princess, as well as meeting the prime minister and Mrs Aso. With all the senior politicians and business figures he met, the prince discussed his initiative to preserve the rainforests, and got positive reactions. Three walkabouts, in Tokyo and Nara, were marked by genuine warmth and enthusiasm from Japanese people of all ages.

The press coverage of the trip was dominated by the environmental messages, as well as the prince's exposure to the cutting edge of Japanese innovation. At the Miraikan, he saw a four-foot high humanoid robot, Asimo, who performed a disco dance, standing on one leg, then the other, and bidding the royal visitor 'bye-bye'. From this exhibition of robotic terpsichore, as the *Daily Telegraph* correspondent commented, 'the Prince kept a safe distance of more than ten feet'. The content of the programme brought home how royal visits today can never be pure ceremonial, but have to supplement and exemplify broader political and social themes.

THE VISIT OF PRINCE WILLIAM, DUKE OF CAMBRIDGE, TO JAPAN, FEBRUARY 2015

A new generation was coming to the fore. Prince William, Duke of Cambridge, the elder son of the Prince of Wales and second in line to the throne, increasingly assumed royal duties substituting on occasions for his father and grandmother. He did not know Japan and the Japanese imperial family had not been invited to send a representative to Prince William's wedding to Kate Middleton. It was time to reconfirm Britain's commitment to close relations with Japan and the importance attached to relations between the two monarchies.

The advice of the British government was that the prince should undertake substantial visits to both China and Japan. Given the complex relations between the two countries at the time, the question of order and length of respective visits was highly contested. The final decision was that, given the important links between the imperial and royal families, Japan was the natural first leg; and the length of the two legs was kept very similar to avoid any criticism.

The original plan had been for Prince William and his wife to go to Japan together, but the duchess was seven months pregnant with their second child and could not accompany her husband. Prince William arrived on Thursday 26 February 2015 for a four-day visit. Rather than the conventional road trip from

Haneda Airport into the city centre, Prince William chose to travel by speed boat through Tokyo harbour, passing through the Rainbow Bridge, so that the first images of his arrival would be set against the modern Tokyo skyline and the newly-developed waterside. The governor of Tokyo, Masazoe Yōichi, kindly provided the boat and showed him places that were to host aquatic events in the 2020 Olympic Games. Prince William alighted at the Hama Detached Palace where the first British royal visitor to Japan, Prince Alfred, Duke of Edinburgh and second son of Queen Victoria, had stayed in 1869. He was greeted by large crowds as well as by rain – and joked that he was an *ameotoko* (a man upon whom rain often falls). Some of those who greeted him perhaps remembered his mother, Princess Diana, who had become a popular icon for young Japanese. In the grounds, now a public park, the prince took part in a Japanese tea ceremony.

His first engagement on Friday 27 February was a visit to the Commonwealth War Graves Cemetery at Hodogaya. In choosing to make this visit he was following a long-standing royal tradition. Previous visitors had included the queen and Prince Philip as well as his father and mother. (Princess Diana had repeated earlier visits to the cemetery by going there on her last visit to Japan in 1995, and the prince was shown an album of pictures recording her visits.)

Prince William went from Yokohama to the imperial palace in Tokyo where he was entertained to lunch by the emperor and empress, whom he had met previously when they attended the queen's diamond jubilee. In the afternoon he had tea with Crown Prince Naruhito. In the evening he was guest of honour at a dinner hosted by the British ambassador and Mrs Hitchens. One of the guests was a top sumo champion (*yokozuna*) who arrived in a Bentley, which is a status symbol in Britain although the company is now German-owned.

The prince had a busy day on Saturday 28 February. He visited two shopping malls in Tokyo where British products were on display, including a shiny Aston Martin car into which the prince climbed together with the chief executive of the company. He also found time to visit NHK studios, where he was induced to put on the glittering helmet and red coat of a samurai in service to the shogun and to watch three geisha actresses dance. The press gleefully took photos of the prince in this amusing attire.

Later the prince proceeded to the Fukushima area with the Japanese Prime Minister Abe Shinzō to pay tribute to the victims of the Tōhoku 2012 earthquake and tsunami. Together they visited an athletic centre in the city of Motomiya, which had been opened in 2012 as a safe place for recreation in an area where there was less danger of radiation. The prince talked with local children, who were said to have been impressed with his juggling skills. The prince and the prime minister also took part in a tree-planting ceremony to express the wish for a quick recovery in the devastated area. In the evening the prime minister invited the prince and his entourage to a Japanese restaurant in Kōriyama where, dressed informally in *yukata*, they ate a dinner made from local ingredients. This was doubtless intended to demonstrate that local produce whose sales had suffered badly in the aftermath of the tsunami was once again safe to eat.

On the Sunday, the last day of his visit before he left for China, Prince William visited a local newspaper office in Ishinomaki on the coastline which had stayed open throughout and in the aftermath of the disaster, providing information and consolation to those left alive. He also visited a community centre in Onagawa, where the Japan Society and other UK-connected organizations had quickly responded to reports of the disaster; they had launched an appeal for donations and did their best to ensure that donations reached the grass roots.

There was some criticism in the media that Prime Minister Abe was using the prince's visit to boost his own agenda, but the prince made a good impression on all the Japanese he met by his unstuffy and genial attitude. The decision to visit the disaster area demonstrated British sympathy for the sufferers who had benefitted from the help given by British charities. As the prince left Sendai *Shinkansen* station, he was mobbed by several hundred young people from the city, eager to wish him farewell.

OTHER BRITISH ROYAL VISITORS TO JAPAN

Prince Philip, Duke of Edinburgh, first visited Japan in September 1945 while serving in the British Pacific Fleet. From 1987, at his suggestion, Duke of Edinburgh prizes have been awarded every other year by the Japan Academy to a Japanese scientist for outstanding achievements in the area of wildlife protection and species preservation.[73]

In addition to accompanying the queen on her state visit in 1975 and representing her at the funeral of the Showa emperor in 1989 (both visits described above), Prince Philip made three other visits in October 1982, October 1984 and October 1986. These visits were primarily in support of the WWF (World Wide Fund for Nature) and the preservation of endangered species. The duke was president of WWF International from 1981 to 1996 and has been president emeritus since 1997.

The duke and WWF were much concerned about the preservation of species of wild life in Japan which were in danger of extinction. Three endangered species in Japan in particular had been brought to his attention. The first of these was the *tanchōzuru* (red-crested crane), which had feeding stations in Hokkaido. The second was the Iriomote *yamaneko* (Iriomote wild cat), a subspecies of the leopard cat, which survives only on Iriomote island in the Nansei-Shotō island group. (It had been listed as a critically endangered species, as only a small number of adult animals remain.)[74] The third was the *toki* (Japanese crested ibis) of which only a very few had survived on the island of Sado in the Japan Sea.

During his first WWF visit in 1982 (31 October-4 November), the duke took the opportunity to visit the feeding sites of the *tanchōzuru* (Japanese red crested crane) near Kushiro in Hokkaido. As British ambassador at the time, I accompanied the duke to Hokkaido making use of a British Aerospace HS146, which the company were anxious to sell in Japan. On this visit the duke met the emperor as he did on his two subsequent visits in 1984 and 1986. The crown prince and princess as well as Princess Chichibu came to the British embassy for a reception that I hosted in his honour.

During his visit in October 1984, the duke spoke at a seminar on conservation of wild life in the Nansei Shotō island group, which has a unique collection of animals including the Iriomote wild cat and to which he made a short visit.[75] He made a speech at a WWF fund-raising dinner at the Okura Hotel at which Crown Prince Akihito and Crown Princess Michiko were present. He also spoke at a WWF forum on 'The plight of wildlife - the panda as one example'.

The duke's visit from 7 to 11 October 1986 was made on behalf of the *Fédération Equestre Internationale* of which he was president 1964–86. He also gave a speech during this visit at another WWF fund-raising dinner in which he welcomed Prince Fumihito (Akishino) as president of WWF Japan. He drew attention to the increasing threats to the natural environment and the vital need for effective conservation measures.

□

Anne, The Princess Royal, made three official visits to Japan in 1983, 1990 and 1999. In 1991 she went to Japan for five days in her capacity as the president of the *Fédération Équestre Internationale* (she held this post from 1986 until 1994). In 1998 she attended the winter Olympics in Nagano.

Her first official visit was from 22 April to 6 May 1983. On this occasion she was accompanied by her first husband, Captain Mark Phillips. Their principal royal engagements were lunch at the palace hosted by Emperor Hirohito and attended by Crown Prince Akihito and Princess Michiko and other members of the imperial family, dinner with the crown prince and princess and lunch with Princess Chichibu. As British ambassador I gave a dinner in her honour which was attended by Princess Chichibu.

The main event of their visit was a gala performance of *Manon* by the Royal Ballet at Tokyo Bunka Kaikan, which was attended by the crown prince and princess, Prince Hiro (Naruhito), Princess Chichibu and other members of the imperial family. This was followed by a reception at the embassy. The princess and Captain Mark Phillips supported British economic interests by visiting Fujitsu and Honda and the Mitsukoshi department store. They were also given a guided tour of Nikkō and, in view of their equestrian interests, of the imperial stock farm.

The second official visit to Japan by the Princess Royal took place from 16 to 23 September 1990. The first part of her stay was devoted to attendance at sessions of the International Olympic Committee and supporting a bid by Manchester to host the Olympic Games. The main purpose of the princess's visit on this occasion was to give royal support for UK90, a major promotion of British culture. Her first engagement was to attend a gala reception at the British embassy and a showing of the film of Henry V. She visited the Isetan department store in Shinjuku to view a Victoria and Albert Museum exhibition and went to the Mitsukoshi department store to see a British fashion show and design exhibition. At the Tokyo Museum of Western Art, she opened a William Blake exhibition. She also attended a performance of Shakespeare's *Richard III* at the National Theatre.

The final day of her visit, Saturday 22 September, was a very busy one. She lunched at the imperial palace with Emperor Akihito and Empress Michiko. Before and after lunch she made various visits in support of UK90. She went to the Setagaya Museum of Modern Art to see a 'British Art for Now' exhibition, to the Tōkyū department store to see a Rossetti exhibition and to Takashimaya department where she was received by the winner of the 'Miss Alice look-alike' competition and viewed an exhibition of British Contemporary Art and a Peter Rabbit exhibition. In all the stores she visited she encouraged by her presence the efforts of British consumer goods exporters. In the evening she attended a concert given by the Academy of St Martin in the Fields conducted by Sir Neville Marriner.

The princess's third official visit to Japan took place from 8 to 11 March 1999. She concentrated during this visit on support for some of the charities of which she is the royal patron. In Tokyo, she visited HELP Asian Women's shelter for battered wives and Grace House, a maternity centre for pregnant women in need. Later she went to the National Welfare Centre for Disabled Persons. In Osaka, she visited another centre for the disabled where she viewed performances by the disabled of drumming, dancing and judo. She also met representatives of Save the Children Fund and other charities including the Missions to Seamen, Animal Refuge and aid for victims of the Hanshin earthquake that had caused so much damage and casualties in the Kobe/Osaka area in 1995. Other engagements included attendance at a Commonwealth Day reception at the British embassy, a Liberty Style exhibition, the Millennium Science Forum exhibition and a 'Noble Horse' reception. The princess had tea with the emperor and empress and dinner with Prince Tomohito of Mikasa and Princess Nobuko. The British ambassador, Sir David Wright, gave a dinner for the Princess Royal, which was attended by Princess Nori, the daughter of the emperor, who left the imperial family when she married.

□

Prince Edward, Duke of Kent, made seven official visits to Japan between February 1971 and May 2000. On each of his visits he had an audience with the emperor and also took the opportunity of his visits to renew contacts with other members of the imperial family. He remembers in particular how friendly Princess Chichibu had been. These visits were all trade-related and made primarily in his capacity as Vice-Chairman of the British Overseas Trade Board (i.e, the royal adviser on overseas trade to the British government).[76] The purpose of his official visit with the Duchess of Kent in September 1973 was to open the British Export Marketing Centre on Aoyama-dōri in Tokyo.[77] In this capacity he welcomed the hundred-strong Japanese import promotion mission to Britain in March 1979.

□

Prince Richard, Duke of Gloucester, first visited Japan in 1969, when he was known as Prince Richard of Gloucester, as part of a round the world trip. He stayed with his elder brother, Prince William of Gloucester (see above), who was serving in the embassy at the time. Prince William, who had his own aeroplane, took him to Kyushu and other parts of Japan. Prince Richard, who qualified as an architect having studied architecture at Cambridge, also visited Japan privately on a couple of occasions, as well as in his capacity as president of the then British Consultants Bureau, leading one trade mission during the 'Action Japan' campaign in the 1990s.

He and the Duchess of Gloucester made an official visit to Japan in 1998 to give royal support for the UK 98 Festival. During their stay in Tokyo they were received by the emperor and empress and called on the crown prince and princess. On 22 July 1998 the duke opened the Science Museum and Lifestyle Exhibition at Tokyo International Forum. Among their other engagements were visits to the Science for Life Exhibition at Tokyo University and to an exhibition and reception given by British Telecom. They also attended receptions for British JET Programme participants. Outside Tokyo, the duke visited the British Industry Centre of the British Chamber of Commerce in Japan at Yokohama as well as a Virtual Reality Techno designed by Richard Rogers and partners near Gifu and as a British designed housing project. The duke and duchess also visited Kyoto. Since 1995, the duke has been the patron of the Japan Society.

RELATIONS BETWEEN THE TWO MONARCHIES IN THE TWENTY-FIRST CENTURY

The assumption must be that the monarchical system will survive in both countries. There is very little support in either Britain or Japan for replacement of the monarchy by a republican system and in neither country is there a credible leader with the following and charisma needed to replace the monarch. But it is undeniable that monarchical systems are now the exception and exist in only a few countries apart from Britain and Japan. In Western Europe the only monarchies left, in addition to Britain are in Denmark, Norway, Sweden, the Netherlands, Belgium and Spain (plus the Grand Duchy of Luxembourg and the principalities of Liechtenstein and Monaco). In Asia the only monarchies now are those in Thailand, Bhutan, Cambodia, Tonga and Brunei, and the only others in the world are a few in the Middle East (Bahrain, Jordan, Saudi Arabia and Oman) and in Africa (Swaziland, Lesotho and Morocco).

The popularity of the monarchy depends on its ability to adapt to the changing world. The queen, during her long reign, has managed this task with great success. Her only misreading of public opinion was over the death of Princess Diana, largely because of the breakdown of the princess's marriage to Prince Charles. The queen and her family were saved by a combination of their response to popular opinion and a well-judged intervention of the Prime Minister, Tony Blair. Prince Philip's occasional politically incorrect remarks have done no harm to his image as a loyal and supportive consort; indeed, they have endeared him to many. Prince Charles is increasingly seen as a worthy and socially-aware successor.

The queen has been very careful not to become involved in political controversies. The palace denied that she was a supporter of Brexit, but she could not totally hide her hope that the union of Scotland with England would be maintained. Her firm belief in the British Commonwealth of Nations has never wavered, as she made clear in her expressed wish that Prince Charles should succeed her as head of the Commonwealth: this was agreed at the Commonwealth Heads of Government meeting in London in 2018.

Through her weekly audiences with the prime ministers who have come and gone during her reign and through the state papers which she reads conscientiously, she has maintained a close understanding of political, economic and social developments. We do not know how far she may have influenced the policies of her governments by her judicious private advice.

The Prince of Wales has strong views on many issues from the environment to architecture and his letters to ministers urging certain courses of action have leaked out, causing some consternation. When he succeeds his mother, he will need to ensure that as a constitutional monarch he maintains a strictly neutral position on political issues, which he shows every sign of understanding. But to achieve this outcome he will need guidance and perceptive advice from his staff.

The future lies with Prince Charles's two sons, Prince William, the Duke of Cambridge, who will in due course become Prince of Wales, and Prince Harry, who, on his marriage on 19 May 2018 to Meghan Markle, became Duke of Sussex. Princess Kate, Duchess of Cambridge, comes from a middle-class English family while Princess Meghan is an American of mixed race. They bring the royal family into the twenty-first century, reflecting the growing diversity in British society. They will increasingly have to perform royal duties as their uncles, cousins and aunt gradually bow out and the focus increasingly is on the immediate family of the monarch.

The monarchy in Japan was forced to change as a result of the Second World War and the new constitution of 1947. The emperor became a symbol with no political power and precluded from taking any initiatives that could remotely be interpreted as political; in this respect, he has even less power than the queen currently has.

A new generation is also taking over in Japan. Crown Prince Naruhito, who while studying at Oxford was known as Prince Hiro, is due to become the next emperor in May 2019 following the carefully planned and politically approved abdication of his father, Emperor Akihito, who will be known as the Heisei Emperor after the name of the era marked by his reign as emperor.

His brother, Prince Akishino (Fumihito), will become the heir apparent and his son, the young Prince Hisahito, born in 2006, will be second in line of succession. As there are no other male princes in the imperial family and since, under the current rules, princesses have no right to succession and must leave the imperial family on marriage, the succession and thus the imperial dynasty can be said to 'hang by a thread'.

Until Prince Hisahito was born in 2006, it seemed likely that the Imperial Household Law of 1947, which had retained the exclusion of females from the succession as in the original Imperial Household Law of 1889, would have to be altered to allow a female to succeed. Crown Princess Masako seems to have been subjected to considerable psychological pressure to produce an heir and there was disappointment among conservative elements in the Japanese establishment when, after the birth of her daughter Princess Aiko (Toshi) in 2001, it seemed unlikely that she would produce a further child. This made a change in the succession law imperative.

In January 2005, the then Prime Minister Koizumi Junichirō accordingly appointed a special panel of judges, academics and officials to study possible amendments to the law and make recommendations. The adoption of a male child by the emperor from one of the branches of the imperial family which had lost their status after the Second World War was considered but not adopted. The group of experts appointed by the government instead recommended that succession follow the rule of absolute primogeniture, as is the case in Britain today. But this was strongly opposed by conservative lawmakers who abhorred the possibility that Japan might have an empress instead of an emperor. There have in fact been some eight empresses in Japan's recorded history. The first of these was the Empress Suiko, who reigned between 593 and 628, and the last was Empress Go-Sakuramachi, who reigned 1762–1771.

The birth of Prince Hisahito in 2006 was greeted with relief in Japan, particularly among conservatives who show misogynist tendencies. The then Prime Minister Abe Shinzō took this as an excuse to drop the proposals to alter the succession law. Debate about the need to amend the law and allow Japanese princesses to retain their imperial status on marriage has, however, continued, and a majority in Japan now probably favours allowing a female to succeed should there be no male heir.

The requirement that princesses lose imperial status on marriage has meant that the imperial family has shrunk in numbers thus reducing the opportunities for the development of relations with foreign royalty. The conservative elements in the imperial household have generally been resistant to efforts to popularize and humanize the monarchy, preferring to maintain their life 'above the clouds'. They are critical of the scandals, which have at times affected the prestige of the British royal family, in which three of the queen's four children have divorced. The marriage of Prince Harry to Meghan Markle of mixed race attracted much attention in Japan. The general reaction was that no member of the imperial family could possibly marry anyone who was not Japanese, but it reignited the internal debate on the role of a monarchy being solely symbolic and largely isolated from the everyday life of the Japanese people.

The role of the emperor and the crown prince has, however, not remained totally static since 1947. Emperor Hirohito was not by training and temperament able to make easy contacts with ordinary Japanese people, although he tried hard on his post-war journeys throughout Japan. He did not believe in his own divinity. He preferred his scientific research to ceremonial duties, for which in any case in post-war Japan there were few funds. He was pleased to be able to make his state visits abroad in 1971 and he retained a friendly interest in Britain.

Emperor Akihito grew up in the aftermath of a war which had nearly destroyed his country and which might under other circumstances have led to his father being tried as war criminal. His wife, Empress Michiko, unlike the consorts of previous emperors, did not come from an aristocratic family, but from a middle-class business background. She was educated at the Sacred Heart, a Catholic school in Tokyo. Both the emperor and the empress have been conscientious in trying to move the Japanese monarchy into the modern world. They are friendly and courteous to all they meet and have no monarchical arrogance. They have travelled widely throughout the world including a number of visits to Britain. Through his visits to countries and places which suffered acutely during the last war and through his expressed sympathy for their sufferings he has given a silent rebuke to Japanese revisionist politicians.

The emperor's rare televised address after the 2011 Great Eastern earthquake and tsunami – the worst disaster to hit Japan since World War Two – and his and the empress's visits to the worst affected regions made a great public impact. He and the empress have been solicitous over the years to show their sympathy and understanding of the difficulties which have affected Japanese people in disaster hit areas whether from earthquakes, floods or typhoons. The many visits they have made to show their sympathy and understanding for the sufferers have given solace to many. The way in which they have knelt on the ground to speak on the same level with those directly affected (and have been photographed so doing) has demonstrated their humility and human understanding. Some Japanese legalists have criticized these visits as a contravention of the strict interpretation of emperor's role as a symbol arguing that paying these visits and voicing sympathy are in themselves political acts and therefore unconstitutional. Such a legalistic interpretation would limit the emperor's role to that of a ceremonial puppet and would mean that the Japanese monarchy would cease to be relevant to the people. The emperor and empress have shown that while remaining a symbol they can have a meaningful role helping and consoling the unfortunate. By so doing they have helped to bring the Japanese monarchy into the twenty-first century and to ensure its survival.

Crown Prince Naruhito, who becomes emperor in 2019 on the abdication of his father, as authorized by a law of 2018, was at the end of April 1983 permitted to widen his horizons and pursue his historical studies and research at Oxford, probably encouraged by his parents and by the Imperial Household Agency. As his memoir of his life there shows, he is an unassuming, studious and sensitive man who will doubtless conscientiously perform the duties that will fall to him. His wife, Crown Princess Masako, who was a member of the Japanese diplomatic service and in that capacity also studied at Oxford University, appears to have found the pressures on her too much at times. She must be sad that her only child Princess Aiko will leave the imperial family on marriage.

The Imperial Household Agency is not monolithic and many of its staff have come from the Japanese diplomatic service. The progressive members of the Agency would like to see the Japanese court and members of the imperial family become more accessible and popular, but have often been inhibited by hidebound traditions and constrained by conservative elements in politics and the Japanese establishment. They are frightened of any whiff of scandal and, through the *kisha* club system of journalists who have privileged access to the Agency, make sure that reporting on the activities of members of the imperial family is anodyne and non-controversial. This may best, they feel, be maintained by secluding members of the imperial family 'above the clouds' in private compounds and out of the limelight. This is helped by the fact that the imperial family lost all its accumulated wealth at the end of the war and the budget of the imperial household is limited.

CONCLUSION

The Japanese imperial family value highly the relationship with the British royal family and close and special efforts are made to welcome British royal visitors. The emperor, after heart surgery in 2012, went to the UK to see the queen to congratulate her on her long reign. But the continuance of close and friendly relation between the two monarchies cannot be taken for granted. There have been fewer visits by British royalty to Japan since the start of the new millennium than there were in the final decades of the last century and it is unfortunate that Crown Prince Naruhito has not visited Britain since 2001. It is a pity that he was not apparently invited to make an official visit as crown prince if only in reciprocation for the official visits to Japan of the Prince of Wales to Japan in 1986 and 2008. If close relations between the two monarchies are to continue to play a role in cementing political, economic and cultural understanding, they need to be cultivated and contacts planned. The limited number of members of the Japanese imperial family reduces the opportunities for meeting, but the future emperor (Naruhito), his wife and his brother, Prince Akishino, all studied at Oxford. They know Britain better than any of our royal family know Japan, and that imbalance will need to be addressed.

ENDNOTES

1 See Sir John Pilcher's despatch of May 1971 entitled 'The Emperor of Japan: the Man and his Life' (FEJ 26/1, paras 16–19), reproduced as chapter 35 in Hugh Cortazzi (ed.), *The Growing Power of Japan 1967–1972: Analysis and Assessments from John Pilcher and the British Embassy, Tokyo* (Folkestone: Renaissance Books, 2015). Sir John Pilcher's dispatches about the Showa Emperor as reproduced in chapters 34–37 are all worth reading by anyone interested in the Japanese emperors.

2 The diary of a Filipino student in Tokyo during the war recorded that the Emperor went around in his maroon Rolls Royce and refused pressure from the military to use a Mercedes Benz, see Leocadio de Asis, *From Bataan to Tokyo: Diary of a Filipino Student in Wartime Japan 1943–1944*, edited by Grant K. Goodman (Kansas: Center for East Asian Studies, University of Kansas, 1979). On p. 138, discussing the emperor's appearance at Yoyogi Parade Ground on 28 April 1944, he mentions seeing 'His Imperial Majesty's car (maroon and black Rolls Royce)' pass just 20 metres away from where he was standing.

3 Quoted from a lecture by Stephen Large of Cambridge University to the Japan Society in 1998 on 'The Role of the Emperors under the Meiji and Showa Constitutions,' *Japan Society Proceedings* 131 (1998).

4 See note 1.

5 See Antony Best, 'We Cannot Pretend That the Past Did Not Exist: The Windsor Dynasty and Japan, 1941–1971', in Matthew Glencross, Judith Rowbotham and Michael D. Kandiah (eds), *The Windsor Dynasty 1910 to the Present: Long to Reign Over Us'?*, (London: Palgrave Macmillan, 2016), p.244, quoting a Foreign Office minute by Arthur de la Mare of 5 December 1945.

6 The National Archives, Kew (TNA), FO 371/69820 F4930/44/23, Gascoigne (Tokyo) to Dening (Foreign Office), 15 March 1948, no. PA10/13/48, cited in Best, 'We Cannot Pretend That the Past Did Not Exist', p.245.

7 Best, 'We Cannot Pretend That the Past Did Not Exist', p.246, quoting TNA FO371/99411 FJ1051/16, Dening (Tokyo) to Eden, 24 March 1952, no.83.

8 TNA FO372/7133 TD10051/2, Eden minute n.d. [November 1952].

9 The account of this visit is based on Hugh Cortazzi, 'Crown Prince Akihito in Britain' in Hugh Cortazzi (ed.), *Britain and Japan: Biographical Portraits*, vol. V (Folkestone: Global Oriental, 2005). The endnotes to this chapter provide sources and references.

10 Cited in Cortazzi, 'Crown Prince Akihito in Britain', in Cortazzi (ed.), *Britain and Japan*, vol. 5, p. 38.

11 Cited in Cortazzi, 'Crown Prince Akihito in Britain', in Cortazzi (ed.), *Britain and Japan: Biographical Portraits*, vol. 5, p. 39.

12 TNA CAB130/165 GEN/693, 'Royal Visits Overseas and Visits by Foreign Heads of State committee' 3rd meeting, 4 November 1960.

13 Hugo Vickers, *Royal Orders: The Honours and the Honoured* (London: Bextree, 1994), p.49.
14 Dorothy Britten (Lady Boucher) in the obituary she wrote for the Japan Society: *Japan Society Proceedings*, 126 (winter 1995). See also *Prince and Princess Chichibu: Two Lives Lived Above and Below the Clouds, Including a Complete Translation of Setsuko, Princess Chichibu's Memoir The Silver Drum*, 2nd edition, (Folkestone: Global Oriental, 2010).
15 TNA PREM11/3853 TS1231/43 Home to Morland (Tokyo) 15 August 1962 no.78: 'It was apparent throughout the arrangement of the tour that the Japanese authorities had some different views from the Princess herself.'
16 See Nicolas Maclean, 'The Great Japan Exhibition, 1981–1982', in Hugh Cortazzi (ed.), *Britain and Japan: Biographical Portraits*, vol. IX (Folkestone: Renaissance Books, 2015), pp. 1–14.
17 See TNA FO372/8012 Stewart to Rundall (Tokyo) 3 December 1965 no. 113.
18 TNA FO372/8012 Makgill (Protocol Dept) to Rundall, 30 November 1965.
19 TNA FO372/8012 Stewart to Rundall 3 December 1965 no. 113.
20 I was working at the Foreign Office at the time and was summoned as Japanese interpreter at the lunch. I recorded the following in my memoir *Japan and Back and Places Elsewhere* (Folkestone: Global Oriental, 1998): 'He [Prince Hitachi] and the Duke of Edinburgh were interested in ornithology. I had some difficulty with the vocabulary. During the luncheon I sat behind the Prince. When Prince Hitachi told the Queen that he had just been visiting Waterloo where Nelson had defeated Napoleon I substituted Wellington for Nelson and a gaffe was avoided. When the fruit came round, Prince Hitachi took grapes but was not sure how to eat them and asked me what he should do. I told him he could eat them in any way he liked. Princess Alexandra who was sitting on the Prince's right and who recognized me from her visit to Japan heard this exchange and to my embarrassment forced me to interpret it to her. Fortunately, she agreed with the advice I had given the Prince.'
21 TNA FO372/8012 Stewart to Rundall 3 December 1965 no. 113.
22 See Ben Thorne, 'British Week in Tokyo, 1969', in Cortazzi (ed.), *Britain and Japan:* vol. IX, pp. 77–88.
23 Sir John Pilcher's despatch about Expo 70 was reprinted in Cortazzi (ed.), *Britain and Japan:* vol. 9, pp. 89–94.
24 Hugh Cortazzi (ed.), *Japan Experiences, Fifty Years, One Hundred Views; Post-War Japan through British Eyes* (Richmond: Japan Library, 2001), p. 334.
25 This account is based on Hugh Cortazzi, 'The Showa Emperor's State Visit to Britain, October 1971', in Cortazzi (ed.), *Britain and Japan*, vol. V, pp. 53–62. The endnotes provide sources and references.
26 TNA FO371/187138 FJ1941/1, Denson minute, 13 April 1966.
27 TNA FO371/187138 FJ1941/5, Rundall to de la Mere (FE Dept), 18 August 1966.
28 TNA FCO21/923 FEJ26/4, Mayall (FE Dept) to Pilcher (Tokyo), 5 May 1971.

29 TNA FCO57/330 TXVII/306/1 Pilcher to Douglas-Home 19 May 1971.

30 Sir John, who accompanied a BBC television journalist at an audience on 8 June 1971, recorded:

> 'The Emperor was very ill at ease to begin with and at first had some difficulty in getting any words out at all...A prodigious number of er's and ah's went on before His Majesty brought himself to offer some words of greeting.' Pilcher noted that the Emperor 'is nearly always obliged to end up with "I remain with this hope", whether it follows on logically or not'. At the subsequent luncheon, 'Nobody made any attempt to converse and the Emperor had the usual difficulties before bringing himself to use "the voice of the crane" at all.' However, Their Majesties exuded kindness and consideration throughout.' Pilcher commented that 'the art of conversation as such has never been generally practised in Japan... Silence is the correct refuge when in doubt and embarrasses nobody.'

31 According to Best (see note 6), the speech 'went through two drafts. The first by the Foreign and Commonwealth Office was ultra-bland. While it did acknowledge the past it emphasized only the positive, focusing on how technology transfer from Britain had helped Japan in the nineteenth century and how the close relationship between the two countries had culminated in the Anglo-Japanese Alliance. Prince Philip who saw the draft realized that more needed to be said and inserted the following important passage:

> We cannot pretend that the past did not exist. We cannot pretend that our two peoples have always been peaceful and friendly. However, it is precisely this experience which should make us all the more determined never to let it happen again.

32 TNA FCO21/926 FEJ/26/4 Pilcher to Douglas-Home 5 November 1971 no.26/8.

33 The press coverage of the visit is reviewed by the FCO in TNA FCO/26/664 PBA 12/306/1 'Japanese State Visit' Walker (News Dept) note 19 October 1971.

34 TNA FCO21/926 FEJ26/4 Morgan to Pilcher, 9 November 1971.

35 TNA FCO21/926 FEJ26/4 Morgan to Pilcher, 9 November 1971.

36 TNA FCO21/926 FEJ26/4 Pilcher to Douglas-Home, 5 November 1971, no. 26/6.

37 TNA FCO21/926 FEJ26/4 Pilcher to Douglas-Home, 5 November 1971, no. 26/6.

38 TNA FCO21/926 FEJ26/4 Pilcher to Douglas-Home, 5 November 1971, no. 26/6.

39 Sir Nicholas Barrington, who was responsible in the embassy for the detailed arrangements, was particularly gratified when he was presented to the queen, for she immediately said 'you are the one who signed all the letters'.

40 Sir Fred Warner, the British ambassador, in his official report of 12 June 1975, described Princess Chichibu as 'a tower of strength throughout the visit', see TNA FCO21/1448 FEJ26/1 Warner (Tokyo) to Callaghan 12 June 1975 no.26/10.

41 Barrington, who was counsellor and head of chancery at the time of the state visit, recorded in his memoir, *Envoy: a Diplomatic Journey* (London: Radcliffe Press, 2013), that it had required a great deal of effort to get the different masters of the art of ikebana to agree to exhibit together: 'The prima donnas had never been so close to each other before.'

42 Memo by Ben Thorne, see fn.59.

43 Barrington commented that royalty were not as punctual as he had been led to expect.

44 Beautifully maintained by the Imperial War Graves Commission.

45 Barrington had suggested that the queen would enjoy a piece of kabuki action rather than a stylized dance, but the conservative-minded courtiers who had been led to think that kabuki was populist and vulgar opted for Japanese classical culture.

46 Many who hoped to be invited were per force disappointed. Simone Lady Warner, the wife of the British ambassador, in a contribution to *Japan Experiences* (see note 22, above) recorded that one Japanese lady tried to bribe her to get an invitation by sending her a string of pearls on a diamond clasp.

47 Barrington recorded in his memoir *Envoy* that in order to ensure that the train was not delayed at Kyoto station while the queen's luggage was removed this was dispersed through various carriages so that it could be unloaded without upsetting the train schedule.

48 Barrington had pressed for the inclusion of Ryōanji in the programme. The garden was, of course, shut to tourists during the visit, thus enabling the royal visitors to enjoy a moment or two of contemplation.

49 Barrington had hoped for a demonstration of *yabusame*, archery on horseback, but the Japanese had turned down this suggestion.

50 A small Japanese group protested to the Japanese government and the British embassy at the inclusion of this visit in the programme. They alleged that the visit would encourage 'reactionary forces such as militarists, the Liberal-Democratic Party and those who advocate revival of the autocratic Emperor system and state Shintoism': *Japan Times*, 9 May 1975.

51 See for instance TNA FCO 21/1448 FED26/1 Haskell (FE Dept) to Cleverly 25 April 1975.

52 TNA FCO 21/1448 FEJ 26/1 Bentley to Nishikawa 17 April 1975.

53 In his memoir cited above, Barrington recorded that, 'The Queen looked radiant in a long dark dress with flowers, garnished with a string of fine pearls given to her by Mr Mikimoto. The Duke was on good form discussing many issues freely.' As he left the table with the queen he went to inspect a tank of fish outside the restaurant but didn't notice that it was surrounded by a small moat of water, so

he put his foot into the water half way up to his knee. The queen stood back and roared with laughter: "Don't laugh, woman," he said, "Take me up to bed. I've got to change my socks!'"

54 TNA, FCO 21/1448 FEJ 26/1 Warner to Callaghan 12 June 1975, no.26/10.

55 Ben Thorne, the commercial counsellor, in a note about the visit which he copied to me, recorded that there were some eighty reporters and cameramen from Britain and something like 4,000 members of the Japanese media had been accredited to the press department of the Japanese foreign ministry to cover the tour.

56 Barrington in a note which he wrote for *Japan Experiences* p. 562, wrote, 'The Imperial Household was not easy to deal with. Being even more officious in that respect, in those days, than the Lord Chamberlain's Office in London.' Simone, Lady Warner, wife of Sir Fred Warner, British ambassador at the time of the State Visit, recorded in the same volume (pp. 584–5) that, 'The Queen's private office were very efficient and very modest. Whereas the preparation for Gerald Ford's two-day trip to Japan [he was the US President] necessitated the visit of some three hundred personnel on a special plane, the royal household sent only two people, one of the Queen's senior Private Secretaries and a most sympathetic but sharp-eyed private detective.'

57 See Simone Warner in *Japan Experiences*, p. 585.

58 TNA, FCO 21/1448 FEJ 26/1, Warner to Callaghan 12 June 1975.

59 The Crown Prince wanted to see a rabbit in the wild. We found one for him in an enclosure in Kensington Gardens.

60 See James Rawlins, 'William Anderson, 1842–1900: Surgeon, Teacher and Art Collector', in Cortazzi (ed.), *Britain and Japan*, vol. V, pp. 3–12.

61 On his time in England, see the papers contained in TNA FCO 21/4386. No foreign guests were invited to the wedding, but the Queen and Prince Philip sent a message of congratulation, as did the prime minister and Denis Thatcher. The British embassy reported that the wedding ceremony had been held at a Shinto shrine within the Imperial Palace grounds. The prince and his bride wore traditional royal costumes. In accordance with Japanese tradition, neither the emperor nor the empress attended the wedding, but received the couple afterwards in a reception at the palace and gave them the title of Prince and Princess Akishino. The Japanese media gave the wedding saturation coverage and among young girls there was 'Kiko-fever', many wanting to copy her dress and hairstyle. But there was no sign of great popular enthusiasm; this, as the British Embassy reported on 4 July, was due 'to a conscious decision by the Imperial Household Agency not to indulge in too much hype'. They see the Imperial Family as still being remote from everyday life. It was particularly striking that the IHA heavily criticized the one photograph of the couple to show any humanity (Princess Akishino smoothing Prince Akishino's hair during a photo session).

62 The prince conducted field research in Indonesia in 1993 and 1994, and in Yunnan Province in the People›s Republic of China. According to Wikipedia, he introduced

tilapia to Thailand as an important source of protein. Tilapia can be easily cultured and Prince Fumihito, who is also known as a 'catfish specialist,' has managed to maintain and expand aqua-cultural cooperation with the people of Thailand.

63 It was published by Global Oriental in 2006 with a foreword by the Prince of Wales. It took me years of argument to get the permission of the Imperial Household to undertake this translation.

64 The Prince had not experienced life in Japan before modern central heating, when one had to rely on a small charcoal *hibachi* or tuck oneself under a *kotatsu.*

65 For an account of the Nissan decision to invest in Britain see Robin Mountfield, 'Nissan Investment in Britain: History of a Negotiation', in Hugh Cortazzi (ed.), *Britain and Japan: Biographical Portraits*, vol. VI (Folkestone: Global Oriental, 2007) pp. 107–121.

66 For a detailed account of the funeral and its aftermath see Carolyn Whitehead and David Powers, 'Death of the Showa Emperor 7 January 1989: The Start of a New Era', in Cortazzi (ed.), *Japan Experiences*, pp. 230–247.

67 Hugh Cortazzi (ed.), *Carmen Blacker: Scholar of Japanese Religion, Myth and Folklore* (Folkestone: Renaissance Books, 2017).

68 Published in *Japan Society Proceedings* 119 (Spring 1992).

69 See 'Opening Celebrations For the Japan Festival 1991', *Japan Society Proceedings* 118 (Autumn 1991).

70 See Christopher Purvis, 'Japan 2001 in Retrospect', *Japan Society Proceedings* 140 (Winter 2002).

71 The other was King Albert II of the Belgians.

72 In 1989 former prisoners of war had protested about the Duke of Edinburgh's attending the funeral of Emperor Hirohito. Under article 16 of the peace treaty with Japan signed at San Francisco in 1951, funds from Japanese property in allied countries had provided some £76 compensation to each former prisoner. This was a pitiful amount even at that time. The Japanese government had refused over many years to make any other funds available in compensation, insisting on sticking legalistically to the terms of the treaty. The British government for their part took the line that the needs of the former prisoners of war were covered by pensions and the health service and that they could not lobby the Japanese government to make *ex-gratia* payments. Eventually, after an early day motion in the House of Lords, the British government announced in parliament on 7 November 2000 that *ex-gratia* payments £10,000 would be made by the British government to each surviving FEPOW, civilian internee, captured merchant seaman and widow, thus settling a long-standing grievance against Japan. For a full account of this saga see Phillida Purvis, 'Philip Malins', in Hugh Cortazzi (ed.), *Britain and Japan: Biographical Portraits*, vol. VII (Folkestone: Global Oriental, 2007) pp. 620–7.

73 The Japan Academy (Nippon Gakushi-in), which operates under the auspices of the Ministry of Education, Culture, Sports, Science and Technology, is an

organization that accords special recognition to researchers with the most eminent records of academic and scientific achievement. The academy's primary purpose is to carry out programmes that contribute to the advancement of academic knowledge.

74 In 1977 Prince Philip, Duke of Edinburgh wrote a letter addressed to Crown Prince Akihito about the preservation of the Iriomote cat. The report attached to the letter (written by Professor Leyhausen) suggested outlawing any further migration to the island as well as banning the cultivation of the land. In response, the crown prince said that he wished for a way that would allow for the preservation of the cats and the continued habitation of people on the island. He also explained that the prime minister at the time, Takeo Fukuda, was considering the implementation of a wildlife sanctuary on Iriomote.

75 Next to the car park below Yuwan-dake there is a sign commemorating the planting of a tree by the Duke of Edinburgh during his visit to the island in 1984 to observe its unique wild life.

76 The Duke of Kent confirmed this to me on 23 May 2018 when I called on him. He was vice-chairman of British Trade International, formerly known as the British Overseas Trade Board, and later acted as the United Kingdom's Special Representative for International Trade and Investment.

77 See Paul Dimond, 'The British Export Marketing Centre and the Promotion of British Exports to Japan from 1972', in Cortazzi (ed.), *Britain and Japan*, vol. IX, pp. 95–109.

Chronology of Royal and Imperial Visits 1868–2018

Year	British visits to Japan	Japanese visits to Britain
1869	Prince Alfred, Duke of Edinburgh	
1871		Prince Yoshihisa of Fushimi (Prince Kitashirakawa from 1873)[1]
1871–72		Prince Higashi-Fushimi (Prince Komatsu from 1882)
1871		Prince Yoshihisa of Fushimi[2]
1872		Prince Yoshihisa of Fushimi[3]
1872		Iwakura Mission
1881	Prince Albert Victor and Prince George	
1881–83		Prince Takehito of Arisugawa (Prince Arisugawa from 1895)
1882		Prince Arisugawa
1884–87		Prince Yorihito of Yamashina (Prince Yorihito of Komatsu from 1885, Prince Higashi-Fushimi from 1903)
1886–87		Prince Komatsu[4]
1889		Prince and Princess Arisugawa
1890	Prince Arthur, Duke, and Duchess of Connaught	
1892		Prince Kikumaro of Yamashina (Prince Yamashina from 1898)[5]
1893		Prince Yorihito of Komatsu Prince Kikumaro of Yamashina [6]

Year	British visits to Japan	Japanese visits to Britain
1894		Prince Yorihito of Komatsu
1897		Prince Arisugawa
1900		Prince Kan'in
1902		Prince Komatsu
1905		Prince and Princess Arisugawa
1906	Prince Arthur, Duke of Connaught	
1907		Prince Fushimi
1908–10		Prince Hiroyasu of Fushimi (Prince Fushimi from 1923)
1909		Prince Kuni Kuniyoshi and Prince Nashimoto Morimasa
1911		Prince and Princess Higashi-Fushimi
1912	Prince Arthur, Duke of Connaught	
1918	Prince Arthur, Duke of Connaught	
1918–19		Prince Higashi-Fushimi
1921		Prince Kan'in Crown Prince Hirohito
1922	Edward, Prince of Wales	
1925		Prince and Princess Asaka Prince Chichibu
1926	Prince George	
1929	Prince Henry, Duke of Gloucester	
1930		Prince and Princess Takamatsu
1934		Prince and Princess Kaya
1937		Prince Chichibu
1953		Crown Prince Akihito
1961	Princess Alexandra	
1962		Princess Chichibu
1965	Princess Alexandra	
1965		Prince and Princess Hitachi
1967		Princess Chichibu

Year	**British visits to Japan**	**Japanese visits to Britain**
1968–70	Prince William	
1968–70		Prince Tomohito of Mikasa
1969	Princess Margaret and Lord Snowden	
1970	Charles, Prince of Wales Prince Richard, Duke of Gloucester	
1971	Prince Michael, Duke of Kent	Prince Tomohito of Mikase Prince Katsura Emperor Hirohito and Empress Nagako
1973	Prince Edward, Duke of Kent and Katherine, Duchess of Kent	
1974		Princess Chichibu
1975	Queen Elizabeth II and Prince Philip, Duke of Edinburgh	Prince and Princess Mikasa
1976		Crown Prince Akihito and Crown Princess Michiko Prince Tomohito of Mikasa
1978	Princess Margaret	Norhito, Prince Takamado
1979	Prince Edward, Duke of Kent	Princess Chichibu
1980		Prince and Princess Mikasa
1981		Prince and Princess Tomohito of Mikasa Crown Prince Akihito and Crown Princess Michiko Princess Chichibu
1982	Prince Philip, Duke of Edinburgh	
1983	Anne, Princess Royal	Prince Tomohito of Mikasa
1983–85		Prince Hiro (Crown Prince Naruhito from 1989)

Year	British visits to Japan	Japanese visits to Britain
1984	Prince Philip, Duke of Edinburgh	Princess Nori
1985		Prince Akishino Prince Takamado
1986	Charles, Prince of Wales, and Diana, Princess of Wales Prince Philip, Duke of Edinburgh	Prince Hiro
1987	Prince Edward, Duke of Kent, and Katherine, Duchess of Kent	
1988–90		Prince Akishino
1989	Prince Philip, Duke of Edinburgh	Princess Nori
1990	Anne, Princess Royal Charles, Prince of Wales, and Diana, Princess of Wales Prince Philip, Duke of Edinburgh,	
1991	Prince Michael of Kent	Crown Prince Naruhito
1992	Prince Edward, Duke of Kent	
1994		Prince and Princess Takamado Prince and Princess Mikasa
1995	Diana, Princess of Wales	
1996	Prince Edward, Duke of Kent	
1997	Prince Philip, Duke of Edinburgh, Princess Alexandra	Princess Tsuguko of Takamado
1998	Prince Edward, Earl of Essex Prince Richard, Duke of Gloucester and the Duchess of Gloucester Anne, Princess Royal	Prince and Princess Tomohito of Mikasa Emperor Akihito and Empress Michiko Princess Tsuguko of Takamado
1999	Anne, Princess Royal	Princess Tsuguko of Takamado
2000	Prince Edward, Duke of Kent	
2001		Crown Prince Naruhito
2001–02		Princess Akiko of Mikasa
2002		Princess Noriko of Takamado

Year	British visits to Japan	Japanese visits to Britain
2003	Prince Edward, Duke of Kent	Princess Takamado Princess Tomohito of Mikasa Princess Akiko of Mikasa
2004		Prince Tomohito of Mikasa and Princess Akiko of Mikasa Princess Noriko of Takamado
2004–08		Princess Tsuguko of Takamado
2004–10		Princess Akiko of Mikasa
2005		Princess Takamado Princess Noriko of Takamado
2007		Emperor Akihito and Empress Michiko
2008	Charles, Prince of Wales, and the Duchess of Cornwall	
2009		Princess Takamado
2011		Princess Akiko of Mikasa Prince and Princess Hitachi
2012		Emperor Akihito and Empress Michiko Princess Mako of Akishino
2013		Princess Ayako of Takamado Princess Akiko of Mikasa
2014		Princess Mako of Akishino
2015	Prince William, Duke of Cambridge	
2016		Princess Mako of Akishino Princess Akiko of Mikasa
2017		Princess Akiko of Mikasa Princess Kako of Akishino
2018		Princess Toshi Princess Akiko

ENDNOTES

1 Prince Kitashirakawa Yoshihisa, who was then known as Prince Fushimi Yoshihisa but took the name Kitashirakawa in 1873, spent several weeks in London from 25 January 1871 before proceeding to Germany for military studies.

2 Prince Kitashirakawa Yoshihisa was then studying in Germany but paid a visit to his brother, Prince Higashi-Fushimi, in Warminster: *Frome Times,* 12 April 1871, p. 3.

3 He came over to Britain in connection with the arrival of the Iwakura Mission.

4 Prince Komatsu left London early in January 1887, spent some time in Germany, and then returned to London in June 1887 for the Golden Jubilee.

5 The online version of Victoria's journals (http://www.queenvictoriasjournals.org/home.do), entry for 23 July 1892, states: 'saw the Cadets of the [German] Training Ship "Stosch" which is at Cowes. A Japanese Prince was amongst them.' This must have been Prince Yamashina Yasumaro, who in 1889 had stopped in Southampton for a few hours on his way to Germany (*The Times*, 30 December 1889, p. 10) and remained in Germany until 1894 studying at the German Imperial Naval School and then the Naval Academy. The training frigate *Stosch* was at anchor at Cowes for several days in July 1892 and the officers and cadets visited Osborne House and were inspected by the Queen: *The Times*, 21 July 1892, p. 11, 25 July 1892, p. 9.

6 He made a brief trip to London from Germany to see the Japanese cruiser *Yoshino* which had just been completed at the Armstrong Whitworth dockyard in Newcastle: *Yorihito shinnō* (Tokyo: Shun'yōdō, 1927), pp. 75–6.

Bibliography

PUBLISHED OFFICIAL DOCUMENTS, DIARIES, LETTERS AND MEMOIRS

A Guide to the Works of Art and Science Collected by Captain His Royal Highness The Duke of Edinburgh, K.G., during his Five-Years' Cruise round the World in H.M.S. "Galatea" (1867–1871) and Lent for Exhibition in the South Kensington Museum, February, 1872 (London: John Strangeways, 1872).

Arisugawa Takehito shinnō [Prince Arisugawa Takehito], 2 vols (1927; facsimile published by Yumani Shobō of Tokyo in 2010).

Arisugawa Taruhito shinnō nikki [Diary of Prince Arisugawa Takehito] (Takamatsu no miya, 1936).

Aston, Sir George, *His Royal Highness the Duke of Connaught and Strathearn: A Life and Intimate Study* (London: George G. Harrap, 1929).

Atholl, Katherine, Duchess of, *Working Partnership: Being the Lives of John George, 8th Duke of Atholl, and of his Wife, Katharine Marjory Ramsay* (London: Arthur Baker Ltd, 1958).

Baba Tatsui zenshū [Complete Works of Baba Tatsui], 4 vols (Tokyo: Iwanami Shoten, 1987–1988).

Barrington, Nicholas, *Envoy: A Diplomatic Journey* (London: Radcliffe, 2013).

Beach, William R., *Visit of His Royal Highness the Duke of Edinburgh, K.G., K.T., G.C.M.G., to Hongkong in 1869* (Hong Kong: Noronha & Sons, 1869).

Bennett, Terry (ed.), *Japan and the Illustrated London News: Complete Record of Reported Events, 1853–1899* (Folkestone: Global Oriental, 2006).

Bennett, Terry, Hugh Cortazzi and J. E. Hoare (eds), *Japan and The Graphic: Compete Record of Reported Events, 1870–1899* (Boston: Global Oriental, 2011).

Beresford, Charles William De la Poer, *The Memoirs of Admiral Lord Charles Beresford*, 2 vols. (London: Methuen & Co., 1914).

Black, John Reddie, *Young Japan: Yokohama and Yedo*, 2 vols. (London: Trubner & Co., 1881).

British Parliamentary Papers Japan, 10 vols. (Shannon: Irish University Press, 1971).

Buckle, George Earl (ed.), *The Letters of Queen Victoria: Second Series. A Selection from Her Majesty's Correspondence and Journal between the Years 1862 and 1878*, 2 vols. (London: John Murray, 1926).

Colvin, Ragnar, *The Memoirs of Sir Ragnar Colvin KBE CB 1882–1954* (Durley: Wintershill Publications, 1992).

Cortazzi, Hugh, *Japan and Back and Places Elsewhere* (Folkestone: Global Oriental, 1998).

Cortazzi, Hugh (ed.), *Mitford's Japan: The Memoirs and Recollections 1866–1906 of Algernon Bertram Mitford the first Lord Redesdale* (London: Athlone, 1985).

Cortazzi, Hugh (ed.), *Japan Experiences, Fifty Years, One Hundred Views; Post-War Japan through British Eyes* (Richmond: Japan Library, 2001).

Cortazzi, Hugh (ed.), *The Growing Power of Japan 1967–1972: Analysis and Assessments from John Pilcher and the British Embassy, Tokyo* (Folkestone: Renaissance Books, 2015).

Dai Nihon gaikō monjo [Diplomatic documents of Great Japan], vol. 2, book 2 (Tokyo: Nihon Kokusai Kyōkai, 1938).

Dajōkan nisshi [*Dajōkan* Journal] no. 81 (Meiji 2.7.1–10), no. 83 (Meiji 2.7.22–30), no. 100 (Meiji 2.9.18)

Daniell, J.J., *The History of Warminster* (London: Simpkin, Marshall & Co., 1879).

De Asis, Leocadios, *From Bataan to Tokyo: Diary of a Filipino Student in Wartime Japan 1943–1944*, edited by Grant K. Goodman (Kansas: Center for East Asian Studies, University of Kansas, 1979).

Dickins, F.V., and S. Lane-Poole, *The Life of Sir Harry Parkes*, 2 vols. (London: Macmillan, 1894).

Eggermont, Isidore, *Voyage autour du globe: Japon* (Paris: Delagrave, 1900).

Eikokushi [History of England] (Nagato: Onchisha, 1861).

Fraser, Mary, *A Diplomatist's Wife in Japan: Sketches at the Turn of the Century*, ed. Hugh Cortazzi (New York: Weatherhill, 1982).

Fukuzawa Yukichi zenshū [Complete Works of Fukuzawa Yukichi] vol. 1 (Tokyo: Iwanami Shoten, 1958).

Futada, Yoshinori, and Setzsuzo Sawada, *The Crown Prince's European Tour* (Osaka: Osaka Mainichi, 1925).

Guranto shōgun to no gotaiwa hikki [Record of the Emperor's Conversation with General Grant] (Kokumin Seishin Bunka Kenkyūjo, 1937; facsimile edition published by Honpō Shoseki, 1980).

Hōki bunrui taizen [Collected Laws and Regulations] *(dai ippen)*, Gaikōmon 3 (Tokyo: Naikaku Kirokukyoku, 1890)

Japan Punch (facsimile edition) (Tokyo: Yūshōdō Shoten, 1975).

Kageyama Muneyasu, *Atagoshita no zu* [Map of Atagoshita] (Edo: Owariya Seishichi, 1861), in *Edo kiriezu shūsei*, vol. 4 (Tokyo: Chūōkōronsha, 1982), pp. 88–9.

Keppel, Sir Henry, *A Sailor's Life Under Four Sovereigns*, 3 vols. (London: Macmillan and Co., 1899).

Kume Kunitake, *The Iwakura Embassy 1871–73*, vol. 2 Britain, trans. Graham Healey (Matsudo: The Japan Documents, 2002).

Lensen, George A. (ed.), *The D'Athenan Despatches from Japan, 1894–1910* (Tallahassee: Diplomatic Press, 1967).

Linzee, John William, *The Linzee family* (Boston, MA: privately printed, 1917).

Matthew, H. C. G. (ed.), *The Gladstone Diaries*, vol. 7 (Oxford: Clarendon Press, 1982).
Meiji nyūsu jiten [Dictionary of Meiji News], vol. 1 (Tokyo: Mainichi Komyūnikeeshonzu, 1983).
Meiji tennō ki [Record of Emperor Meiji], 12 vols (Tokyo: Yoshikawa Kōbunkan, 1968–77).
Milner, John, and Sir Oswald Walters Brierly, *The Cruise of H.M.S. Galatea, Captain H.R.H. the Duke of Edinburgh, K.G., in 1867, 1868* (London: W. H. Allen & Co., 1869).
Nagai Hiroshi, *Koshashin de miru Bakumatsu Ishin to Tokugawa ichizoku* [The End of the Bakufu and the Meiji Restoration, and the Tokugawa Family, as seen in Old Photographs] (Tokyo: Kadokawa, 2018).
Navy List, 1881, vol. iv (London: John Murray, 1881).
Nihon shoki shinbun zenshū [Collected Early Newspapers of Japan], vol. 24 (Tokyo: Perikansha, 1990).
Ōkubo *Toshimichi nikki* [Diary of Ōkubo Toshimichi], 2 vols. (Tokyo: Nihon Shiseki Kyōkai, 1927).
Oranda fūsetsugaki shūsei [Collected Dutch Reports], 2 vols (Tokyo: Yoshikawa Kōbunkan, 1976–79).
Phillips, Sir Percival, *The Prince of Wales' Eastern Book: A Pictorial Record of the Voyages of 'HMS Renown'* (London: Hodder & Stoughton, 1922).
Plomer, William (ed.), *Kilvert's Diary: Selections from the Diary of Francis Kilvert*, 2 vols. (London: Jonathan Cape, 1938).
Redesdale, Lord, *The Garter Mission to Japan* (London: Macmillan, 1906).
Redesdale, Lord, *Memories*, 2 vols. (London: Hutchinson & Co., 1915).
Riddell, Lord, *Intimate Diary of the Peace Conference and After 1918–1923* (London: Gollancz, 1933).
Rosen, Baron Roman, *Forty Years of Diplomacy*, 2 vols. (London: George Allen and Unwin, 1922).
Russell, Sir Herbert, *With the Prince in the East: A Record of the Royal Visit to India and Japan*, (London: Methuen, 1922).
Ruxton, Ian (ed.), *The Diaries of Sir Ernest Satow: British Envoy in Peking (1900–1905)* vol.1 (Morrisville NC: Lulu Press, 2006).
Ruxton, Ian (ed.), *A Diplomat in Japan, part II: The Diaries of Ernest Satow, 1870–1883* (Morrisville NC: Lulu Press, 2009).
Sadanaru shinnō jiseki [The Life of Prince Sadanaru] (Fushimi no miya, 1931).
Satow, Ernest, *A Diplomat in Japan* (New York: Oxford University Press, 1968).
Schäfer, Bernd, Uta Wallenstein and Michaela Appel (eds), *Ein Prinz entdeckt die Welt. Die Reisen und Sammlungen Herzog Alfreds von Sachsen-Coburg und Gotha (1844–1910)* (Gotha: Stiftung Schloss Friedenstein, 2008).
Scott, Admiral Sir Percy, *Fifty Years in the Royal Navy* (London: John Murray, 1919).
Shinbun shūsei Meiji hennenshi [Chronology of the Meiji Period with Newspapers], 2nd edition, vol. 1 (Tokyo: Rinsensha, 1936).
Society of British Artists: the forty-ninth annual exhibition (1872).

Sōseki zenshū [Complete works of Sōseki], vol. 19 (Tokyo: Iwanami Shoten, 1995).

Tada Kōmon (ed.), *Iwakura kō jikki* [Diary of Lord Iwakura], 3 vols. (Np: Iwakura-kō kyūseki hozonkai, 1927).

Tanaka Akira (ed.), *Tokumei zenken taishi Beiō kairan jikki* [Diary of the Visit of the Ambassador Extraordinary to America and Europe], (Tokyo: Iwanami Shoten, 1985).

The Cruise of Her Majesty's Ship "Bacchante" 1879–1882: Compiled from the Private Journals, Letters, and Note-books of Prince Albert Victor and Prince George of Wales with additions by John N. Dalton, 2 vols. (London: Macmillan, 1886).

The King to his People (London: Williams and Norgate, 1935).

Windsor, The Duke of, *A King's Story* (London: Cassell, 1951).

Yorihito shinnō [Prince Yorihito] (Tokyo: Shun'yōdō, 1927).

Ziegler, Philip (ed.), *The Diaries of Lord Louis Mountbatten 1920–22: Tours with the Prince of Wales* (London: Collins, 1987).

SECONDARY SOURCES

Ayers, John, *Chinese and Japanese Works of Art in the Collection of Her Majesty The Queen*, 3 vols (London: Royal Collection Trust, 2016).

Beasley, William G., *Great Britain and the Opening of Japan, 1834–1858* (London: Luzac & Co., 1951).

Behr, Edward, *Hirohito: Behind the Myth* (London: Hamish Hamilton, 1989).

Bennett, Gill, 'British Policy in the Far East 1933–1936: Treasury and Foreign Office', *Modern Asian Studies*, 26 (1992): 545–68.

Bergamini, David, *Japan's Imperial Conspiracy* (New York: William Morrow, 1971).

Best, Antony, *Britain, Japan and Pearl Harbor: Avoiding War in East Asia, 1936–41* (London: Routledge, 1995).

Best, Antony, 'The Role of Diplomatic Practice and Court Protocol in Anglo-Japanese Relations, 1867–1900', in Markus Mosslang and Torsten Riotte (eds), *The Diplomats' World: The Cultural History of Diplomacy, 1815–1914* (Oxford: Oxford University Press, 2008) pp. 231–53.

Best, Antony, 'We Cannot Pretend That the Past Did Not Exist: The Windsor Dynasty and Japan, 1941–1971', in Matthew Glencross, Judith Rowbotham and Michael D. Kandiah (eds), *The Windsor Dynasty 1910 to the Present: 'long to reign over us'?*, (London: Palgrave Macmillan, 2016) pp. 239–58.

Bix, Herbert, *Hirohito and the Making of Modern Japan* (New York: Harper Collins, 2000).

Bräutigam, Herbert, *Schätze japanischer lackkunst auf Schloß Friedenstein (Gotha:* Schlossmuseum, 1998).

Breen, John, 'Shintoists in Restoration Japan (1868–1872): Towards a Reassessment', *Modern Asian Studies*, 24 (1990): 579–602.

Breen, John, 'The Rituals of Anglo-Japanese Diplomacy: Imperial Audiences in Early Meiji Japan', in G. Daniels and C. Tsuzuki (eds), *The History of Anglo-Japanese Rela-*

tions 1600–2000, vol. 5, *Social and Cultural Perspectives* (London: Palgrave, 2002) pp. 60–76.

Breen, John, 'Meiji tennō no kunshō gaikō to kyūtei bunka no kokusaisei', *Kikan yūkyū* 153 (2018): 105–116.

Britton, Dorothy, 'Prince and Princess Chichibu', in Hugh Cortazzi, (ed.), *Britain and Japan: Biographical Portraits*, vol. 5 (Folkestone: Global Oriental, 2005) pp. 23–32.

Britton, Dorothy, *Prince and Princess Chichibu: Two Lives Lived Above and Below the Clouds, Including a Complete Translation of Setsuko, Princess Chichibu's Memoir The Silver Drum*, 2nd edition (Folkestone: Global Oriental, 2010).

Chow, Phoebe, *Britain's Imperial Retreat from China, 1900–1931* (London: Routledge, 2017).

Cobbing, Andrew, *The Japanese Discovery of Victorian Britain: Early Travel Encounters in the Far West* (Richmond: Japan Library, 1998).

Cook, Andrew, *Prince Eddy: The King Britain Never Had* (Stroud: Tempus, 2006).

Cortazzi, Hugh, 'Royal Visits to Japan in the Meiji Period, 1868–1912', in Ian Nish (ed.), *Britain and Japan: Biographical Portraits*, vol. II (Richmond: Japan Library, 1997) pp. 79–93.

Cortazzi, Hugh, 'Crown Prince Akihito in Britain', in Hugh Cortazzi (ed.), *Britain and Japan: Biographical Portraits*, vol. V (Folkestone: Global Oriental, 2005) pp. 205–215.

Cortazzi, Hugh, 'The Showa Emperor's State Visit to Britain, October 1971', in Hugh Cortazzi (ed.), *Britain and Japan: Biographical Portraits*, vol. V (Folkestone: Global Oriental, 2005) pp. 77–86.

Cortazzi, Hugh (ed.), *Carmen Blacker: Scholar of Japanese Religion, Myth and Folklore* (Folkestone: Renaissance Books, 2017).

Dimond, Paul, 'The British Export Marketing Centre and the Promotion of British Exports to Japan from 1972', in Hugh Cortazzi (ed.), *Britain and Japan, Biographical Portraits*, vol. IX (Folkestone: Renaissance Books, 2015), pp. 95–109.

Fox, Grace, *Britain and Japan 1858–1883* (Oxford: Clarendon Press, 1969).

Fujitani, Takashi, *Splendid Monarchy: Power and Pageantry in Modern Japan* (Berkeley: University of California Press, 1996).

Fung, Edmund S. K., *The Diplomacy of Imperial Retreat: Britain's South China Policy, 1924–1931* (Hong Kong: Oxford University Press, 1991).

Goto-Shibata, Harumi, *Japan and Britain in Shanghai, 1925–31* (Basingstoke: St. Antony's/Macmillan, 1995).

Guth, Christine, *Longfellow's Tattoos: Tourism, Collecting, and Japan* (Seattle: University of Washington Press, 2004).

Hagihara Nobutoshi, '*Baba Tatsui zenshū* henshū yoroku' [Editorial Afternotes to the Collected Works of Baba Tatsui], in Ōkubo *Toshikane rekishi chosakushū*, vol. 6 furoku geppō (Yoshikawa Kōbunkan, 1988), pp. 4–6.

Hamill, Ian, *The Strategic Illusion: the Singapore Base and the Defence of Australia and New Zealand* (Singapore: Singapore University Press, 1981).

Harris, Steve, *The Prince and the Assassin: Australia's First Royal Tour and Portent of World Terror* (Melbourne: Melbourne Books, 2017).

Hatano Masuru, 'Taishō junen kōtaishi hoō – sono kettei e no porosesu to saika [The Crown Prince's visit to Europe in Taishō 10 – the process and result of the decision], *Hogaku Kenkyū*, 66 (1993): 30–58.

Heinrichs, Waldo, *American Ambassador: Joseph C. Grew and the Development of the United States Diplomatic Tradition* (New York: Oxford University Press, 1966).

Hoare, J.E., 'John Frederick Lowder (1843–1902): Consul, Counsel and *O-Yatoi*', in Hugh Cortazzi (ed.), *Britain and Japan: Biographical Portraits*, vol. X (Folkestone: Renaissance Books, 2016) pp. 300–2.

Hope, Robert, *A History of the Lord Weymouth School, Warminster* (Warminster: [Lord Weymouth] School Parents' Association, 1970).

Hosoya Chihiro, '1934-nen no nichi-ei fukashin kyōtei mondai,' [The Question of the Anglo-Japanese Non-Aggression Pact, 1934], *Kokusai Seiji*, 58 (1977) 69–84.

Ishizuki Minoru, *Kindai Nihon no kaigai ryūgakushi* [History of Study Abroad in Modern Japan] (Tokyo: Minerva Shobō, 1972).

Kawamura, Noriko, *Emperor Hirohito and the Pacific War* (Seattle: University of Washington Press, 2015).

Kashima Shigeru, *Miyake no jidai: sepiairo no kōzoku arubamu* [The Age of the Princely Houses: A Sepia Album of the Imperial Family] (Tokyo: Asahi Shinbunsha, 2006).

Keene, Donald, *Emperor of Japan: Meiji and his World, 1852–1912* (New York: Columbia University Press, 2001).

Kennedy, Greg, 'The Keelung Incident and Britain's Far Eastern Strategic Foreign Policy, 1936–37' , in Greg Kennedy and Keith Neilson (eds) *Incidents and International Relations: People, Power, and Personalities* (Westport: Praeger, 2002) pp. 135–157.

Kerry, Simon, *Lansdowne: The Last Great Whig* (London: Unicorn, 2017).

Kimizuka Naotaka, 'Itō Hirobumi no Roshia homon to Nichi-Ei domei: Igirisu seifu shunōbu no taiō o chushin ni' [Itō Hirobumi's Visit to Russia and the Anglo-Japanese Alliance: Concentrating on the Response of the British Government], *Kanagawa-ken ritsu gaigo tanki daigaku kiyo*, 23 (2000): 33–44.

Kimizuka Naotaka, *Joō Heika no Buru Ribon: Gātā Kunshō to Igirisu Gaikō* [Her Majesty's Blue Ribbon: the Order of the Garter and British Diplomacy], Tokyo: NTT Shuppen, 2004).

Kimizuka Naotaka, 'Nicho-Ro sensō to Nichi-Ei oshitsu gaikō: Meiji Tenno e no gata kunshō juyo o megutte' [The Russo-Japanese war and Anglo-Japanese court diplomacy: concerning the conferment of the Order of the Garter on the Meiji Emperor], *Gunji Shigaku*, 40 (2004): 112–22.

Kinmonth, Earl H., *The Self-Made Man in Early Japanese Thought: From Samurai to Salaryman* (Berkeley: University of California Press, 1981).

Kornicki, P.F., 'General Sir Ian Hamilton (1853–1947) and the Russo-Japanese War', in Hugh Cortazzi (ed.), *Britain and Japan: Biographical Portraits* vol. VII (Folkestone: Global Oriental, 2010) pp. 168–73.

Koyama, Noboru, 'Three Meiji Marriages between Japanese Men and English Women', in Hugh Cortazzi, (ed.), *Britain and Japan: Biographical Portraits*, vol. IV (Abingdon: Routledge, 2002) pp. 383–396.

Koyama, Noboru, 'Japanese Tattooists and the British Royal Family during the Meiji Period', in Hugh Cortazzi (ed.), *Britain and Japan: Biographical Portraits*, vol. VI (Folkestone: Global Oriental 2007), pp. 71–80.

Koyama Noboru, *Nihon no shisei to Eikoku* ōshitsu*: Meijiki kara daiichiji sekai taisen made* [Japanese Tattoos and the British Royal Family: From the Meiji Period to the First World War] (Tokyo: Fujiwara Shoten, 2010).

Large, Stephen, *Emperor Hirohito and Showa Japan: A Political Biography* (London: Routledge, 1992).

Large, Stephen, 'The Role of the Emperors under the Meiji and Showa Constitutions,' *Japan Society Proceedings*, 131 (1998).

Lee, Bradford A., *Britain and the Sino-Japanese War, 1937–1939,* (Stanford: Stanford University Press, 1973).

Lowe, Peter, *Great Britain and the Origins of the Pacific War: A Study of British Policy in East Asia, 1937–1941* (Oxford: Clarendon, 1977).

Maclean, Nicolas 'The Great Japan Exhibition, 1981–1982', in Hugh Cortazzi (ed.), *Britain and Japan: Biographical Portraits*, vol. IX (Folkestone: Renaissance Books, 2015) pp. 1–14.

Masuda Wataru, *Japan and China: Mutual Representations in the Modern Era*, trans. and ed. Joshua Fogel (Richmond: Curzon Press, 2000).

Matsukata Fukuyo, *Oranda fūsetsugaki to kinsei Nihon* [The Dutch reports and Early Modern Japan] (Tokyo: Tōkyō Daigaku Shuppankai, 2007).

Miller, Delia, *The Victorian Watercolours and Drawings in the Collection of Her Majesty The Queen*, vol. 1 (London: Philip Wilson Publishers 1995).

Miwa Hideo, 'Kunisawa Shinkurō no gareki to sakuhin' [Kunisawa Shinkurō's Career as an Artist and his Works], *Bijutsu kenkyū*, 321 (1982): 25–32.

Miyama Jun'ichi, 'Enryōkan no jidai: Meiji Nippon omotenashi kotohajime' [The Age of the Enryōkan: the Beginning of Imperial Hospitality in the Meiji Period], Ākaibuzugaku *kenkyū*, 26 (2017): 107–109.

Mori Ōgai, 'Yoshihisa shinnō jiseki' [The Life of Prince Yoshihisa], in Ōgai *zenshū*, vol. 3 (Tokyo: Iwanami Shoten, 1972), pp. 497–620.

Morton, Robert, *A.B. Mitford and the Birth of Japan as a Modern State: Letters Home* (Folkestone: Renaissance Books, 2017).

Mosley, Leonard, *Hirohito Emperor of Japan* (London: Weidenfield and Nicolson, 1966).

Mountfield, Robin, 'Nissan Investment in Britain: History of a Negotiation', in Hugh Cortazzi (ed.), *Britain and Japan: Biographical Portraits*, vol. VI (Folkestone: Global Oriental, 2007) pp. 107–21.

Nagakuni Jun'ya, *Tosa-han ryūgakusei ibun* [Forgotten Stories of the Tosa Domain Students] (Kōchi: Tosa Shuppansha, 1989).

Newall, Sir Paul, *Japan and the City of London* (London: Athlone, 1996).

Harold Nicolson, *King George V: His Life and Reign*, vol. 1 (London: Constable & Co., 1952).

Nish, Ian, *The Anglo-Japanese Alliance: The Diplomacy of Two Island Empires, 1894–1907* (London: Athlone 1966).

Nish, Ian, *Alliance in Decline: A Study in Anglo-Japanese Relations 1908–1923* (London: Athlone, 1972).

Nish, Ian, 'Crown Prince Hirohito in Britain, May 1921', in Ian Nish (ed.), *Britain and Japan: Biographical Portraits*, vol. 2 (Richmond: Japan Library, 1997) pp. 205–215.

Nish, Ian, 'Echoes of Alliance, 1920–30' in Ian Nish & Yoichi Kibata (ed.), *History of Anglo-Japanese Relations: The Political and Diplomatic Dimension*, Vol. 1, 1600–1930 (Basingstoke: Macmillan, 2000), pp. 255–78.

Nish, Ian 'Yoshida Shigeru (1887–1967): Difficult Times for Anglo-Japanese Relations, London (1936–38)', in Ian Nish (ed.), *Japanese Envoys in Britain, 1862–1964* (Global Oriental, Folkestone, 2007) pp. 163072.

Nish, Ian (ed.), *Japanese Envoys in Britain, 1862–1964: A Century of Diplomatic Exchange* (Folkestone: Global Oriental, 2007).

Oka Yoshitake, *Reimeiki no Meiji Nihon: Nichi-Ei kōshōshi no shikaku ni oite* [The Dawn of Meiji Japan: from the point of view of Anglo-Japanese Negotiations] (Tokyo: Miraisha, 1964).

'Opening Celebrations for the Japan Festival 1991', *Japan Society Proceedings* 118 (Autumn 1991).

Purvis, Christopher, 'Japan 2001 in Retrospect', *Japan Society Proceedings* 140 (Winter 2002).

Purvis, Phillida, 'Philip Malins', in Hugh Cortazzi (ed.), *Britain and Japan: Biographical Portraits*, vol. VII (Folkestone: Global Oriental, 2007) pp. 620–7.

Rawlins, James, 'William Anderson' in Hugh Cortazzi (ed.), *Britain and Japan: Biographical Portraits,* vol. V (Folkestone: Global Oriental, 2005) pp. 3–12.

Roberts, Christopher, *The British Courts and Extra-territoriality in Japan* (Leiden: Brill, 2014).

Shillony, Ben-Ami, '"Restoration", "Emperor", "Diet", "Prefecture": Or How Japanese Concepts were Mistranslated into Western Languages', in Adriana Boscaro, Franco Gatti & Massimo Raveri (eds), *Rethinking Japan*, vol. 2 (Folkestone: Japan Library, 1990), pp. 300–310.

Shimazu, Naoko, *Japan, Race and Equality: The Racial Equality Proposal of 1919* (London: Routledge, 1998).

Thorne, Ben, 'British Week in Tokyo, 1969', in Hugh Cortazzi (ed.), *Britain and Japan: Biographical Portraits*, vol. IX (Folkestone: Renaissance Books 2015) pp. 77–88.

Thorne, Christopher, *The Limits of Foreign Policy: The West, the League and the Far Eastern Crisis of 1931–1933* (London: Hamish Hamilton, 1972).

Trotter, Ann, *Britain and East Asia, 1933–1937* (Cambridge: Cambridge University Press, 1975).

Uchiyama Masakuma, 'Meiji kyūtei gaikō no enkaku: Meiji ninen no eikoku ōji raichō o kiten to shite' [The History of Meiji Court Diplomacy: Focusing on the visit of an English Prince in 1869], *Hōgaku kenkyū*, 50/12 (1977): 43–68.

Verlustdokumentation Der Gothaer Kunstsammlungen, 2 vols. (Gotha: Schloß Friedenstein, 1997 and 2011).

Vickers, Hugo, *Royal Orders: The Honours and the Honoured* (London: Bextree, 1994).

Yabuki, Hiraki, 'Britain and the Resale of Argentine Cruisers to Japan before the Russo-Japanese War', *War in History*, 16/4 (2009): 425–446.

Yokoyama, Toshio, *Japan in the Victorian Mind: A Study of Stereotyped Images of a Nation 1850–80* (London: Macmillan, 1987).

Yoshimura Michio, 'Nichi-Ei kyūtei kōryu shi no ichimen: sono seijiteki seikaku to hiseijiteki seikaku' [One Face of Anglo-Japanese Imperial Court Relations: Their Political and Non-Political Character], in Yoichi Kibata, Ian Nish, Chihiro Hosoya and Takahiko Tanaka (eds), *Nichi-Ei kōryu shi,* vol. 1, Seiji-Gaikō [The History of Anglo-Japanese Relations: Politics and Diplomacy] (Tokyo: Tokyo University Press, 2000) pp. 309–14.

Yoshimura Michio, 'Jōji go-sei taikanshiki zengo no kokusai jōsei to Nihon no taiō' [Japan's response to the international situation at the time of George V's coronation], *Seiji Keizai Shigaku*, 370 (1997): 61–78.

Ziegler, Philip, *King Edward VIII: The Official Biography* (London: Collins, 1990).

Index

For Product Safety Concerns and Information please contact our EU representative GPSR@taylorandfrancis.com Taylor & Francis Verlag GmbH, Kaufingerstraße 24, 80331 München, Germany

Batch number: 10347035

Printed by Printforce, the Netherlands